HOLD'EM HANDS I PLAYED BADLY

HOLD'EM HANDS I PLAYED BADLY

MICHAEL HESSE

CARDOZA PUBLISHING

Cardoza Publishing is the foremost gaming and gambling publisher in the world with a library of more than 200 up-to-date and easy-to-read books and strategies. These authoritative works are written by the top experts in their fields and with more than 10,000,000 books in print, represent the best-selling and most popular gaming books anywhere.

Copyright © 2012 by Michael Hesse

Library of Congress Catalog Number: 2011933353
ISBN 10:   1-58042-298-5
ISBN 13: 978-1-58042-298-7

Visit our website or write for a full list of Cardoza Publishing books and advanced strategies.

CARDOZA PUBLISHING
P.O. Box 98115, Las Vegas, NV 89193
Toll-Free Phone (800)577-WINS
email: cardozabooks@aol.com
www.cardozabooks.com

About The Author

After getting degrees from MIT and UCLA, Michael Hesse went to work as a policy analyst for The Rand Corporation. He always loved games and became a nationally-ranked chess player and tournament bridge player. When he realized that people were making money playing poker, he read every book he could find and began playing professionally in the card rooms of Los Angeles.

After he married, he realized he needed a more stable lifestyle, and set up Helix Information Services, Inc. to consult in mathematical analysis and systems analysis. In addition to consulting for banks, insurance companies and hedge funds, he began applying his skills to the gaming industry. For the last 35 years, his clients have included professional poker players, blackjack players, casinos, proposition player services, and game inventors. Throughout this time, he has continued to play poker, both live and online.

Mr. Hesse also invents casino games and has been awarded seven U.S. patents, including a patent for EasyPoker®, which has been played at the Hustler Casino in Los Angeles since 2004.

ACKNOWLEDGEMENTS

Several poker-playing friends have taught me a lot about poker and they helped me improve this book, often by challenging what I had written. This book would is much better because of their contributions. I want to particularly thank and acknowledge Louis Werman, Daniel Koizumi, Lary Kennedy, and Bob Sevy.

I would also like to thank my daughter Danielle for her help in editing this book. She may need to work on her poker face, but her writing and editing skills are outstanding. I also need to thank my amazing wife, Marianne, for her incredible patience in putting up with me while I finished this book and spent WAY too many hours at the card table. Finally, I need to acknowledge the many authors of poker books that I learned so much from. They have helped mold me into a better player.

TABLE OF CONTENTS

11. HOW TO PLAY WHEN YOU'RE RUNNING BAD   214

12. PLAYING KILL-POT HOLD'EM GAMES   221

INTRODUCTION

I wish someone else had written this book! Why? Because he would have saved me many years of struggle at the poker tables. Can you really benefit by studying the mistakes I made? Yes. I did and you can too. You may lose money making mistakes, but if you gain new insights on how to improve your game, you have earned something of value from your losses. The trick is to take your hard-earned lessons to the next level—playing better poker by eliminating your mistakes. And that's what this book is all about—how to play mistake-free hold'em.

Not all the ideas in this book are new, but many have never been published before, which is too bad because it would have saved me from learning these concepts the hard way, losing a lot of hands and a bundle of money. My goal here is to save you the trouble and trauma I endured at the start of my poker career by showing you how *not* to make the mistakes I made.

Three skills make you a successful poker player:

1. Knowing the math and strategies of the game
2. Observing everything and everybody at the table
3. Using psychological insights to your advantage

My approach to winning at poker emphasizes the first skill, the math and strategies of limit hold'em cash games. This book will probably be most valuable to people who play middle-limit hold'em. It is not meant to be your first poker book, although it covers many of the basic concepts of any poker game—pot odds, implied odds, outs, check-raising, and value betting. One friend begged me not to publish "The Rule of 42" because he felt it would give his opponents the edge. However, I assured him that there are plenty of donkeys out there that will never crack a poker book, and even more who won't be able to get through one like this because they're not willing to make the effort it takes to think through their mistakes—in this book, my mistakes—to learn how to make more money at the poker table.

The new information you'll find in the chapter on how to play suited and unsuited connectors should be very useful to you, especially in playing those multiway pots that are so common in middle limit and low limit games. I also give you multiple charts that show you exactly how specific types of hands stack up against other hands and against different numbers of opponents.

If you enjoy playing kill-pot hold'em games, you'll benefit from a special chapter devoted to the best strategies to use when you're the killer and when you have a leg up. And if you're an online player who likes to play several games at once, the chapter on multi-tabling online gives you important tips on how to handle the action competently, competitively, and profitably.

Poker is a wonderful game. No other game combines the mathematical sophistication with the psychological challenges of hold'em. At the poker table, you learn a lot about other people and how they think, and you learn even more about yourself. Poker exposes your psychological weaknesses and forces you to examine yourself. With the strategic information and logical approach I give you in this book, you will become a stronger and wiser player.

And a whole lot wealthier.

1

HOW TO IMMEDIATELY IMPROVE YOUR GAME

When I first started playing poker, I attended a poker seminar conducted by legendary author Mike "The Mad Genius of Poker" Caro. Afterward, a group of us hung around talking with Mike. He told the following story.

CARO'S TALE

A number of years ago a poker player in his eighties went on a monster winning streak and ended up with $4 million. A few of his friends pulled him aside and told him, "You're not young anymore. Why don't you take $1 million and put it into a trust account that will guarantee that you have an income for the rest of your life. You'll still have $3 million to gamble with."

"I've always been a gambler. Every time I sit down, I put all my money on the table," said the old-timer. Six months later he was broke.

"Wow!" said one of Caro's students. "If I had $4 million, there's no way I'd be broke six months later."

"And that's exactly why you'll never make $4 million playing poker," was Mike's instant reply.

IS LIMIT HOLD'EM THE RIGHT GAME FOR YOU?

Some of the greatest no-limit hold'em players of all time are Doyle Brunson and Phil Ivey, plus the late Stu Ungar. What do they all have in common? They love to gamble! Ungar went broke time and time again after winning huge sums playing cards and then losing it all at the craps table or betting sports. Brunson has done a better job of managing his life, but as he says in the first edition of *Super System,* "I've won millions playing poker. Lost most of it betting on sports and golf."

In televised cash games, Ivey is likely to be heavily involved in large prop bets, which are side bets on what will come on the flop. It's not unusual to see him betting $50,000 on whether the next flop will have more red cards than black cards. Often the action on these side bets dwarfs the action on the poker game. While this is hardly conclusive, it is interesting that the best no-limit hold'em players love to gamble—and gamble b-i-g. Everyone who plays poker has to gamble sometimes, but these guys are fearless at the table and they welcome the big gamble.

Perhaps you are already very good at limit hold'em, and are considering switching to no-limit. Though no-limit and limit hold'em require some of the same skills—in both games, you need to understand the math of the game and be able to accurately read both flops and people—making the switch is not a simple matter of learning some new strategies. It requires that you be emotionally equipped to handle the game.

It is apparent that the most successful no-limit pros seem eager to take very large risks in their pursuit of very large rewards. Make no mistake about it—if that's not you, you will neither enjoy yourself playing the game nor will you be as successful as players who love to gamble.

> Unless you can emotionally handle large losses and big swings and really enjoy gambling, you are better off playing limit hold'em than no-limit.

If that description doesn't fit you, you're far better off playing the equally exciting game of limit hold'em. You won't have to risk your entire bankroll every time you play a hand. You won't get squeezed out of the action by an aggressive player's huge bet on the flop. And your bankroll won't suffer the extreme roller-coaster fluctuations so common in no-limit hold'em.

WHY READ ABOUT MISTAKES?

This book describes a lot of big and medium mistakes I have made. Does that mean I am a bad player? You surely wouldn't want to read a book by a bad player, right? I may not be a world-class player, but I am very successful at poker. I have been a consistent winner for the past 30 years, and have won at many forms of poker, including five-card draw, lowball, Omaha, seven-card stud high-low, as well as limit hold'em.

It used to be a running joke in my regular live game that my first poker book would be called *Hold'em Hands I Played Badly*, my second book would be *More Hands I Played Badly*, and my third book would be *Even More Hold'em Hands I Played Badly*. What I didn't tell the rest of the players is that I was keeping a journal of my bad plays—and that was the start of this book.

Usually when I left the table, I kicked myself for the two or three hands I had messed up, and promised that I would never make those mistakes again. I noticed that in spite of this, I was repeating the same errors. Finally, I started jotting down my mistakes at the table, and then analyzing them more carefully at home. In the heat of battle, there just isn't the time to consider everything—I analyzed hands better away from the table. I reviewed my errors every week or two, and stopped making many of them. I still wasn't playing mistake-free poker, but I was playing better. And as my game improved, I started to see new mistakes that I wouldn't have recognized before. My game analysis resulted in a very big benefit: I was thinking deeper and analyzing better during the games. The best thing was that my play was improving.

SOMETIMES WE ALL PLAY HANDS BADLY

We play a hand badly for a lot of reasons. Sometimes it is ignorance: We simply have never learned how to play a situation correctly. Poker books can be very helpful with opening our eyes to something we have never considered before. Sometimes, we don't take enough time to think a hand through at the table. That is where thinking about hands away from the table can help. If you think a lot about a hand at home or in the car, you will be better equipped to play a similar situation at the table.

Then there are the other factors such as fatigue, tilt, and frustration. Nobody plays his best all the time. Sometimes we just make a bad play, even though we know better. Preparation can help with some of this. The more you have prepared for a situation, the more likely you are to get it right, even when you are not at your best.

> It isn't the close decisions that affect your profit or loss the most. It's avoiding the big mistakes.

You are probably familiar with the articles in the poker magazines that show a "brilliant" play that illustrates what a great player the author is. The author was faced with a very close decision: If it were an easy decision, there would be nothing brilliant about it. They explain the profound reasoning they used to make the decision. They get it right and rake in the big pot.

Are they really that brilliant? I don't know. Perhaps they get it right most of the time; if so, they are brilliant. Perhaps they don't write about all the times they get it wrong. In that case, they just guessed right this time. Perhaps they really went through the analysis they describe at the table. Perhaps the analyzing occurred after the fact.

However, brilliant plays don't really matter all that much to you in the long run. If they are close decisions, then you could play either way. Sometimes you'll get it right; sometimes you won't. In the long run, it will all even out, and you won't make or lose much money. Unless you are a poker genius, you probably won't get enough close decisions right over your poker career to make much difference in your results.

HOW CAN YOU ELIMINATE MISTAKES?

Malcolm Gladwell's book *Outliers* discusses the "Ten-Thousand Hour Rule." The basic idea is that to become an expert in most fields, whether it is computer programming or playing the cello, you must put in 10,000 hours of work or practice. That's about five years of full-time work.

That may well be true in poker too. To be a world-class player, you probably need many, many hours of play. However, just playing a lot of hours won't guarantee success. Lots of very experienced players continue to lose. You also need to be determined to win and find ways to keep learning. Some players will play 10,000 hours and still be losers. Others will be winners in far fewer hours. A world-class basketball player didn't just play a lot. The player also got coaching to learn fundamentals and correct mistakes. Unless you have the luxury of a poker coach, you have to be your own coach. You have to review your play and find out what you are doing wrong. Even the best players in sports review their own game films and look for opportunities to fix flaws in their game. Going over hands you have played is the equivalent if reviewing the game film.

Reviewing hands is one of the single best ways to improve faster. Studying your mistakes is not beating yourself up for them. You need to analyze the hand to be sure you made the wrong play. Many times I am sure I blew it, but after further analysis, I realize my play was reasonable. When you do find a mistake, think about how you could recognize the situation in the future.

How else do you improve as fast as possible? There are many good poker books that can help immeasurably. Read a lot of poker books, but think about the quality of their advice. It is not always right. Sometimes, authors recommend the wrong play. Other times, they are playing a very different game from the ones you frequent. Visit the online poker forums, but take the advice with even more caution.

LOOK FOR A FEW GOOD HANDS

While putting in a lot of hours at the tables is imperative, it will help you far more if you spend some time on your game away from the tables. Pick out key hands and think more deeply about them. (I have done some of that picking and thinking for you.) Take a hand or two and spend a lot of time figuring out the best play.

In some places in this book, you will see a lengthy mathematical analysis of a situation. You cannot do this at the table. However, going through the numbers will help you to make better judgments in the heat of battle. A small group of poker friends and I have an e-mail group where we send each other hands and discuss them. Sometimes the debate on one hand can go on for days. I cannot tell you how much I have learned from these discussions.

When you read this book, don't try to cover it as quickly as possible. Take some time to think about the hand we are discussing. Try to figure out what is right or wrong with our analysis. It will pay dividends!

Another thing that pays big dividends in any form of poker is knowing exactly how good your hand is. In other words, how much can you expect to win (or lose) by making a specific play? The next chapter covers "expected value" in detail.

2 UNDERSTANDING THE STRENGTH OF YOUR HAND

In poker, we express the strength of a hand in terms of its expected value (EV). Expected value is a concept from statistics that not every poker book explains. This book uses it a lot, so a brief explanation is in order.

EXPECTED VALUE

Expectation or **expected value** (**EV**) is how much you can expect to win or lose on average if you repeat the same contest a very large number of times.

Here is a common way to calculate EV:

1. List the possible outcomes.
2. Determine how often each occurs
3. Determine how much you win or lose when each outcome occurs.
4. Multiply the probability of each outcome by the win or loss.
5. Add up the values.

Suppose someone offers to pay you $5 every time you roll a 6 on a die, but you have to pay him $1 every time you roll any other number.

EXPECTED VALUE			
OUTCOME	PROBABILITY	WIN/LOSS	NET
You roll 6	1/6	$5	$0.83
You roll 1-5	5/6	-$1	-$0.83
YOU MAKE			**$0.00**

This is a fair bet. In the long run, you shouldn't win or lose on it.

Now let's look at a poker example. Suppose you have 3♠ 2♠ and the board is A♠ 10♥ 8♠ 6♦. Your opponent isn't very careful with his cards and you have seen that he has an ace and king in his hand. Therefore, you are sure that if a spade comes on the river, you will win; otherwise, you will lose. You are sure that he will call a bet on the river, so you will win six bets if you get there. There are five bets in the pot and you have to decide whether to call.

EXPECTED VALUE			
OUTCOME	PROBABILITY	WIN/LOSS	NET
You make flush	9/44 = 20.4%	$6	$1.27
You miss flush	35/44 = 79.5%	-$1	-$0.80
YOU MAKE			**$0.43**

On average you make 43 cents every time this occurs; thus, 43 cents is your expectation. You may miss nine flushes in a row or make nine in a row, but over the long run, calling is a profitable play. As we will see in the next section, there is an easier way to make this particular decision (6 x 9 is greater than 42), but we will make a lot of expectation calculations in this book.

A PRACTICAL EXAMPLE

Here's a more practical example. Suppose there are 3.25 bets in the pot on the turn. Your aggressive opponent has checked and you happen to know that he has a gutshot straight draw. Let's make two assumptions:

- If you check, he will bet the river whether or not he hits his draw.
- If you bet, he will fold.

Do you want to bet? If you bet, you always win the 3.25 bets in the pot, since he will always fold. If you check, the outcome will be:

EXPECTED VALUE			
OUTCOME	PROBABILITY	WIN/LOSS	NET
He makes straight	4/44 = 9.1%	-1	-0.09
He misses	40/44 = 90.9%	4.25	3.86
YOU MAKE			3.77

Since you make 3.77 bets by checking and 3.25 bets by betting, you are better off checking. Betting has a positive expectation, but checking has a bigger positive expectation.

Following closely on the heels of the expected value of an event occurring is your ability to count the number of outs you have before you decide your next action during a hand at the poker table. The next chapter explains the nature of outs and how to count them in a variety of poker scenarios.

3 THE IMPORTANCE OF OUTS

If you have been playing for a while and studying, you probably think you know how to count outs and you may be tempted to skip this section. Don't! Very few players understand all the important subtleties of counting outs.

What is an **out**?

An out is a card that comes on the turn or river that improves your hand when you are behind and wins the pot for you. Let's be clear. Three factors are necessary for a card to be an out:

1. You are behind.
2. The card improves your hand.
3. You win when the card appears.

Why is this so important? A lot of players seem to think that any card that improves their hand is an out. For example, when they hold A-5 they assume that any ace is an out. However, if another player has an ace with a bigger kicker, the ace is not an out.

There are also players who seem to think that a card that gives them a chance to improve their hand is also an out. Suppose you have K♥ J♥ and the flop is Q♠ 7♥ 4♣. I have heard players say that any heart is an out since it gives them a flush draw, and that aces or tens are outs since they give them a straight draw. These are not outs. You do have some backdoor draws, and we will discuss how to count those when counting outs. However, those cards are not outs—by themselves, they don't improve your hand.

The chart pictured below shows how big a pot is needed to justify calling based on the number of clean outs you have. It also shows how often you will improve. A **clean out** is a card that makes your hand a winner if that card shows up. On the chart, "L" is the number of outs you have times the number of bets in the pot.

THE OUTS CHART				
CLEAN OUTS	**POT ODDS NEEDED**	**IMPROVE W/2 CARDS TO COME**	**IMPROVE W/1 CARD TO COME**	**L**
1	46	4.5%	2.3%	46
2	23	8.8%	4.5%	46
3	15	13.0%	6.8%	45
4	11	17.2%	9.1%	44
5	8	21.2%	11.4%	40
6	7	25.2%	13.6%	42
7	6	29.0%	15.9%	42
8	5	32.7%	18.2%	40
9	4	36.4%	20.5%	36
10	4	39.9%	22.7%	40
11	3	43.3%	25.0%	33
12	3	46.7%	27.3%	36
13	2.5	49.9%	29.5%	32
14	2.5	53.0%	31.8%	35
15	2	56.1%	34.1%	30

If your outs aren't clean, you need to discount them. If an out has a 50 percent chance of giving you a winner, it is really only half an out. Naturally, you will only be guessing at how clean your outs are, but you need to make your best estimate. This chart shows the breakeven point. If you have six outs and there are seven bets in the pot, it doesn't really matter whether you call or fold (assuming no further action). If you think you will make money after you call, either because you are a better player than your opponent(s) or you will make a big hand, you should play. If you *don't* think you will make money after the next card, you should fold.

THE RULE OF 42

If you don't want to memorize the odds chart, there is a much easier way to get approximately the right answer. To repeat, "L" is the number of outs times the number of bets in the pot. Therefore, L = Outs x Bets in Pot. The "Rule of 42" says that if L is 42 or higher, you may have a playable hand. For example, if you have six outs, there should be seven bets in the pot to consider continuing (6 x 7 = 42).

THE RULE OF 42
If L is 42 or higher, you may have a playable hand.

Notice that you *may* have a playable hand. You still might not. This is a breakeven situation. If you are in doubt, you should not play unless your number is higher than 42. Here are some reasons to not play if it is close:

- You are not closing out the action, and you might get raised.
- Your outs are to hands that are not pretty sure to win. You could hit your hand and lose quite a bit on the later rounds.
- You have a lot of cards that improve your hand but you don't know which ones you want to hit.
- You have poor position.

A quick review of the table in the previous section shows that this is a crude rule. If you want to be more accurate, use the following rules as well:

- With four outs or fewer, you need an L of 45
- With nine outs or more, you need an L of 35

If you really want to play as accurately as possible, you can just learn the entire table, of course.

DISCOUNTED OUTS

What if a card doesn't always give you the best hand? In that case, it is a **tainted out** and you need to count that card as less than a full out. Suppose you have 9♥ 8♣ and the board is J♠ 10♦ 3♠. Eight cards will make you a straight: four sevens and four queens. The biggest problem is that the Q♠ or 7♠ could make someone else a flush.

Suppose you estimate there is a 50 percent chance that someone else has two spades in their hand. Then there is only a 50 percent chance that the Q♠ or 7♠ will win for you. So each of those is worth half an out, and you have a total of seven outs after you discount them, not eight outs. Observant readers will have noticed that there are other ways to make your straight and lose. If a queen comes you will lose to A-K. If you make your straight with a spade on the turn, you could still lose if another spade comes on the river. Or if the board pairs, your straight could lose to a full house. The turn and river could be Q and 9, and you could split the pot to anyone with an 8 in his hand. This leads us to a key law about outs:

> You never have quite as many outs as you think.

For simplicity, we will often talk as though you do, since it is hard to quantify all the ways you can make a good hand and still lose. Just remember that before you make a call based on outs, include an extra safety factor.

Four factors affect the strength of an out:

1. How strong a hand will you make if the out comes?
2. How scary is the board?
3. How sure are you which cards are outs?
4. Do you have position?

Let's look at each of these factors.

UNDERSTANDING THE STRENGTH OF OUTS

1. HAND-STRENGTH PRINCIPLE

Consider a pot that offers you odds of 8 to 1. The board is 10♥ 6♦ 2♣. Which hand would you rather have?

 HAND (1)   **HAND (2)**

Hand (1) gives you two overcards and six ways to improve. Hand (2) only has five ways to improve. At first glance, it might seem that Hand (1) is the better hand to draw to. However, Hand (2) has three big advantages:

With Hand (1) you are trying to improve to one pair. With Hand (2) you are trying to improve to two pair or trips. Your hand is much more likely to win if you improve.

With Hand (1) you are more likely to be dominated. If someone has K-10 or Q-10, you are drawing thin; improving your hand and still losing could be costly. It is quite a bit less likely that someone has played 10-7, than K-10.

There is a better chance you will win the pot without improving with a pair than with a king high.

This is not to say you should never play overcards or always play when you pair on the flop. However, overcards are among the most overrated hands in limit hold'em.

> Outs to a big hand are worth more than outs to a smaller hand.

2. SCARY-BOARD PRINCIPLE

Use some common sense here. If there are two pair on the board, most "outs" are extremely weak. If the board is K-K-7-7 and you have a pair of nines, you have two outs to a full house, but if anyone has a king you are drawing dead. Or if the board is K♥ Q♥ 7♥ 3♥ and you have J♣ 10♣, you shouldn't draw to the straight unless all the stars align. The pot should be very big, and you should be heads up against a player who will bet without a heart.

3. UNCERTAINTY PRINCIPLE

In some cases you may have a lot of outs, but you may not know which ones are winners for you. Here's an example: Four players limp, and you raise from the small blind with A♥ 9♦, The big blind raises. One limper folds and three call. You call (15 bets, four players). The big blind is a very tight player who only three-bets here with a big pair, A-K, or A-Q suited.

The flop is 7♠ 5♥ 2♦. You check, the big blind bets, and everyone folds to you (16 bets, two players). Do you call? Let's start with how many outs we have:

- If he has A-K or A-Q, three nines are outs.
- If he has K-K, Q-Q, J-J, or 10-10, three aces are outs.
- If he has A-A, you have no outs (other than backdoor draws).

So you have a little less than three outs on average (2.8 outs, if you do the math). You need pot odds of 15 to 16 to break even. You are getting a little more than this, so it looks like a marginal call. However, the uncertainty hurts your implied odds. If an ace or a nine comes, you cannot raise. He can bet when he has the best and check when he has the worst of it. You will typically lose two big bets when you improve and lose. You will only win one big bet when you make the best hand.

Suppose a 9 comes on the turn. Do you bet? Based on his range, you are ahead 24 times and behind 27 times. Your opponent isn't going to fold the best hand. You have to check. Now he can bet twice when he is ahead, and bet or call once when he is behind. The following chart shows two possible ways the hand can play out when you are ahead. In both scenarios, you win one bet.

HIS HAND	TURN ACTION	HIS RIVER ACTION	YOUR WIN/LOSS
A-K or A-Q	You check, he bets, you call	You check, he checks	Win 1 bet
	You check, he checks	You bet, he calls	Win 1 bet

Now, here is what is likely to happen when he is ahead. Unless you are prepared to fold the river, you are going to lose two bets.

HIS HAND	TURN ACTION	HIS RIVER ACTION	YOUR WIN/LOSS
A-A to 10-10	He bets, you call	He bets, you call	Lose 2 bets

You will lose money on the later rounds. The fact that you will never be very certain if you are ahead or behind puts you at a big disadvantage, particularly when you're playing out of position. If you catch your other "out," the situation is similar. If an ace comes, you will typically lose two bets when you lose, and only win one bet when you make the best hand. Because of the bad implied odds, what appears to be a close call is actually a fold.

> **Outs are less valuable if you don't know which ones give you the best hand.**

When you improve, if you still don't know whether you have the best hand, your uncertainty will cost you money. That is, you will win less money when you win, or lose more money when you don't. Either way, your outs are less valuable than when you improve and are still unsure that you have the best hand. The bottom line is: Don't make marginal calls if you don't know which outs are winners.

4. OUTS AND POSITION

Position affects your implied odds. With good position, you will win more money when you win, and you will lose less money when you lose. When the pot is offering around the right price to call based on the number of outs, you should tend to call with good position and fold with bad position.

> **Don't make marginal calls when you are out of position.**

OUTS AND OVERCARDS

Naturally, outs to a strong hand are much more valuable than outs to a weaker hand. This might seem ridiculously obvious, but you will see people drawing to weak hands all the time. Let's look at this concept in a little more detail.

Overcards are generally weak outs, since even if you improve you still only have one pair. One pair wins a lot of pots, but nothing is worse than drawing to a hand, getting there, and still losing. Most people draw to overcards far too often and lose more money drawing to them than they make when they hit.

> If you never draw to overcards, you will probably come out ahead.

Overcards can give you six outs. You need pot odds of 7 to 1 to break even with six outs. However, you will frequently have fewer than six outs. Here are six things that can reduce your number of outs.

SIX FACTORS THAT WILL REDUCE YOUR OUTS

1. There can be a flush draw on the board, and two of your "outs" can make someone a flush.
2. Someone can have one of your out cards with a better kicker. If you have K-10, you are in trouble if someone else has A-K, K-Q, K-J, or A-10. On your really bad days, two players will have both of your outs dominated and you are virtually drawing dead.

3. Someone has already flopped a set, two pair or holds an overpair.
4. One of your outs could make someone a straight.
5. If there are quite a few players in the pot, some of them will have big cards and they may be using up your outs. (If you have K-10 and someone has J-10, one of your tens is gone and you have only five outs at best.)
6. If you are not last to act, someone might raise behind you, killing your pot odds.

WHAT YOU NEED TO DRAW TO OVERCARDS

I am not recommending you never draw to overcards. Just be very selective. To draw to overcards:

- The pot should be big.
- Your cards should be high.
- The board should be uncoordinated.
- You would prefer to be last to act.
- It helps a lot if you have other draws.
- It helps if there is a chance you have the best hand without improving.

Let's look at each of these requirements in more detail.

1. BIG POT

I will usually not call with just two overcards unless I am getting pot odds of 9 to 1 or more. Odds of 7 to 1 is break even, but given all the risks if you improve, it is better to be getting really good pot odds. However, remember that if the pot is big because there was a lot of raising before the flop, you may be facing a big pocket pair that might beat you even if you hit one of your outs, or take away some of your outs.

> With just two overcards to the flop, you usually want at least 9 to 1 pot odds to call.

2. BIG CARDS

If you are going to play overcards, the higher they are the better. An A-Q is significantly stronger than a K-Q, which may seem ridiculously obvious, but plenty of players seem to ignore this fact and treat all overcards the same.

3. COORDINATED BOARD

A coordinated board is bad for overcards. If you have A♠ K♠, you would rather see a board like 8♦ 6♣ 2♥ than a board like 10♥ 9♥ 8♣. And J♥ 10♥ 9♣ is even worse. If you catch a king, anyone with a queen in his hand has made a straight.

4. LAST TO ACT

When you call with overcards, it is much better to be the last to act. If someone raises behind you, you might find that you are getting only 5 to 1 odds on your draw instead of 9 to 1.

5. OTHER DRAWS

Overcards get much better if you have some other draws. If you have A♠ K♣ and the flop is J♥ 10♠ 3♦, you have 10 possible outs, since any queen gives you the nut straight. This is going to almost always be playable, and there are plenty of situations where you might raise with this hand.

Backdoor draws help, too. If you have A♠ K♠ and the flop is J♥ 8♠ 3♦, you have 8.5 possible outs. You get two outs for the backdoor flush and half an out for the backdoor straight. Two overcards with a backdoor flush draw is usually playable. A backdoor straight draw is typically not going to make a big difference.

6. WHAT IF YOU DON'T NEED TO IMPROVE?

All this assumes that you need to improve to win. With strong overcards like A-K against one or two opponents, your A-K may be the best hand without improving. Depending on the board and your opponents, you should sometimes play unimproved overcards to a showdown.

When you have position, it is often correct to raise with two overcards, even if it might not be correct to call. For example, suppose you have K♥ Q♦ and call a limper. Everyone folds to the big blind, who raises. You and the limper call (6.5 bets, two players). The flop is 9♥ 7♠ 4♦. The big blind bets and the limper folds (7.5 bets). What do you do?

If you are 100 percent sure that a king or queen will win the pot, you should call since you are getting the right price with six outs. However, you are not sure of that. The big blind could have a big pair or A-K or A-Q. You could also fold. If the big blind is extremely tight and will only raise with a very big hand, you probably should. However, you have another option: You could raise. If everything goes well, the big blind will call and then check the turn. If you miss, you can take a free card and try to improve on the river. You are now investing two bets for a chance to win 8.5 bets. You are getting 4.25 to 1 on your raise. You need around nine outs to justify your play. However, you are getting two chances to improve your hand. Getting two chances to hit five outs is as good as getting one chance to hit 10 outs. This is a profitable play. Your implied odds are pretty good since you can check the turn if you miss, and you can bet if you hit.

There is also a small chance that the big blind will fold to your raise on the flop, and you will win the whole pot right there. And if the big blind looks weak when he calls your flop bet, you can bet the turn. You might still win the pot without improving. You should not do this automatically. Many things can go wrong. The big blind can reraise on the flop. Not only does this ruin your pot odds, you now face a difficult decision.

If he has a big pair or A-K, you are in bad shape. He might also just call the flop and bet the turn. You lose the free card you invested so much to get.

Though this play should be a part of your arsenal, you need to be careful when you make it and against whom. When it fails, it still helps your image: Your raises are more likely to get paid off in the future. There is nothing nicer than raising on the flop, hitting on the turn, and getting paid off all the way. When someone asks, "How could you raise with nothing on the flop?" you can smile and say, "I knew it was coming."

If you make this play, it is very important to pause before checking the turn. If you check quickly, you are advertising you have a draw. Stop and act like you are considering your action. You might even want to act like you are checking reluctantly.

To summarize, raise with overcards when:

- You have around the right pot odds to call.
- You are against one opponent.
- You have position.
- Your opponent is passive and unlikely to reraise you.

OUTS & HANDS

OUTS TO TWO PAIR OR TRIPS

This situation occurs when you flop a pair and you think that you will need to improve to win the pot. For example, if you have 7♠ 6♠ and the flop is K♥ Q♦ 7♣, you have three outs (sixes) to make two pair, and two outs (sevens) to make trips. With five outs, you need pot odds of over 8 to 1 to call a bet or raise.

These are usually pretty strong outs and don't need to be discounted much, but things can go wrong. Someone could have or make a bigger two pair. Someone could have a 7 with a bigger kicker—and there are possible straight draws out there. On the other hand, in many cases, your pair of sevens might be the best hand, so if you are getting the right price, you can usually play this hand.

If the board is suited, your outs get weaker. For example, if the board is K♥ Q♦ 7♥, you should treat this hand as having closer to four outs than five outs, and you need pot odds of over 10 to 1 to continue.

OUTS TO A SET OR FULL HOUSE

You have outs to a set or full house when you have a pocket pair and you need to improve to win the pot. They are usually very strong outs, but since you only have two of them, you need *very* big pot odds to try to hit your hand. Occasionally, you will get the pot odds of more than 23 to 1 that you need to play your pair.

OUTS TO A STRAIGHT OR FLUSH

Outs to a straight or flush come in two varieties: one-card straight or flush draws, and two-card straight or flush draws. **Two-card draws** mean that you will need to use both your cards to make the complete hand.

	HAND	FLOP
2-Card Flush Draw	K♥ Q♥	9♥ 7♥ 5♠
1-Card Flush Draw	10♠ 8♥	9♥ 7♥ 5♥
2-Card Straight Draw	K♣ Q♣	J♦ 10♥ 4♣
1-Card Straight Draw	A♦ 10♦	J♣ 9♠ 8♠

Two-card draws are much stronger than one-card draws. A two-card flush draw is far less likely to lose to a bigger flush, and a two-card straight draw is far less likely to lose to a bigger straight or to split the pot with someone who has the same straight card that you have. Also, with a two-card draw, you are more likely to get paid off if you have the best hand.

Of course, if you have the highest outstanding card in a flush suit, a one-card flush draw is very strong. For example, these are very strong one-card flush draws:

HAND	FLOP
A♥ Q♣	9♥ 7♥ 5♥♠
K♠ 10♥	A♠ 7♠ 5♠

COUNTING FLUSH AND STRAIGHT OUTS

The most valuable outs are outs where one more card makes you a straight or flush. Here is a standard draw to the nut flush:

YOUR HAND   **THE BOARD**

YOUR OUTS: 9

There are nine hearts that give you an almost unbeatable hand (if the board pairs you could lose to a full house).

Now look at the following hand:

YOUR HAND   **THE BOARD**

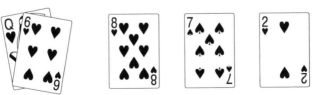

YOUR OUTS: 9

With Q♥ 6♥, you still have nine cards that make you a flush, but there are more ways to make the flush and still lose. You could lose to a bigger flush draw such as A♥ 3♥ or K♥ J♥. Even if no one has two hearts with an ace or king, you could still make your flush on the turn and lose on the river if anyone has the A♥ or K♥. If no one has those hands, you may make less money on the river if a fourth heart comes. You still have a strong draw, but it is weaker than the draw to the nut flush.

Now look at the following hands and determine how many straights can beat each one.

	HAND	BOARD	# BIGGER STRAIGHTS
TWO OVERCARDS	K♣ Q♥	J♥ 10♠ 2♦	0
With this hand, you have the nut straight draw.			
OVER & UNDER	Q♣ 9♥	J♥ 10♠ 2♦	1
With this hand, you lose to A-Q if a king comes.			
OVER & MIDDLE	K♣ J♥	Q♥ 10♠ 2♦	0
With this hand, you have the nut straight draw.			
MIDDLE & UNDER	J♣ 9♥	Q♥ 10♠ 2♦	1
With this hand, you lose to A-J if a king comes.			
TWO UNDER	9♣ 8♥	J♥ 10♠ 2♦	2
With this hand, you lose to A-K or K-9 if a queen comes.			
DOUBLE GUTTER #1	10♣ 9♥	Q♥ 8♠ 6♦	0
With this hand, you have the nut straight draw.			
DOUBLE GUTTER #2	J♣ 5♥	9♥ 8♠ 7	Many
With this hand, if you catch a 10, you lose to Q-J and split the pot with anyone who has a jack. If you catch a 6, you lose to any 10 and split if anyone has a 5.			

Why is the second double gutshot draw so much worse than the first one? In the first case, you use both of your cards to make a straight. In the second case, any straight will only use one of your cards. A draw to a one-card straight is far more vulnerable, so those outs need to be significantly discounted.

Straight outs are worth a bit more than flush outs. When you make a straight, your hand is usually better disguised and you can win more money. However, straight outs are draws to a weaker hand. If you make a straight and end up facing a flush, your outs will cost you.

COUNTING BACKDOOR FLUSH OUTS

A **backdoor flush draw** is a draw where you will need two cards of the right suit to make a flush. Generally, a backdoor flush draw is worth two outs. However, if it is a one-card draw, you need to discount it heavily unless you have one of the top two outstanding cards in the flush suit. Here are some backdoor flush draws and how I recommend counting the outs after discounting:

HAND	FLOP	NEEDED	FLUSH OUTS
K♥ Q♥	9♥ 7♣ 5♠	2 Hearts	2
10♠ 8♥	9♥ 7♥ 5♠	2 Hearts	0
K♥ Q♣	J♥ 10♥ 4♠	2 Hearts	1
A♥ 10♦	J♥ 10♥ 4♠	2 Hearts	2

Backdoor flush outs usually have better implied odds than regular flush outs. Most players don't expect you to draw to a backdoor flush, so when you hit your hand, you are likely to get more action.

COUNTING BACKDOOR STRAIGHT OUTS

A **backdoor straight draw** is worth one-half an out for each two-card combination that makes your straight (before any discounting). A backdoor straight draw is a draw where you will need two different cards to make a straight. Normally, the number of gaps will tell you how many outs you have.

CARDS IN DRAW	GAPS	CARDS THAT MAKE A STRAIGHT	2-CARD COMBOS	OUTS
8-7-6	0	10-9, 9-5, 5-4	3	1.5
8-7-5	1	10-6, 6-4	2	1.0
8-6-4	2	7-5	1	0.5
8-7-4	2	6-5	1	0.5

However, when your straight cards are high or low, counting gaps may not be accurate. If you count each two-card combination as one-half of an out, you will always get an accurate number.

CARDS IN DRAW	GAPS	CARDS THAT MAKE A STRAIGHT	2-CARD COMBOS	OUTS
A-K-Q	0	J-10	1	0.5
A-K-J	1	Q-10	1	0.5
K-Q-J	0	A-10, J-10	2	1.0
K-Q-10	1	A-J, J-9	2	1.0
A-2-3	0	5-4	1	0.5
A-2-4	1	5-3	1	0.5
2-3-4	0	A-5, 6-5	2	1.0
2-3-5	2	4-5	1	0.5

The next chapter shows you seven action hands that illustrate how to evaluate your outs in different types of situations.

4 EVALUATING YOUR OUTS

EIGHT GAME SCENARIOS

GAME SCENARIO #1

You are on the button with A♥ Q♥. An unknown player in the hijack raises, you reraise, the blinds fold, and he calls (7.5 bets, two players). The flop is 10♠ 7♥ 6♦. He bets (8.5 bets in the pot). How many outs do you have? Should you call?

OUT CARDS	# OF OUTS	WORRIES
Ace	3	A-K, A-A, A-10, 10-10, 7-7, 6-6
Queen	3	A-A, K-K, 10-10, 7-7, 6-6
Running Hearts	2	None
K-J	0.5	None

As noted earlier, a runner-runner flush draw is worth around two outs. Your draw is to the nut flush so you don't have to worry about discounting these outs. Only one two-card combination, K-J, makes you a straight. Each combination like this is worth around one-half of an out, so you have 8.5 outs before you discount them. Since he didn't reraise before the flop, you probably don't need to discount them much. Most players will put in another raise with A-A, K-K, or A-Q. You only need five outs to call, and you have up to 8.5. You should call here, and you could even consider raising to get a free card on the turn.

GAME SCENARIO #2

Let's change the previous hand a bit. You are in the big blind with A♥ Q♥. An unknown player in the hijack raises, you reraise, and he reraises again. You call (8.5 bets, two players). The flop is 10♠ 7♥ 6♦. You check and he bets (9.5 bets in the pot). How many outs do you have? Should you call?

OUT CARDS	# OF OUTS	WORRIES
Ace	3	A-K, A-A, A-10, 10-10, 7-7, 6-6
Queen	3	A-A, K-K, 10-10, 7-7, 6-6
Running Hearts	2	None
K-J	0.5	None

You still have 8.5 outs before you discount them. However, since he raised preflop, you need to worry a lot more about A-A, K-K, Q-Q, and A-K. If they make up half of his four-bet range, you now have three or four overcard outs instead of six. Since hitting a big card and losing is expensive, I tend to be conservative in counting these outs. Count an ace or queen as 1.5 outs each, for a total of 5.5 outs.

You only need five outs to call, so you should call here. However, this is a fairly close decision. Against a tight player who will rarely four-bet preflop, you should fold. Against an aggressive player, you should definitely call. Against an unknown player, this is a close call.

GAME SCENARIO #3

Suppose an early player limps and everyone folds to you in the small blind. You call with 9♦ 8♣. The big blind raises, and you and the limper call (6 bets, three players). The flop is 10♣ 6♣ 5♦. You check, the big blind bets, and the limper calls (8 bets). What do you do? First, how many outs do you have? An optimist would say you have six outs: four sevens make a straight and you have a backdoor flush draw worth two outs.

With six outs and eight bets in the pot, you would have an easy call. If you are even more optimistic, you might speculate that a 9 or 8 might give you the best hand. After all, the big blind is just putting in a continuation bet and the limper didn't raise. If neither of them has a 10, a 9 or 8 might give you the best hand. That's six more outs. With 14 outs, you should raise. (Don't laugh: This kind of reasoning is common on the Internet.)

Let's look at these 14 "outs." Remember that an out is a card that gives you the best hand, not a card that improves your hand. Improving to second best is going to cost you. We'll start with the four sevens. Any 7 makes you a straight, but the 7♣ could also make someone a flush. Since limpers love suited cards and the limper called the flop bet, you have to seriously worry about a club draw. Call this 3.5 outs.

What about the backdoor flush draw? This is a one-card backdoor flush draw to a weak flush. There are four clubs higher than your 9♣. This is a worthless draw. In the long run, drawing to this flush will cost you more money than you make.

Finally, there are the six nines and eights. Two of them are clubs that could make someone a flush. However, the bigger problem is that they are too likely *not* to make you a winning hand. The big blind could have a 10, an overpair, or even a set. The limper could have a big hand and he might be waiting to raise, or he might be too timid to raise with a 10. A 9 or an 8 could make someone a straight. Sometimes, a bunch of weak draws combine to make a strong draw. This is not one of those cases! Your only solid draw is to the straight and you don't have enough outs to continue with only eight bets in the pot. Fold.

GAME SCENARIO #4

You have 7♦ 5♦ in the big blind. An early player raises and another early player calls. Everyone else folds and you call (6.5 bets, three players). The flop is 9♥ 8♦ 5♥. You pass, the opener bets and the next player raises (9.5 bets, but two bets to call).

What should you do? This is a fairly complex problem. Here are the steps you should take:

1. What pot odds are you getting?
2. How many outs to you have?
3. How much should you discount your outs?
4. Do you have good position?
5. Do the implied odds hurt you or help you?
6. Is the pot offering the right price?

Let's examine each step in detail.

THINKING TO FIGURE OUT THE RIGHT PLAY

1. POT ODDS

First, let's look at our pot odds. Right now the pot is offering 4.25 to 1. The opener will probably call, so you might get better pot odds. On the other hand, the opener might reraise, making your pot odds worse. Let's keep it simple and figure that those will cancel each other out, and just take the pots odds you are getting right now.

2. COUNT YOUR OUTS

Let's look at our outs:

OUT CARDS	# OF OUTS	WORRIES
7	3	Any 6 would give someone a straight. The 7♥ could give someone a flush
5	2	The 5♥ could give someone a flush
Running Diamonds	2	A bigger flush
6	4	10-7 gives someone a bigger straight. You are splitting with anyone else who has a 7

While none of your outs is all that powerful, you have a strong hand with 11 possible outs when you put them all together. You only need pot odds of 3 to 1 to call.

3. DISCOUNTING OUTS

So we have an easy call, right? Hold on a minute! Let's look at those "worries." How big a worry are they?

OUT CARDS	WORRIES	COMMENT
7	Any 6 would give someone a straight. The 7♥ could give someone a flush	With an early opener and caller, it is not very likely either has a 6 in his hand. The flush is possible. Discount the outs from 3 to 2.5.
5	The 5♥ could give someone a flush	This is a serious worry. Discount the fives from 2 to 1.5.
Running Diamonds	A bigger flush	This could happen, but flush-over-flush is fairly rare.
6	10-7 gives someone a bigger straight. You are splitting with anyone else who has a 7	10-7 or any hand with a 7 isn't too likely for an early opener and early caller.

With a little discounting, you are down to 10 outs.

4. POSITION

You will be acting first on the turn and river. You don't have good position.

5. IMPLIED ODDS

You also have pretty good implied odds. When you hit one of your outs, you are likely to have a strong hand. With the betting so far, you can expect to get action.

6. IS THE PRICE RIGHT?

Here are the factors:

- 10 outs
- 4.25 to 1
- Bad position
- Good implied odds

With 10 outs, we only need odds of around 4 to 1 to call, so we are getting the right price. The other factors seem to cancel each other out. It's not a huge overlay, but this is worth a call, even for two bets. However, if you fold here, you are not making a big mistake.

THE OUTCOME

On this actual hand, the hero and the opener both called. The turn was the 5♠. The hero checked, the opener bet, the next player folded, and the hero check-raised. The opener called. The river was the 10♣, the hero bet, and the opener disgustedly folded, saying she had A-Q. The implied odds worked out great, with the hero getting another five small bets.

Can you really do all of this at the table? It may seem like a lot to go through at the table, but with some practice it gets easier. Take your time if you need to. Otherwise, write the hand down and analyze it the next day. Analyzing outs is a very important skill, and is worth investing some time in.

GAME SCENARIO #5

You have 8♦ 6♠ in the big blind. An early player limps, a middle player raises, the button and the small blind call. With good pot odds, you call, as does the early limper (10 bets, five players). The flop is A♠ 6♥ 4♠. The small blind checks and you check. The early limper bets and everyone except the small blind calls (13 bets, four players). What do you do?

With four players and an ace on the board, your pair of sixes probably isn't the best hand. What are your chances of improving? You have:

EVALUATING YOUR OUTS

OUT CARDS	# OF OUTS	WORRIES
8 (two pair)	3	Someone could have or make a bigger two pair. The ace on the board is a serious concern
6 (trips)	2	Not much. Someone could have a 6 with a bigger kicker.
Running 7, 5 (straight)	0.5	Anyone else with an 8 splits the pot.

You have around 5.5 possible outs. You need to discount the eights, so call it 4.5 outs. With thirteen bets in the pot, you only need 2.5 outs, so you have an easy call. Note that you should not count the backdoor flush. You could catch running spades, but the 6♠ is too weak to draw to. The turn is the 5♣.

YOUR HAND

THE BOARD

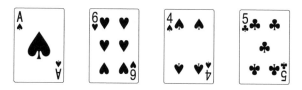

BETS IN THE POT: 7

The turn card gives you more outs. You now have:

OUT CARDS	# OF OUTS	WORRIES
8 (two pair)	3	Someone could have or make a bigger two pair. With an ace on the board, this is a serious concern.
6 (trips)	2	Not much. Someone could have a 6 with a bigger kicker.
7 (straight)	4	Anyone else with an 8 splits the pot. 9-8 gives someone a bigger straight.

You check, the early player bets, the middle player folds, and the button calls (9 bets, three players). What do you do?

With nine bets in the pot, you need around four to five outs to call. You have as many as nine. Even though they should be discounted, you have plenty for a call. The river is the 2♦, missing you completely. You check, the limper bets and the button calls. With a bet and a call, a pair of sixes isn't worth much, and you fold. If the button had folded, you should call with ten bets in the pot.

The limper had A♦ 4♥. He flopped two pair. The button had J♥ J♣. You only had around 2.5 outs on the flop, so you had a marginal call. You had six outs on the turn, so the call was correct.

GAME SCENARIO #6

You raise from middle position with Q♥ 10♥. The next player reraises. You are playing online, so you check her stats and she three-bets 19.5 percent of the time, which is extremely high. "Normal" is around 6 percent. You are the only one who calls (7.5 bets, two players). The flop is J♥ 4♦ 3♦. You check and she bets (8.5 bets). What do you do?

At first glance, it may appear that you have missed the flop. It looks like you just have some backdoor draws. But you also have an overcard, and it is possible that a 10 is an out if the raiser has a small pair. You need around five outs to play on. First, we have to decide what you should consider an out. You have two backdoor draws, one to a flush and one to a straight. Is a queen or a 10 an out? The top 19.5 percent of her hands consist of 6-6, A-4 suited, K-8 suited, Q-9 suited, J-9 suited, 10-9 suited and A-9. If she has any of these hands, your 10 is not an out (A-10, K-10, A-A, K-K, Q-Q, J-J, 10-10). But with most of those hands, your 10 is an out. A queen is even more likely to be an out.

OUT CARDS	# OF OUTS	WORRIES	DISCOUNTED OUTS
Queen	3	She could have a big pair or a queen with a bigger kicker.	2.5
10	3	She could have a big pair or a 10 with a bigger kicker.	2
Backdoor flush	2	No worries.	2
Backdoor straight	1.5	No worries.	1.5

That's 8.5 outs. Even if you discount the queen and 10, you easily have enough outs to play. By the way, if you play your hand against the three-bettor's range you win around 24 percent of the time. That is plenty to play a pot offering 8.5 to 1. What if the three-bettor is tighter? If you think a queen or 10 will win at least half the time, you should still call since you still have around five outs. Unless you are pretty sure the raiser has aces, kings or queens, you will have a call.

In the actual hand, the hero called. The turn was the Q♦. The hero checked and the villain checked behind him. (With three diamonds on the board, it is better to bet. You don't want to let the villain draw out by catching another diamond on the river.) The river was the 2♠, and the hero bet. The villain folded.

GAME SCENARIO #7

The hijack raises, the button calls, and the small blind calls. You call from the big blind with 5♦ 4♦ (8 bets, four players). The flop is 8♠ 6♦ 2♥. The small blind checks, you check, the hijack bets, the button raises, and the small blind calls (13 bets). What do you do?

To start with, the pot is currently offering you 6.5 to 1 pot odds. They may get better if the hijack calls. They may get worse if he reraises. With those pot odds you need around six or seven outs to call. The key here is to recognize that you have a double gutshot straight draw. Any 7 or 3 makes you a straight. That's eight outs right there. In addition, you have a backdoor flush draw worth two more outs. That's 10 outs total. Do you need to discount them? The straight outs are very strong. Your flush cards are low, but flush-over-flush isn't all that common. Even if you discount your backdoor flush a bit, you have plenty of outs to call.

On the actual hand, the hero called. The turn was the Q♦ and the river was the 3♠. The hero won the pot on the river with his straight. The other two hands on the river were the 8♦ 7♦ and 7♠ 7♣. As it turned out, the hero had a lot fewer outs than he thought. There was a bigger flush draw out there, so his flush outs were worthless. Three of his straight cards were in other hands, and the 3♦ (one of the straight outs) would have lost to a bigger flush. He actually had only five outs, and on the turn, he had only four outs. While this is clearly a call, this hand shows that you need to constantly be discounting your outs.

GAME SCENARIO #8

You have 8♥ 8♣ on the button. Two middle players **gypsy** (just call), you raise, and both blinds and the limpers call (10 bets, five players). The flop is 10♣ 9♥ 7♥. It is checked to you, and you bet. (With this coordinated board, you should probably check. You're lucky if you don't get raised.) Everyone calls (7.5 big bets, five players). The turn is the 9♠. The small blind bets, the big blind raises, the first limper calls, and the second limper folds (12.5 bets). What do you do?

This is a good example of having weak outs. In theory, you have 10 outs.

"OUT CARDS"	HOW MANY	BAD HANDS	COMMENTS
Eights	2	10-10, 9-9, 10-9, 9-8, 9-7	Even if you make a full house, yours will be smaller.
Sixes	4	Any hand with an 8, J-8, 7-7	The 6♥ can make a flush.
Jacks	4	Any hand with an 8, Q-8, K-Q, 7-7	The J♥ can make a flush.

You are getting just over 6 to 1 in pot odds. You need around seven outs to break even on a call. The two big questions are:

- How strong are your outs?
- Do the implied odds favor you or hurt you?

HOW STRONG ARE YOUR OUTS?

You should start with the fact that you may be drawing dead. Look at the hands that make a bigger full house. Those are the kinds of hands that limpers and blinds like to play. The other bad hands for you are flush draws and hands with an 8 in them. Limpers and blinds love suited hands and medium cards. It shouldn't shock you if players have these kinds of hands. Also consider that four players called your flop bet, and three of them seemed to love the turn card. This should reinforce your fear that dangerous hands are out there.

IMPLIED ODDS

As for implied odds, you should get some action if you make your hand and win. But there are three bad things that can happen:

1. You can make your hand and lose, which could be costly.
2. You can also make your hand and chop the pot. If anyone else has an 8, your eight straight outs are really only worth four outs, if that many.
3. Finally, someone could still raise on the turn, increasing your cost to see the river.

In the actual hand, the hero folded and the river was a 6. The first limper showed A-8 and won the pot. The hero would have split it with her. Actually, with another 8 out there, a fold is correct.

Now let's look at a recap of the rules for discounting your outs.

THE RULES FOR DISCOUNTING OUTS

1. Discount your outs if you don't know which outs are good.
2. Discount your outs if you have bad position.
3. Discount your outs if you are up against more than one villain and your call doesn't end the action.
4. Discount your outs if your hand may be dominated.

The next chapter discusses how to play drawing hands, which so many limit hold'em players like to play—and for some very good reasons.

5 PLAYING DRAWING HANDS

Playing drawing hands correctly—translate that "profitably"—is an important part of limit hold'em. Occasionally, a situation comes up in which it seems to cost very little to play a draw and the pot is offering attractive odds. The two most common situations are:

- You are in the small blind and several players have limped.
- You are in the big blind, the pot has been raised, and several players have called.

Some people will tell you to play any two cards in those cases. They are wrong. Here's a hand a friend asked about:

"I'm back in Vegas for two days. I played $30/$60 again last night for an hour. This hand was kind of interesting. The structure is $30 big blind and $20 small blind. Middle player limps. Late player limps. I toss in one chip ($10) to make the call from the small blind with 5-3 offsuit. Is there any hand you wouldn't call with?"

This chapter gives us an answer to my friend's question and many more.

THE VALUE OF DRAWS

Most players love drawing to straights and flushes. You have the chance to make a really strong hand. However, missing draws can become expensive. We've all had those nights. We miss draw after draw: 9-outers, 12-outers, and even 16-outers. Meanwhile, it seems like every donkey hits his 2-outer and 4-outer on the river to beat us. On those nights it feels like draws are a big hole that we throw our money into.

How valuable is a draw, really? Let's make a few assumptions:

- A villain has bet the flop.
- If you make it on the turn or river, you will win a big bet on the turn and another on the river, so you will win the current pot plus four more bets.
- If you miss on both streets, you will lose three bets (a small bet on the flop and a big bet on the turn).

Sometimes you will win even more bets when you hit. Sometimes, you will not get paid off on the river, while other times, it will cost you more than three bets to make it to the river, so these assumptions are probably a pretty good average. Here is the expectation for different pot sizes:

POT SIZE (SMALL BETS)	STRAIGHT-DRAW EXPECTATION (SMALL BETS)	FLUSH-DRAW EXPECTATION (SMALL BETS)
2	-0.17	0.15
3	0.15	0.50
4	0.46	0.85
5	0.77	1.20
6	1.09	1.55
7	1.40	1.90
8	1.72	2.25

These results may look pretty good, but remember that unless you were in the big blind in an unraised pot, you paid some money to get to this point. If you paid two bets to flop a straight draw, unless the pot is huge, you are losing money overall. You need pot odds of at least 4 to 1 before the flop to make it (slightly) profitable to flop a flush draw.

SUITED AND UNSUITED CONNECTORS

Suited connectors are very popular hands in no-limit hold'em. You can flop a huge hand or a huge draw, and make the kind of hand that is hard to read. It's the kind of hand that lets you win an opponent's entire stack. The common wisdom in limit hold'em is that these hands play well in volume pots, so you want to play them if there are lots of people in the pot and you can get in cheaply. Is the common wisdom true?

Take a minute to look over this chart. It may seem daunting, but a few minutes of study will pay big dividends. You will probably never look at small connectors quite the same way. Here are three important definitions:

Pair Plus Draw means a pair plus an open-ended straight draw or a flush draw.

Strong Hand means two pair or better, but does not include a pair or three-of-a-kind on the board. A board of Q-Q-7 does not qualify as giving you a strong hand when you have 8-7. This is treated as a pair.

Strong Draw means no pair and a draw with at least 12 outs.

The chart shows how often you will make various hands on the flop. The top part of the table shows how likely you are to make strong hands. You are just as likely to make hands like two pair, three of a kind, a full house, or four of a kind with any non-pair hand. You are also just as likely to make a flush with any two suited cards.

> The quality of your connectors is in the straights, strong draws, and pair-plus-draw hands.

THE CONNECTORS CHART
% CHANCE OF MAKING VARIOUS HANDS ON THE FLOP

	SUITED				UNSUITED			
	8-7s	8-6s	8-5s	8-4s	8-7	8-6	8-5	8-4
Straight Flush	0.02	0.015	0.01	0.005	0.00	0.00	0.00	0.00
Quads	0.01	0.01	0.01	0.01	0.01	0.01	0.01	0.01
Full House	0.09	0.09	0.09	0.09	0.09	0.09	0.09	0.09
Flush	0.82	0.83	0.83	0.84	0.00	0.00	0.00	0.00
Straight	1.29	0.96	0.64	0.32	1.31	0.98	0.65	0.33
Trips	1.35	1.35	1.35	1.35	1.35	1.35	1.35	1.35
Two Pair	2.02	2.02	2.02	2.02	2.02	2.02	2.02	2.02
Pair Plus Draw	3.06	2.60	2.14	1.68	2.00	1.52	1.04	0.56
Pair	25.90	26.36	26.82	27.28	26.96	27.44	27.92	28.40
No Pair w/Outs								
15 Outs	1.15	0.93	0.63	0.32	0.24	0.19	0.13	0.07
12 Outs	1.93	1.71	1.68	1.47	0.39	0.35	0.35	0.31
9 Outs	6.00	6.47	6.86	7.42	1.02	1.11	1.18	1.30
8 Outs	6.98	5.66	3.80	1.93	8.01	6.50	4.36	2.21
Strong Hand	8.66	7.88	7.10	6.32	6.78	5.97	5.16	4.36
Strong Draw	3.08	2.65	2.31	1.79	0.62	0.54	0.48	0.38
Ordinary Draw	12.98	12.14	10.65	9.35	9.03	7.61	5.54	3.51
Strong Hand or Strong Draw	11.74	10.53	9.41	8.11	7.40	6.51	5.64	4.74
Strong Hand or Any Draw	21.64	20.02	17.75	15.67	15.81	13.58	10.70	7.87
Strong Hand, Pair, Any Draw	47.54	46.38	44.57	42.94	42.77	41.02	38.62	36.27

To repeat, the quality of your connectors is in the straights, strong draws, and pair-plus-draw hands. This is important because the really profitable hands are the strong hands (including pair plus draw), and the strong draws. Every one of these three profitable categories decreases as your connectors get weaker; therefore, the hands that you really want become less frequent as your connectors get weaker. This shouldn't be news to most players, but the following table allows you to see how much weaker the different draws are.

COMPARISON OF VARIOUS DRAWS % CHANCE OF MAKING VARIOUS HANDS ON THE FLOP								
	SUITED				UNSUITED			
	8-7s	8-6s	8-5s	8-4s	8-7	8-6	8-5	8-4
Straight	1.29	0.96	0.64	0.32	1.31	0.98	0.65	0.33
Strong Draw	3.08	2.65	2.31	1.79	0.62	0.54	0.48	0.38
Pair Plus Draw	3.06	2.60	2.14	1.68	2.00	1.52	1.04	0.56

Here are the hands you are really hoping for:

MOST DESIRED HANDS % CHANCE OF MAKING THE HAND ON THE FLOP								
	SUITED				UNSUITED			
	8-7s	8-6s	8-5s	8-4s	8-7	8-6	8-5	8-4
Strong Hand or Strong Draw	11.74	10.53	9.41	8.11	7.40	6.51	5.64	4.74

As you can see, even in the best of circumstances, they aren't that frequent. When you start playing weaker hands, the good hands drop off. Playing 8-7s is almost three times as likely to put a smile on your face as playing 8-4 (assuming you are playing online and don't have your poker face on). 8-7s is 50 percent better than 8-4s.

Of course these aren't the only playable flops for you. Most of the draws you will flop will be ordinary straight or flush draws, and they are more frequent than big hands or big draws until you get to the really weak connectors. However, as we noted in the previous section, flopping a draw isn't all that profitable unless the pot is pretty big.

ORDINARY HANDS							
% CHANCE OF MAKING THE HAND ON THE FLOP							
	SUITED				UNSUITED		
	8-7s	8-6s	8-5s	8-4s	8-7	8-6	8-5	8-4
Ordinary Draw	12.98	12.14	10.65	9.35	9.03	7.61	5.54	3.51

Other than missing entirely, the single most common outcome is to flop a pair. Now, let's apply these results.

PLAYING CONNECTORS
IN MULTIWAY POTS

Two players limp. You are on the button with 8♠ 7♠. The small blind is very tight and probably won't play, so the pot is offering you 3.5 to 1. Should you call?

COMPARISON OF VARIOUS DRAWS							
% CHANCE OF MAKING VARIOUS HANDS ON THE FLOP							
	SUITED				UNSUITED		
	8-7s	8-6s	8-5s	8-4s	8-7	8-6	8-5	8-4
Strong Hand	8.66	7.88	7.10	6.32	6.78	5.97	5.16	4.36
Strong Hand or Any Draw	21.64	20.02	17.75	15.67	15.81	13.58	10.70	7.87

You make a strong hand that is likely to win the pot only 8.7 percent of the time. The other 13 percent of the time, you are on a draw. Assume that when you win, you will win a bet on every street. The following chart shows how it works out.

OUTCOME	PROBABILITY	WIN/LOSS	EXPECTATION
Big Hand	8.7%	8.5	0.74
Flop a Draw/ Win	4.3%	8.5	0.37
Flop a Draw/ Lose	8.7%	-4	-0.35
Miss the Flop	78.3%	-1	-0.78
TOTAL			-0.02

It's pretty close, but it's a small loser. Some good things could happen. You might get more action when you hit your hand or you might win with only 1 pair. If the small blind calls, this adds another half a bet to the pot and it becomes profitable. But bad things can happen, too. You could also get raised before the flop. You could make your hand and lose.

The next chart lists my suggestions for the pot odds you need to play different hands.

POT ODDS NEEDED TO PLAY VARIOUS HANDS

HAND	POT ODDS NEEDED
8-7s	4
8-6s	4.5
8-5s	5.5
8-4s	7.0
8-7	6.5
8-6	8.0
8-5	10.0
8-4	13.5

Keep these points in mind:

- **Position matters**. You would prefer to play these hands from the button rather than from the small blind, but you are more likely to get the right price when you are in the blinds. However, keep in mind that position matters more in small pots than in big ones.

- **Size matters**. J-10s is better than 8-7s. If you make one pair or two pair, you are more likely to have top pair or top two pair. If you make a straight, you are more likely to have the nut straight. If you make a flush, you are less likely to lose to a bigger flush, particularly if a fourth card of the flush suit comes down.

- **Connectedness matters**. The bigger the gap between your two cards, the harder it is to flop a big hand or big draw.

The issue of the size of your hand isn't just theoretical. Consider this example of a hand I recently played. Everyone folds to me in the small blind. I raise with 5♥ 2♥. The big blind calls (4 bets, two players). The flop is A♠ 7♦ 4♦. I make the continuation bet and he calls (3 big bets). The turn is the lovely 3♠. Again I bet and he calls (5 bets). The river is the ugly 5♠. I bet and he calls. He turns over 7♥ 6♥. First I curse my bad luck in losing, and then I thank the poker gods that he didn't find the nerve to raise me. I throw in another prayer of gratitude that hearts didn't come. This hand illustrates how bigger cards can lead to having the good end of a straight-versus-straight contest.

Now let's return to the question we started this chapter with: "I'm back in Vegas for two days. I played $30/$60 again last night for an hour. This hand was kind of interesting. The structure is $30 big blind and $20 small blind. Middle player limps. Late player limps. I toss in one chip ($10) to make the call from the small blind with 5-3 offsuit. Is there any hand you wouldn't call with?"

Looking at the chart above, with 5-3 offsuit, you need 8 to 1 to call. With 14 bets in the pot, this is an easy call. But what about 7-2, the worst hand in hold'em? If we look at The Connectors Chart, we see a hand that almost cannot flop a draw. (You could flop a weak draw if the board came 6-5-4.) Without going through all the numbers, you need pot odds of around 22 to 1 to call.

The answer to the question is: You should not call with any two cards.

PLAYING CONNECTORS HEADS UP

Since good connectors play better in big pots than in medium pots, many people assume that they are not very good hands against one opponent. This is not necessarily true. Let's look at part of The Connectors Chart.

COMPARISON OF VARIOUS DRAWS								
% CHANCE OF MAKING VARIOUS HANDS ON THE FLOP								
	SUITED				UNSUITED			
	8-7s	8-6s	8-5s	8-4s	8-7	8-6	8-5	8-4
Ordinary Draw	12.98	12.14	10.65	9.35	9.03	7.61	5.54	3.51
Strong Hand, Pair, Any Draw	47.54	46.38	44.57	42.94	42.77	41.02	38.62	36.27

Suppose a player raises in middle position. Everyone folds to you on the button and you have 8♦ 7♦. What should you do? You can make a good case for folding, calling or raising.

THE CASE FOR FOLDING

- You have less than a 50 percent chance of making a hand you will play on with.
- Many of your playable hands are draws, which you will miss two-thirds of the time.
- According to PokerStove, a free program you can download and use to compare hands, you only win around 35 percent of the time against most openers.

THE CASE FOR CALLING

- You have position on the opener.
- If an ace or big cards come on the flop, you can get away from the hand cheaply.
- If small cards come on the flop, you can frequently steal the pot by raising on the flop.

THE CASE FOR RAISING

- You have position on the opener.
- You usually keep out the blinds, improving your chances of winning with one pair.
- It is easier to steal.
- Stealing costs the same as calling preflop and raising on the flop, but is more likely to succeed.
- If you win and show the hand, others will think of you as a wild and unpredictable player. You will get more calls with your legitimate hands.

WHAT'S THE RIGHT ANSWER?

There is no right answer here. It depends on your style, your table image, your assessment of the opener, and so on. Note that if the opener is tight, you should lean toward raising. It is far easier to steal the pot when small cards flop. Tight players frequently don't like calling without a hand, particularly after they get three-bet.

Strong, aggressive players often like to raise with suited connectors. Some of them may do it with one-gap and two-gap connectors as well. When you see someone make this play, don't assume that they are maniacs, unless you see them make other "wild" plays as well. Raising could indicate a maniac, but it could also mean that the villain is a strong player. Suited connectors in position play better heads-up than is commonly believed.

HOW MUCH IS BEING SUITED WORTH?

Let us calculate the gain in expected value from being suited. How much more expectation can you expect against an aggressive player if your hand is suited? If you go back to the Connectors Chart, you will see that by playing 8-7s instead of 8-7, you will increase your chance of making these hands:

HAND	MORE LIKELY WHEN SUITED
STRONG HAND	1.88%
STRONG DRAW	2.46%
FLUSH DRAW	3.95%

How likely are you to win with each of these types of hands? Let's assume that each of these hands wins 90 percent of the time when it hits.

HAND	MORE LIKELY WHEN SUITED	MAKES A GOOD HAND	WIN/ LOSS	WIN %	LOSE %
Strong Hand Wins	1.88%	100%	90%	1.69%	
Strong Hand Loses	1.88%	100%	10%		0.19%
Strong Draw Improves/Wins	2.46%	51.5%	90%	1.14%	
Strong Draw Improves/Loses	2.46%	51.5%	10%		.012%
Strong Draw Misses	2.46%	48.5%	100%		1.19%
Flush Draw Improves/Wins	3.95%	36.4%	90%	1.29%	
Flush Draw Improves/Loses	3.95%	36.4%	10%		0.14%
Flush Draw Misses	3.95%	63.6%	100%		2.51%

Overall, we win 4.13 percent and lose 4.16 percent when our suited cards help us. Remember that we win 7.25 bets when we win, and lose 6.0 bets when we lose. So overall, a suited hand is worth around 0.05 big bets. We don't want to play a lot more hands just because we are suited.

Now, let's look at a few action hands in which connected cards are being played.

CONNECTED CARDS: FOUR GAME SCENARIOS

GAME SCENARIO #1

An aggressive player opens from the hijack. The hero reraises with 5♣ 4♣ from the cutoff. Everyone else folds (5.5 bets, two players). The flop is J♠ 7♣ 4♥. The villain checks, the hero bets and the villain calls (3.75 big bets, two players). The turn is the 3♦. The villain checks, the hero bets, and the villain calls (5.75 bet, two players). The river is the 2♣. The villain checks, and the hero checks behind him. When the hero shows his pair of fours, the villain mucks K♠ Q♥. This hand shows the power of having one pair heads-up.

GAME SCENARIO #2

A middle player opens, and the hero calls from the small blind with 8♠ 7♠. (You should be less likely to raise with suited connectors out of position.) Everyone else folds (5 bets, two players). The flop is A♦ K♣ 10♦. The hero checks, the villain bets, and the hero folds. This hand is an example of how easy it is to get away from suited connectors with an unfavorable flop.

GAME SCENARIO #3

A player who raises preflop very aggressively opens from the hijack. He is not usually that aggressive the rest of the way. The hero reraises with 9♦ 8♦. The big blind messes up the strategy of getting heads up with the opener by calling (9.5

bets, three players). However, the flop cooperates by coming 10♣ 9♥ 8♠. They both check to the hero. He bets, and they both call. The turn is the 3♠. They both check, the hero bets, and they both call. The river is the A♦. They both check, the hero bets his two pair, the big blind calls and the opener folds. The big blind loses with A-J.

The big blind probably didn't raise on the river because he was afraid of a hand such as A-K or Q-J, since it would be hard to put the hero on two pair. This illustrates how this type of raise makes it harder for others to read you. And you can be sure that some players will remember this hand. If the hero three-bets later with A-A or K-K, he is likely to get more action. This is the best of all worlds. The hero wins a pot with 10 big bets in it, and he gets to sow seeds of doubt in his opponents' minds. This hand illustrates a successful raise with suited connectors.

GAME SCENARIO #4

Just to keep things in perspective, here is an example of when raising with suited connectors didn't work. A middle player raises, and the hero reraises from the cutoff with J♠ 10♠. Everyone folds back to the opener, who raises again. The hero calls (9.5 bets, two players). The flop is A♥ 5♦ 3♠. Opener bets. The hero has nothing but a couple of backdoor draws, and he folds. This hand cost him four small bets. The hand also points out the danger of overdoing this type of late-position raise: Observant, aggressive players will start to play back at you. This hand demonstrates that raising with suited connectors doesn't always work.

DOUBLE GUTSHOT STRAIGHTS

A **double gutshot straight draw**—also known as a double inside straight draw, double gutter, double belly buster, or double gut buster—occurs when cards of two different ranks will make you a straight, but both are inside straight draws. Double gutshot straights are sometimes hard to recognize. I have seen cases where a player hit a straight and didn't realize it because he didn't realize he actually was drawing to one.

There are two patterns of cards in double gutshot straight draws: the 1-3-1 and the 2-2-2. The 1-3-1 can occur on the flop or turn. The 2-2-2 can only occur on the turn.

PATTERN #1: 1-3-1

A 1-3-1 double gutshot occurs when your cards and the board cards include:

1	3	1
A	Q-J-10	8
K	J-10-9	7
Q	10-9-8	6
J	9-8-7	5
10	8-7-6	4
9	7-6-5	3
8	6-5-4	2
7	5-4-3	A

They key to recognizing these hands is the run of three consecutive cards in the middle of the pattern. Any time you see three consecutive cards when you combine your hand with the board, look for a double gutter.

As with all other draws, whether you use one of your cards or both of them is critical to evaluating how strong your draw is. Look at these two examples:

HAND ONE

THE BOARD

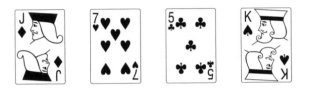

HAND TWO

THE BOARD

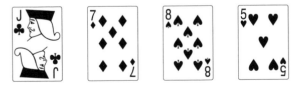

In both cases, you have a double gutshot draw. A 10 or a 6 will make you a straight, but the first hand is much stronger than the second one, since you must use both cards to make your straight. If you make your straight, you will only have to share the pot with someone else who has 9-8. In the second case, you will need to share the pot with anyone who has a nine in his hand. This is much more likely, so you should treat this as a weaker hand.

In addition, the first hand will make your straight harder to recognize, increasing the chance that you will get good action if you hit. A board of J-7-5-K-6 doesn't look that threatening. With the second hand, it will be easier for someone to put you on a straight. With a board of J-7-8-5-10, anyone will recognize that it only takes a 9 to make a straight. This will slow down the action.

PATTERN #2: 2-2-2

A 2-2-2 double gutshot is even easier to miss than a 1-3-1. It happens when your cards and the board cards include:

2	2	2
A-K	J-10	8-7
K-Q	10-9	7-6
Q-J	9-8	6-5
J-10	8-7	5-4
10-9	7-6	4-3
9-8	6-5	3-2
8-7	5-4	2-A

Notice the pattern: two cards, gap, two cards, gap, two cards. For example, K-Q (gap) 10-9 (gap) 7-6. To get a feel for things that can go wrong with draws, let's take a look at three drawing hands in action.

DRAWING HANDS: THREE GAME SCENARIOS

1: CHASING A WEAK DRAW ON A COORDINATED BOARD

A middle player limps into the pot and I look down at 8♥ 8♣. There are two ways to play this hand. First, I can raise the opener, hope no one else calls, and get heads up with a player when I am likely the favorite. The other way to go is to call, hope for a lot of players, pray to spike an 8 and win a big pot with my set. This is a very loose game, and I have been playing tight. If I raise, I am unlikely to get everyone out; and if I call, I am likely to get lots of company and good pot odds. It's an easy decision. I call. The button also calls, as well as both blinds. Five players take the flop of 10♥ 9♦ 7♦ (5 bets).

Both blinds check and the middle player bets. It's on me. Raise, call, or fold? I figure that with this board, he could be on a draw. If I can get everyone else out, I am ahead. That's two big "ifs!" So, I raise. The button calls two bets. Both blinds fold. The bettor reraises. I call again. The button also calls. It costs me three bets to get to the turn, where a blank comes. I finally fold when the middle player bets. The button calls.

MY HAND

THE BOARD

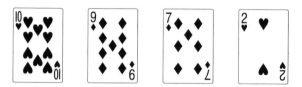

WHAT'S WRONG WITH MY PLAY?

Five players on a draw-heavy board is the wrong time to try to make a play or try to run over the table. Also, I have no diamond. This is important since it makes it a bit more likely that someone has a diamond draw (folks love to limp with suited cards). It's also not a huge pot, with only six small bets in it when it gets to me. So how good is my hand?

I seem to have a lot of outs. A jack or 6 makes a straight, and an 8 gives me a set. That's 10 outs. However, most of those outs aren't very good. First, the J♦ or the 6♦ could make me a straight, but someone else could make a flush. A non-diamond jack or 6 would make me a straight, but then a diamond on the river could kill me. If a jack comes, I lose to anyone with K-Q or Q-8 and chop the pot if anyone else has an 8. Only the three non-diamond sixes are fairly clean outs, but I could be splitting the pot with another 8, and losing to J-8. And I can still lose if a diamond hits on the river.

As for an 8 flopping, that puts four parts of a straight on the board (10-9-8-7). To feel good about flopping an 8, I probably need to flop an 8 and have the board pair. I have no clean outs and few good ones. Once I raise, there are three live players behind me who could reraise. The right play here is to fold. As it turned out, the button had K♦ Q♦ (two overcards, a flush draw, and a gutshot straight draw) and made a straight on the river when a jack came, one of my so-called "outs."

THE LESSON

- **You should mix up your play with middle pairs.**
  The nature of the game and your table image should be deciding factors. In a loose game, where lots of people will call for two bets, there isn't much point to raising. In a tighter game where you are likely to drive people out, raising makes more sense. Also, you should raise more if you have been playing tight and showing a lot of good hands. If you have been more active, lean toward calling. You are less likely to get heads up with the limper.

- **In a loose game, play medium pairs like small pairs.**
  In a tight game, play them like big pairs. If more than one thing has to work well for a play to succeed, don't count on both of them to happen. If there's a 40 percent chance that each event will happen, there is only a 16 percent chance they both will happen.

- **Discount outs that might leave you with the second-best hand if they come in.**
  Discount outs that might be killed if the right card comes on the turn and the wrong one comes on the river. You might put a lot of money in before that river card comes. Chasing with a hand when you aren't too sure you want to get there is a great way to put someone else's kids through college.

2: CALLING A RAISE WITH A FOUR FLUSH ON THE BOARD

I raise with 10♦ 10♣ from three seats off the button. A new player in the next seat reraises. Everyone else folds and I call (7.5 bets, two players). The flop is Q♥ 6♣ 3♣. I check, he bets, and I call. The turn is the J♣. I check, he bets and I call. The river is the A♣. I figure he might pay me off with a smaller club or a hand with an ace or queen in it, and I bet. He raises. I call. He shows K♠ K♣.

MY HAND

THE BOARD

WHAT'S WRONG WITH MY PLAY?

I have to either bet and fold on the river, or just check. Either play is better than my actual line of play. Betting is fine. The pot is big and many players will call with weaker hands. And there are only two cards in the deck I lose to. But following that with a call is not good. If I am not prepared to fold, because I am suspicious of a new player I should just check.

His raise before the flop makes it likely he has big cards. He could have a medium pair, but the big cards are more likely. If he has a club, there is a good chance that it is the K♣ or Q♣. When I bet and get raised, what can he possibly have that I can beat? Very few people will raise in that spot with less than the nuts. Also, it is very difficult for him to make a move here without a big club, since he cannot know that I don't have one.

THE LESSON

- **When a player raises on the river with a four flush showing on the board, he almost always has the top flush.**

  If someone has shown a lot of strength, he is likely to have big cards in his hand. When you value bet on the river with a medium flush that uses only one of your cards, be prepared to fold to a raise. If the opponent is aggressive, tricky or unknown, tend to check and call instead of betting.

3: BACKING OFF A BIG DRAW

A solid player opens on the button. The small blind folds, and I call in the big blind with Q♠ 6♠. The flop is A♠ K♦ 6♠. I check and the button bets. I'm afraid he will reraise with an ace, so I just call. The turn is the 4♣. I check, he bets, and I call. The river is the 10♣. We both check. He shows 10♥ 8♥, winning the pot with a pair of tens.

MY HAND

THE BOARD

WHAT'S WRONG WITH MY PLAY?

Check-raising the flop is not optional; it is mandatory. There are too many hands he could have raised with that he will fold to my check-raise. I'm going to the river anyway, so I need to put him to the test to see if he will fold.

As to my fear of getting reraised, so what? I have nine outs to a flush and five outs to two pair or trips, plus a backdoor straight out worth another half an out. I have 14.5 outs, which means I have a 52 percent chance of getting there by the river—assuming that I don't have the best hand right now. Putting in another bet if he has an ace doesn't cost me money, and it could make me money. The chance of winning the pot far outweighs any loss to a raise. Actually, my failure to raise probably cost me the pot.

THE LESSON

• **When you have a big draw on the flop, *always* raise.**

The next chapter is all about raising—when you can raise, how strong a hand you need, who you can raise against, and who will call you every time.

6 PLAYING RAISING HANDS

RAISING IN MULTIWAY POTS

I recently read an article that made the following recommendations: "If five players limp and you are on the button with 5♣ 5♠, you should raise. If five players limp and you are on the button with J♦ 10♦, you should raise."

I used PokerStove.com and assumed that six players each had 9-9 through 2-2, A-9s through A-2s, K-10s, K-9s Q-9s, J-9s, 10-8s, 9-7s, 8-6s, 7-5s, 6-4s, 5-4s, 4-3s, 3-2s, K-10, Q-10, or J-10. I gave them pretty wide ranges because so many players were in the hand. Here are the results with 5♣ 5♠:

	WIN PERCENT
Limpers	14.4%
You	13.4%

You would be raising when you have the worst hand, but it is even worse. You win 13.4 percent of the time when you go to the river. But will you get to the river? If someone bets, you are getting around 13 to 1 to draw to a two-out hand. You aren't going to be able to call, so you will generally only win when you flop a set, which happens only around 11.5% of the time—and you won't win 100 percent of the time when you do.

It is conceivable that everyone will check to the raiser and give you a free card on the flop, but with five villains, this isn't very likely. That would give you a chance to make a set on the turn. With only an 11 percent chance of having the best hand on the flop, this is not a good time to be raising.

How about raising with J♦ 10♦? The results are almost the same.

	WIN PERCENT
Limpers	14.4%
You	13.7%

This hand is a little better than with the 5♣ 5♠, since: (1) You are more likely to go to the river, so you will win more often; and (2) You are mostly drawing to a straight or a flush that is a bigger hand than a set. It is a little worse with J♦ 10♦, in that your hand is less disguised. Usually, people will suspect a flush if three diamonds hit the board, but will not suspect a set of fives, particularly after you have raised preflop.

RAISING AGAINST SIX LIMPERS

Here are the results of some hands that you have raised against six limpers:

HAND	WIN %	LIMPERS WIN %
5♣ 5♠	13.4%	14.4%
6♣ 6♠	14.1%	14.3%
7♣ 7♠	15.2%	14.1%
8♣ 8♠	16.6%	13.9%
9♣ 9♠	17.7%	13.7%
J♦ 10♦	13.7%	14.4%
Q♦ J♦	15.1%	14.1%
K♦ 10♦	14.8%	14.2%
K♦ J♦	16.4%	13.9%
K♦ Q♦	17.8%	13.7%

You can raise with 7-7, Q-Js, and K-10s or better; however, you don't have to raise if you don't want to increase your variance.

RAISING AGAINST FOUR LIMPERS

What if there are fewer than six limpers?

HAND	WIN %	LIMPERS WIN %
5♣ 5♠	18.5%	20.44%
6♣ 6♠	19.8%	20.0%
7♣ 7♠	21.7%	19.6%
8♣ 8♠	24.0%	19.0%
9♣ 9♠	26.6%	18.3%
J♦ 10♦	19.8%	20.1%
Q♦ 10♦	20.3%	19.9%
Q♦ J♦	22.0%	19.5%
K♦ 10♦	21.6%	19.6%
K♦ J♦	23.8%	19.1%
K♦ Q♦	25.6%	18.6%

The raising hands remain the same, namely 7-7, Q-Js, and K-10s or better. Q-10s is marginal, and I wouldn't raise with it. Note, however, that not everyone limps with as wide a range as I used in this analysis.

RAISING AGAINST THREE LIMPERS

For three limpers, I tightened up their range to: 9-9 through 2-2, A-9s through A-2s, K-10s, K-9s, Q-9s, J-9s, 10-9s, 9-8s, 8-7s, 7-6s, 6-5s, K-10, Q-10, and J-10.

HAND	WIN %	LIMPERS WIN %
5♣ 5♠	23.7%	25.4%
6♣ 6♠	25.5%	24.8%
7♣ 7♠	27.8%	24.1%
8♣ 8♠	30.3%	23.2%
9♣ 9♠	33.5%	22.1%
J♦ 10♦	23.2%	25.6%
Q♦ 10♦	23.9%	25.4%
Q♦ J♦	26.0%	24.7%
K♦ 10♦	26.0%	24.7%
K♦ J♦	28.5%	23.8%
K♦ Q♦	30.1%	23.1%

The raising hands still remain the same: 7-7, Q-Js, and K-10s or better.

RAISING AGAINST TWO LIMPERS

For this calculation, I dropped 6-5s from the limpers' range and included only 9-9 through 2-2, A-9s through A-2s, K-10s, K-9s, Q-9s, J-9 s, 10-9s, 9-8s, 8-7s, 7-6s, K-10, Q-10, and J-10.

HAND	WIN %	LIMPERS WIN %
5♣ 5♠	32.5%	33.7%
6♣ 6♠	34.7%	32.6%
7♣ 7♠	37.6%	31.2%
8♣ 8♠	40.9%	29.6%
9♣ 9♠	45.0%	27.5%
J♦ 10♦	30.4%	34.8%
Q♦ 10♦	31.7%	34.6%
Q♦ J♦	34.4%	32.8%
K♦ 9♦	31.8%	34.1%
K♦ 10♦	35.0%	32.5%
K♦ J♦	38.0%	31.0%
K♦ Q♦	40.9%	29.6%

With only two limpers, 6-6 becomes a raising hand. Therefore, you can raise with 6-6, Q-Js, and K-10s or better.

SOME CONCLUSIONS

I do not recommend that you raise with all of these hands. In particular, I usually would not raise with 7-7, 8-8 or 9-9 in a multiway pot, because I am basically playing them as small pairs. If I don't make a set, I usually fold them; and unless I flop a set, these hands are very difficult to play in a multiway pot.

Even if you end up with an overpair, the flop is likely to hit a bunch of limpers. Suppose you have 8-8 and the flop is 7-6-3. It isn't too hard to see how this could give a limper two pair or a straight draw. If there are two suited cards, it is even more dangerous. Finally, players with two overcards are likely to be drawing against you. You aren't folding 8-8 here, but you will often end up losing on the turn or river with them.

With the other hands listed on the chart, I do recommend raising. There are several advantages to raising with them instead of calling:

- You have a chance to drive out the blinds; dead money is always good.
- You may be able to knock out people behind you, improving your position.
- If you have an above-average hand, you gain additional equity by increasing the pot size.
- By increasing the pot size, you make it more likely that you will get action when you hit your hand. While this increases the chances that someone will draw out on you, it will increase your profit in the long run, even if your volatility increases.
- Raising with a hand like Q-Js will give people the false impression that you are a looser player than you actually are.

- You might be able to get a free card. If you have a hand such as 7-7 and hit a 7 on the turn, it will be worth a lot to you.

WOULD YOU EVER RAISE PREFLOP AND THEN FOLD?

Most of the time, when you put any money in before the flop, you will see the flop. Are there any exceptions? Consider this situation: The game has been very tight with lots of walks, so you raise under the gun with K-Q. The cutoff, a solid player reraises. The small blind, another solid player makes it four bets. These are both players who will respect an under-the-gun raise. The first raiser has a real hand. The second raiser has a real hand. You can figure him for Q-Q, K-K, A-A, or A-K, at the very worst. This is not a guy who makes four-bet moves.

When this happened to me, I looked at my K-Q and I couldn't see how I was anything but a big dog against the small blind. I had never before raised preflop and then folded without seeing the flop—but there's always a first.

Did I play this hand badly? No, not in this case. My read on the small blind was perfect: He had A-A. The other player had 10-10 and put a bad beat on the small blind when the river card was a 10. I gleefully watched the carnage from the sidelines.

Shortly after this hand, a similar situation came up. I opened from middle position with K-Q. The cutoff reraised. The small blind capped it. The button had A♦ J♦. The small blind had A♥ K♦. As the cards lie, the pot is offering my 5.5 to 1 to call (11 small bets), and I have a 23.6 percent chance of winning, so it is an overlay. In this example, I was very fortunate that the capper didn't have a big pair. If he had had one, I would have been in very bad shape. So what is the right play? A lot depends on the ranges of hands your opponents will play.

Look at the following charts to see what I mean.

EIGHT RANGE CHARTS

(1) If both players are tight, you are not getting the pot odds to call.

PLAYER	HANDS	WIN %
You	K-Q	14%
Cap	Q-Q, A-K	54%
3-Bet	9-9, A-10s, K-Qs	32%

(2) Add J-J and 10-10 to the capper's range and you are barely getting the right price. However, I still think you should fold because, unless you flop exactly K-Q-X, K-K-X, or Q-Q-X, you are going to have a hard time playing your hand.

PLAYER	HANDS	WIN %
You	K-Q	18%
Cap	10-10, A-K	47%
3-Bet	9-9, A-10s, K-Qs, A-K	35%

(3) If the three-bettor is weaker, it doesn't help you, but it does help the capper.

PLAYER	HANDS	WIN %
You	K-Q	19%
Cap	10-10, A-K	50%
3-Bet	7-7, A-9s, K-Js, Q-Js, A-Q, K-Q	31%

(4) If the four-bettor is looser, it doesn't help you much either.

PLAYER	HANDS	WIN %
You	K-Q	19%
Cap	9-9, A-Qs, K-Qs, Q-Js, A-K	42%
3-Bet	9-9, A-10s K-Qs, A-K	39%

(5) Even if they are both pretty loose, calling is still not that great a play.

PLAYER	HANDS	WIN %
You	K-Q	20%
Cap	9-9, A-Qs, K-Qs, Q-Js, A-K	45%
3-Bet	7-7, A-9s, K-Js, Q-Js, A-Q, K-Q	35%

(6) If both players are aggressive and the capper is on the button, there will be 11.5 bets in the pot. You need around 15 percent chance of winning to call, so you're getting the right price.

PLAYER	HANDS	WIN %
You	K-Q	21%
Cap	8-8, A-Qs, K-Qs, A-K	44%
3-Bet	6-6, A-10s, K-Js, Q-Js, A-Q	35%

(7) If the capper is the small blind, the pot is a little smaller, and the capper will play a few more hands (11 bets, 15 percent required), again the price is right to call.

PLAYER	HANDS	WIN %
You	K-Q	23%
Cap	6-6, A-Js, K-Qs, A-Q	40%
3-Bet	6-6, A-10s, K-Js, Q-Js, A-Q	37%

(8) When the capper is the big blind, the pot is a bit smaller (10 bets), but you are still winning more than the 16 percent, so you need to call.

PLAYER	HANDS	WIN %
You	K-Q	23%
Cap	6-6, A-10s, K-10s, Q-10s, A-J, K-Q	41%
3-Bet	6-6, A-10s, K-Js, Q-Js, A-Q	35%

SOME CONCLUSIONS

Against aggressive players, you wouldn't fold, but against very tight players you should. Keep in mind that if you flop one pair, however, that you will have a hard time knowing where you stand after the flop. If you are calling aggressive players, you will have a hard time getting away from your hand. If you don't have position on at least one of the villains, you might still consider folding.

SHOULD YOU CHECK-RAISE ON THE TURN?

This hand led to a heated discussion among a group of strong players. The cutoff, the button, and the small blind limp. You take the free play from the big blind with 10♣ 9♠ (4 bets, four players). The flop comes A♦ J♦ 9♣. The small blind bets, you call (which is not a great idea), the cutoff raises, and everyone calls. You call (6 big bets, four players). The turn is the 9♥. The small blind checks. What would you do?

A number of good players heatedly argued for a check-raise on the turn. The argument is that the cutoff is likely to bet and you could trap one or two more players for two bets. You will make a lot more money that way. The other possibility is that the cutoff has a big draw or a hand such as K♦ J♠. In this case, he might check and then it could get checked around. Getting absolutely no action on the turn and giving free cards to everyone is a terrible outcome.

The first question is, "What is your goal here?" Do you want to get more money into the pot? Do you want to eliminate player to decrease the chance that someone will draw out on you? To some extent you want to do both, and it is not clear which option is better for either goal. Let's consider these three likely possibilities:

ACTIONS	BETS IN POT	PLAYERS
You bet and get two callers.	9	3
You check and everyone else checks	6	4
You check, the cutoff bets, one player calls, and you raise. Both players call.	12	3

If the cutoff bets more than half the time, you get more money in the pot with the check-raise. If he doesn't, you lose money. Will he bet more than half the time? It depends on the player. He raised on the flop and got three callers, including a player who called two bets cold. That could easily slow him down, particularly since some people will raise on the flop with a wide range of hands.

There are several reasons I lean toward betting:

- I hate the idea of giving a free card here. If there is any chance to eliminate a player or charge him to draw, I will take it.
- The cutoff still may raise, and I still get to build a pot here.
- If the cutoff flopped a set and turned a full house, the check-raise will cost me more money. If I bet and get raised, I can just call, which only costs me two big bets.
- A check-raise on the turn is a more intimidating move than a bet on the turn. By betting, I am more likely to get paid off on the river, and maybe by more than one person.

This is a lot to think about in the heat of battle. I suggest that when you are torn between betting or trying for a check-raise, usually bet unless you are confident that someone else will bet. A raise on the flop is often not enough to give you that confidence, so don't automatically check to the raiser.

SHOULD YOU FIRE A SECOND BARREL?

One of the most common situations in limit hold'em occurs when you open with a raise and only the big blind calls. Then you bet the flop and the big blind again calls. Then you face a big decision: If you don't have anything, should you bet again on the turn? If your opponent is very predictable, your decision is easy. If the villain tends to fold on the flop unless he has a pair, you should give up. If your opponent frequently calls a bet on the flop but usually folds on the turn, you should always bet the turn.

Frequently, however, your opponent will not be this predictable, or you may not be familiar with his play. In that case, several factors should influence your decision:

- How big is the top card on the board?
- Are there any possible draws on the flop?
- How aggressive is your opponent?
- How loose is he?

Let's look at each factor to see how it works at the table.

FOUR FACTORS TO CONSIDER

1. HOW BIG IS THE TOP CARD?

Obviously, with an ace or king on the board, it is impossible for a player to call your flop bet with two overcards. He is more likely to have a pair. With a flop like 8♥ 5♦ 2♠, the chances that a player has two overcards are much higher. Many players will call a bet on the flop with overcards and give it up on the turn. You should tend to bet again.

2. ARE ANY DRAWS POSSIBLE?

If few draws are possible on the flop, it becomes more likely that your opponent has a pair and will continue to call. You should be more likely to give up a hopeless hand.

3. IS YOUR OPPONENT AGGRESSIVE OR PASSIVE?

There are two reasons you should be more likely to check to an aggressive opponent on the turn, particularly if you have a hand with some showdown value. First, if you bet, there is a chance he will raise, forcing you into a difficult decision.

Second, by checking, you might induce a bluff on the river. Against a passive player, you can fold to a raise on the turn. If the hand progresses to the river, the passive player won't bluff the river.

4. HOW LOOSE IS YOUR OPPONENT?

A loose player will call in the big blind with a wide variety of hands, and call on the flop with a lot of marginal hands. Because of this, a loose player will have a lot more hands that he will need to give up on the turn.

FIVE RULES FOR FIRING
ANOTHER BARREL

Considering each of the four influential factors in deciding whether to fire another barrel, we come up with the following general rules:

1. If the top card on the flop is not too high, tend to bet.
2. With a lot of possible draws and an aggressive opponent, tend to check the turn and call on the river.
3. With a lot of possible draws and a passive opponent, tend to bet.
4. With no possible draws, tend to check the turn and fold on the river
5. Against a loose player, be more likely to bet the turn than against a tight player.

TWO GAME SCENARIOS

GAME SCENARIO #1

You open on the button with 7♣ 6♣ and only a loose, passive player in the big blind calls (4.5 bets, two players). The flop comes J♥ 10♥ 2♠. He checks, you bet, and he calls (3.2 big bets). The turn is the 3♠. He checks. What do you do?

Bet. He could easily have two overcards or a draw. He is passive, so you are unlikely to get check-raised unless he has a big hand. If he calls, you will probably want to bet the river as well.

GAME SCENARIO #2

You open on the button with 7♣ 6♣. Only a loose-passive player in the big blind calls (4.5 bets, two players). The flop comes K♠ 8♦ 2♣. He checks, you bet, and he calls (3.2 big bets). The turn is the 5♥. He checks. What do you do?

Check. He cannot have two overcards and there are no draws, so it is highly likely that he has a pair.

ARE YOU WAY AHEAD OR WAY BEHIND?

Determining whether you are way ahead or way behind is a very important process, and these situations will come up several times in a typical session. How you play them will have a significant effect on your win rate.

Being either way ahead or way behind occurs when:

- **You have a strong hand.**
  If you have the best hand, your opponent has few outs.
- **Your opponent may have a better hand.**
  If your opponent is ahead, you have few outs; for example, when you have a set and a four flush is on the board.

When you are way ahead or way behind, you should normally play cautiously, but not always. If you are way ahead against 80 percent of your opponent's probable hands and way behind against 20 percent of them, you should bet or raise. If it is 50/50, or even 60/40 in your favor, you should *not* raise. The reasons are as follows:

IF YOU HAVE THE BEST HAND

1. You will only win one bet when the villain calls.
2. You will win nothing if the villain folds.
3. You miss the chance to induce a bet or bluff by a weaker hand.

IF YOU HAVE THE WORST HAND

1. You will lose two bets if you call a raise.
2. You lose only one bet if you bet and fold, but:
    a. You risk losing the whole pot if he is bluffing
    b. You risk losing the whole pot (and more) if you might have hit one of your few outs.

In these situations you need to be *very* confident that you have the best hand to bet or raise. This is particularly true when you have position and can take a free card.

Let's examine four game scenarios.

FOUR GAME SCENARIOS

GAME SCENARIO #1

You are in the small blind with A♥ K♦. An early player, a middle player and the cutoff limp. You raise. The big blind folds, and the other three players call (9 bets, four players). You bet the flop of K♣ 6♠ 6♥. The early player raises and the other players fold (12 bets). What do you do?

With no draws on the board, unless the early player is on a total bluff, he has either a king or a 6. If he has a king, you are in great shape, since he has only three outs to improve. If the villain has a 6, you have only two outs. So whoever is ahead now will likely be ahead at the end. This is classic "way ahead or way behind." In general you don't want to put in the extra raise in these circumstances.

GAME SCENARIO #2

A middle player limps, and you raise from the button with A♠ K♠. The small blind folds, and the big blind and the limper call (6.5 bets, three players). The flop is A♦ Q♥ J♠. Both opponents check. You bet and both players call (4.75 big bets). The turn is the K♣. Both opponents check. What do you do?

Before betting, consider what they can call you with. They can only really call you with a straight or a set. And if either of them has the straight you will get raised. A bet is unlikely to be called by a worse hand; and if you get raised, you will have a very difficult decision. You don't have the right pot odds to draw to improve. If they have the straight or a set, you have four outs. If they don't have the straight or a set, they have very few ways to beat you. You should check. You might be ahead and induce a bluff or a bet by a worse two pair. On your really good days, you will make a full house on the river with the free card and beat a player with a straight.

GAME SCENARIO #3

An early player raises and a loose middle player calls. You raise from the big blind with A♦ A♣ and they both call (9.5 bets, three players). The flop is 7♣ 3♣ 3♥. You bet and both players call (6.25 big bets). The turn is the 7♦. You check, the early player bets, and the middle player calls (8.25 bets). What do you do?

You should call. If they don't have a 7 or a 3, there are few cards that will give them the best hand. If either opponent has a full house, you only have two outs. You might argue that an early opener and a middle caller are unlikely to have a 7 or 3 and you are likely to have the best hand. However, you have position for the river. If you raise, it's very hard for either player to stay in without a full house, so it won't make you any money.

GAME SCENARIO #4

Everyone folds to you on the button and you raise with A♥ 3♦. Only the big blind calls (4.5 bets and two players). The flop is 7♣ 4♣ 3♠. The big blind bets and you call (3.25 bets). The turn is the A♣. The big blind bets again. What should you do?

Call. The ace didn't seem to bother him. He could have bet the flop out with a club draw. You are either way ahead or way behind. Let him keep betting. On the actual hand, the hero called. The river was the 5♣. The big blind checked, the hero bet, and the big blind called with 10♠ 7♥. The villain would likely have folded to a raise on the turn.

Now let's turn our attention to playing the river. The next chapter shows you nine action hands with an analysis of the play of the each hand.

7 PLAYING THE RIVER

"Either bet or fold," I've told myself after losing sessions in which I paid people off on the river time after time, and never seemed to win when I called. Was I right about this? I wanted to find out.

The $2/$4 online game is a reasonably tough game—most live $25/$50 games are actually easier. However, it is not a hotbed of crazed bluffing. I decided that calling should be a worse option in the $2/$4 game than it is in bigger games.

But was I right?

To find out, I studied some hand histories from my play in several $2/$4 online games to analyze what had happened when I called on the river. In 68 hands, I won 12, chopped four, and lost 52. I lost almost 80 percent of the time! At one point, I lost on 12 calls in a row. From a psychological standpoint, it's pretty easy to see why I might form that opinion. Suffering 12 losses in a row means that I might play for a few hours, losing every time I called. I would have four negative results by calling for each positive result.

However, I discovered that I would not be ahead if I had always folded on the river. My 12 wins and four chops netted me $449. My 52 calls had cost me $208. On average, I made almost a big bet every time I called. Does this mean that I should call more often? That's hard to say. I might do so well because I am good at picking my spots to call, though I might do even better if I called a bit less often.

WHEN SHOULD YOU CALL ON THE RIVER?

There is no magic formula for when to call on the river. It comes down to how good your "guesses" are. You just need to play a lot and improve your judgment. And don't get discouraged if you are wrong most of the time—you're supposed to be. Some very good players make calls out of curiosity when they are pretty sure they are beaten. I don't recommend making curiosity calls, unless you are sure the information will really help you on a future hand. Information only helps if the player plays for quite a while, or if you will see him or her again. Further, you can usually get plenty of information from other hands without paying for it.

Calling a raise on the river is different from calling a bet. If you bet and get raised, remember that only a small portion of players will raise on the river as a bluff. Calling most players here with one pair is almost certainly a losing play.

THE BOTTOM LINE

Choosing when to call on the river is a matter of judgment. Trust yours. If you are really not sure, you are better off calling than folding. Take into account the type of opponent you are playing against. And don't call down straightforward players when all you have is a marginal holding. Also keep in mind these important tips:

- **Don't give lessons at the table.** Not only is it annoying, it hurts you in the long run. You don't want educated opponents; you want ignorant ones. Pick another time and place to show off how smart you are.

- **Don't show your big hands when you win.** If you make quads or a straight flush and no one calls, there is no reason to show those hands. No one will admire you forever simply because you got very lucky one time.
- **Don't show your bad beats.** You may get a tiny bit of sympathy from some players, but you are not in the game to get sympathy. You are in the game to make money.
- **Don't show your big laydowns.** If you are laying down a hand like pocket kings because you are pretty sure you are beaten, just throw them away. If good players see you folding big hands, they will start bluffing you a lot more often.

Now let's look at some hands I played badly on the river. How would you have played them to avoid making the same mistakes?

SIX GAME SCENARIOS

1. TIED UP ON THE RIVER

I have A♠ 9♠ in the big blind. A middle player limps, the cutoff raises, the button calls, and the small blind folds. I am worried about being up against a bigger ace, but I am suited and am getting great pot odds. I call, but I remind myself to be careful if an ace flops (8.5 bets, four players). The board is 8♣ 8♥ 2♥. I check and it gets checked around. At this point I am pretty sure the raiser has a bigger ace than mine. With a pocket pair, he almost certainly would bet. The turn is the 3♦. It's hard to represent much on this board, and I suspect the opener will call with an ace-high, so I check. It is checked around again. At this point I am pretty sure that no one has a pair.

The river is the 2♣. I suspect that I will be chopping the pot with the opener, so I check. It gets checked around, he shows A♣ 10♣, and we chop the pot.

MY HAND

THE BOARD

WHAT'S WRONG WITH MY PLAY?

I should have bet the river. If I have read the hand right, I am tied for the best hand. Checking will only give me half the pot, while betting will give me a chance at the entire pot. Even if he only folds a tiny fraction of the time, I still show a profit. And he is likely to fold more often than that: His checks on the flop and turn indicate a passive player. Betting also can pay off on future hands, even if I get called. The next time I bet into a possible chop situation, such as a straight on the board, people are much more likely to call me. If I can beat the board, I will get paid off.

Checking gives me a chance to lose on the river. If someone bets the river, I now have to decide whether to call. After that action, I have to call, but I could get it wrong and fold, losing half the pot. A lot of players will criticize my play on the turn. You can make a strong case that a bet there would take down the pot, but that play is far less obvious than the bet on the river.

THE LESSON

- **When you are pretty sure you are chopping the pot, bet!**

2. FOLD ON THE RIVER?

An early player limps. I have A♣ A♥ in middle position. I raise. The button, who is a solid player cold calls, and the big blind and limper both come in (8.5 bets, four players). The flop is 10♣ 9♣ 9♦. The big blind and the limper both check. I hate this flop! Flush and straight draws are possible, and anyone with a 9 has me beat. I bet and everyone calls (6.25 big bets, four players). With all those folks calling, I am worried about someone slowplaying a 9.

The turn is the K♦. The big blind checks and the limper checks. I bet, and the button raises. The big blind folds and the limper stays in for two more bets. The pot is offering me 10.25 to 1. I call. I figure the big blind has a flush draw (11.25 bets, three players). The river is the 6♦. We check to the raiser, who bets. The big blind folds. With 12.25 bets in the pot, I decide that I am beaten and fold.

MY HAND

THE BOARD

WHAT'S WRONG WITH MY PLAY?

This one is pretty embarrassing. Somehow I convinced myself that the player who raised the turn had to have a 9, and so I had to be beaten. However, that isn't really true. He's a solid player, and he called two bets cold before the flop. What hands would he call with that include a 9? A-9s? 9-9? Neither of those is very likely. Does he have Q-J for a straight? Not too likely that he would call two bets with that even if suited. The most likely big hand he would have is 10-10, though this is not very likely.

Another hand that fits his play perfectly is A-K. He might call a raise preflop with it. He would call the flop with two overcards and raise the turn when the king hits. He would bet it on the river. I need an 8-percent chance of winning to justify calling. Is there at least an 8-percent chance he has A-K? Absolutely!

THE LESSON

- **Don't make "brilliant" folds on the river for one bet in big pots, particularly when no one else has called.** If you have to be right 92 percent of the time for a fold to be the right play, it is the wrong play. Nobody is going to guess right 92 percent of the time. This doesn't mean that you should always call on the river in small pots or with weak hands. Sometimes, you need to call on the river with an ace-high, but it is not an automatic play in a smaller pot. When someone raises on the turn, always consider the possibility that they have top pair, top kicker.

3. THIN RIVER BET? DEPENDS

A very loose, very aggressive player raises on the button. I call in the big blind with 7♠ 5♣. The flop is K♥ 6♥ 5♠. I check, he bets, I check-raise, and he calls. The turn is the 2♠. I bet, and he calls. The river is the 8♥. I bet and he calls. He shows Q♦ 6♦ for a pair of sixes and takes the pot.

MY HAND

THE BOARD

WHAT'S WRONG WITH MY PLAY?

I have fourth pair, which is getting into the range of extremely thin value bets. What hand can he call me with that I can beat? If he will call with an ace, there is some value in betting; however, unless I have seen him call with an ace in similar situations, I should not assume that he will. Against a very aggressive player, I should check here. There are two reasons for this: 1) I should give him a chance to bluff me. 2) If I bet and he raises me, I have a difficult choice: Did he make a flush, is he making a move, or does he have a king?

It probably doesn't make any difference. If I check, he will bet, and I will call. The outcome is the same. (Actually, with the heart hitting the board, there is a chance he checks the river, saving me a bet.) The question is whether he will call me with a worse hand more often or bet a worse hand more often. This player is quite likely to call me with an ace high, but he could easily have raised from the button with far less than ace high. Would he have stayed in to the river without a pair and without an ace? It's possible he has a draw, but very aggressive players like to raise with draws.

The key factor is that an aggressive player will jump on perceived weakness. If I check the river, he will bet any garbage. The other factor is that I have such a low pair. If he has a pair, I am likely beat. It is possible he has twos, but he would have had to raise before the flop and call the flop with a deuce and some other card. If he has a pair, it is far more likely I am beaten. So this isn't much of a value bet. Finally, there is the raise danger. Checking and calling avoid a difficult choice, and that is usually a good thing.

THE LESSON

- **Betting fourth pair or bottom pair with a weak kicker on the river for value is a marginal play at best.** With a weak hand such as a low pair, when acting first on the river:
  1. Against aggressive players, tend to check and call; and
  2. Against passive players, tend to bet or check and fold.

4. WHAT IF A SCARE CARD COMES ON THE TURN?

A solid early player opens with a raise. I have K-K and I reraise. He calls and the two of us go to the flop. The flop is Q-8-2. He passes, I bet, he calls. The turn is an ace. He passes,

I bet, he calls. The river is a blank. He passes. I consider that he is a solid early opener, and will frequently have an ace when he opens. I check behind him. He shows Q♦ J♦.

WHAT'S WRONG WITH MY PLAY?

I missed a bet on the river. What hands with an ace would he call with on the flop? He probably doesn't have two overcards, since a queen flopped (and I have two kings). He probably didn't open early with A-8, since he is solid. If he had A-Q, he probably raises on the turn. His most likely hands are K-Q or a medium pair. Since he hasn't shown any strength, I probably still have the best hand.

If he had position, you might be a bit more cautious. He might have a big hand and be waiting until the river to raise. But with the ace on the board, you can probably fold to a check-raise against all but the trickiest players. Bluff raises on the river are far less common than on other betting rounds. But with him acting first, it is going to be hard for him to keep checking a big hand, knowing that you might check behind him. A better way to play this hand is to check the turn and then bet or call on the river. However, once I bet the turn and get called, I am better off firing on the river.

THE LESSON

- **Catching a scare card on the turn shouldn't scare you on the river.** If you are betting a pair, and your opponent keeps calling, you should keep betting—unless there are at least two cards on the board better than your pair. Then consider slowing down, but don't always slow down. You should slow down more often if the two bigger cards came on the flop. It is more likely that the caller stuck around with a bigger pair. Bet for value more often if the original flop was all small cards. Your opponent may have stuck around with overcards.

5. WHAT WAS SHE THINKING?

Here's a hand someone else played badly. I open from early position with A♦ 10♦. A somewhat aggressive lady calls from the button, and the big blind calls. The lady has been picking on the live one at the table, but otherwise has been playing pretty solid. The flop is 8♦ 5♦ 4♣. I bet and only the button calls. The turn is the 6♦. I bet and the button calls. The river is the Q♥. I bet, and the button raises. I reraise and the button puts in another raise. After some thought, I decide to just call in case she has the straight flush. She shows Q♦ J♦.

MY HAND

THE BOARD

WHAT'S WRONG WITH HER PLAY?

Let's start with what's wrong with the play of the lady on the button. Should she put in the last raise? Could she have the best hand? There are three reasons she should not think so.

Unless someone is very, very aggressive, the third bet on the river usually indicates the nuts or very close to it. It's pretty rare that someone puts in the third bet with a medium flush.

If I don't have her beat, I have the fourth-best flush at best. The top diamonds out are the ace, queen, jack, and 10. She has the queen and jack, so if I don't have her beat, the best I can have is a 10-high flush. To make that raise, I have to assume she does not have the ace, queen or jack.

I raised from early position before the flop. I am a pretty tight player. Which I am more likely to have two diamonds headed by the ace or two diamonds headed by the 10? Would I have raised before the flop with 10♦ 9♦? Possible, but not likely.

For her raise to be correct, I have to have made two unlikely plays: I have to have raised from under the gun with 10♦ 9♦, or I have to have put in a third bet on the turn with my flush headed by the fourth-best flush card (as I see it). So what was she thinking when she reraised? Obviously she wasn't thinking. As for me, I have to decide which is more likely:

1. She called an early raise from the button with 9♦ 7♦.
2. She is raising with a weaker flush.

In hindsight, number 2 looks a bit more likely. Neither play is very good on her part. However, risking two more bets to find out seems like a bad idea.

THE LESSON

- **If an opponent three-bets on the river, he usually has the nuts or something very close to it.**

6. DON'T EVEN THINK ABOUT IT!

An early player limps, and another early player raises. The cutoff calls, the button calls, I call from the small blind with 9♠ 9♣ and the big blind calls (12 bets, six players). On the flop of Q♠ 9♦ 5♦, I bet, two players fold, the preflop raiser calls, along with the cutoff and button (8 big bets, four players). On the turn of A♦, with three callers on the flop, I worry about a flush draw getting there. I decide to see what the action behind me looks like: I check, the early player bets, the cutoff folds, and my worst fears seem to be confirmed when the button raises. Even if he has a flush, I have 10 outs to a full house, so I call, along with the early player (14 bets). The river is the K♥. We both check to the button, who bets (16 bets). I am pretty sure he has to have a flush for his action. I consider folding, but I reluctantly call. The other player folds.

MY HAND

THE BOARD

WHAT'S WRONG WITH MY PLAY?

I should not think about folding. I should not reluctantly call. I should call with zest and enthusiasm. I should do my happy dance as I call. Sure I might be beat. But there are sixteen (16!) big bets in the pot. I only need to win 6 percent of the time to make money. And I have a freakin' set! It's okay to feel a twinge of regret, since I am going to lose the pot more often than win. But I should never ever consider folding here. So what did the villain have? He had K♦ Q♣ for a pair and the nut flush draw. I knew I had him beaten all along!

THE LESSON

- **Nobody makes money by making brilliant laydowns on the river in big pots.** Nobody! Folding after a raise on the river is a different matter.

THREE-BETS ON THE TURN OR RIVER

The next three hands illustrate a theme. In every case I have a strong hand, and I get raised on the turn or river. I am faced with either reraising or calling.

GAME SCENARIO #7

A middle player and the cutoff limp. I raise from the small blind with J♥ J♦. The big blind folds and the limpers call (7 bets, three players). On the flop of 8♣ 5♦ 3♠, I bet and both players call (5 big bets, three players). The turn is the 9♣. I bet, the first limper folds and the next limper raises. I reraise, and he raises again. I call (13 big bets, two players). The river is the 2♠, and I check-call when he bet. He shows 9♠ 8♠ for top two pair.

GAME SCENARIO #8

I raise from early position with 9♠ 9♥ and only the button calls (5.5 bets, two players). The flop is A♣ Q♠ 9♦. I bet, he raises and I call (4.75 big bets). The turn is the 4♣. I check, he bets, and I raise. He calls (8.75 bets). The river is the J♥. I bet the river and he raises. I just call. He shows the K♠ 10♣ for the nut straight.

GAME SCENARIO #9

A tight player raises from the hijack, and I reraise from the small blind with A♣ K♦. The big blind folds (5 bets, two players). On the flop of K♠ 6♦ 2♥, I bet and he calls (3.5 big bets, two players). On the turn of the 4♠, I bet and he raises.

I just call (7.5 bets). The river is the 3♦. I check, he bets and I call. He shows K♣ 9♦, and I take the pot.

WHAT CAN WE LEARN FROM THESE HANDS?

In each case, I might have had the best hand when I got raised, and I might not have. The problem with raising is that you have to risk two bets to win one. As we saw in the first hand, when I got raised, I had to either pay off another big bet or fold a very good hand with eight big bets in the pot. I was hoping to win an extra bet, but it cost me two.

Even when you are ahead, the raise may not make you more money. In Example 3, I probably made more money by checking it down. If I three-bet the turn, there is a good chance the tight player will fold. And Example 2 shows how hard it is to put in that extra raise based on a good read. There is no way to put the opponent on K-10. For most players it is not a raising hand before the flop, and he isn't getting good pot odds to call a raise on the turn with just a gutshot.

THE LESSON

- **When you get raised on the turn or river, you need the nuts or close to the nuts to put in the third raise.** You are risking two bets to win one, so you need to be very sure you are going to win. Therefore, tend to not raise when you are either way ahead or way behind.

These nine river hands involved making the correct decision, one that would either make you money or save you some money. The next chapter presents a dozen types of other tricky situations in which you need to use your skills and intuitive powers to decide what you should do to either maximize your profits or minimize your losses.

8 TRICKY HANDS AND HOW TO PLAY THEM

Here are a dozen hands that ask what you should do in certain perplexing situations. Some involve reading your opponents correctly, while others center on counting your outs. Some involve tricky situations where there seems to be more than one answer, and others require close calls in judgment. Let's start with a situation in which you're able to very closely read your opponent's most likely hand.

> The most important factor in your results is not how much you win with your good hands, but how much you don't lose with your bad ones.

TWELVE GAME SCENARIOS

1. WHAT IS YOUR OPPONENT'S MOST LIKELY HAND?

You can't put someone on their exact hand very often, but here is an example. An extremely loose player limps from middle position. She plays almost every hand and rarely folds on the flop. A loose aggressive player raises from the cutoff. You reraise from the button with A♦ Q♦, the small blind folds, and the big blind calls. The big blind is a tight aggressive player who occasionally makes a move, but usually plays a straightforward game. The other two call (12.6 bets, four players).

The flop is A♥ 5♠ 5♦. Everyone checks to you. You bet, the big blind raises, the loose lady calls and the cutoff folds (17.6 bets, three players). What do you do?

Before reading further, try to guess the hand or range of hands the big blind has.

WHAT COULD THE BIG BLIND HAVE?

First, review the key facts about the big blind.

- He is a tight aggressive players.
- He called two raises before the flop, but he didn't put in the third raise.
- He doesn't make moves very frequently.

Could the big blind be bluffing? He occasionally will try to steal, but this hardly looks like a place where a solid player will make a move. There are four players in the pot, and they have shown a lot of strength. He almost certainly has a real hand.

What could he have that beats you? A-K? He probably would have reraised before the flop. A 5? There are few hands where a tight player would call two bets before the flop with a 5 in his hand. There is the highly unlikely 5♥ 5♣, and he conceivably might have A-5 suited. But with the cards out, the only possibility is A♣ 5♣, and whether he would call with either of those hands before the flop is not certain. The chances that he has you beaten are very slim.

Far more likely is an ace with a kicker lower than a king. He probably has a hand like A-Q, A-J, A-10, or A-9. A-Q is possible, but a little less likely because of your queen. A-10 and A-9 are possible, but he might not call with them before the flop. The most likely hand is A-J. Would he check-raise with A-J here? Absolutely! Think about the range he puts you on. You have just three-bet a loose raiser from fairly late position before the flop. You could have a pocket pair as low as 6-6. You might have a weaker ace. You could even have a hand like K-Qs or Q-Js. He probably thinks his ace has an excellent chance of being the best hand.

WHAT SHOULD YOU DO?

Since you are pretty sure you have the best hand, your choices are to raise now or just call to set up a raise on the turn. Without the loose lady in the hand, waiting until the turn would be a good move. It likely gains a big bet instead of a small bet; however, with her in the hand you gain two small bets by raising. (The loose lady isn't going out for one more small bet.) Also, a raise on the turn might convince the big blind he is beat, and you might lose him. Raises on the turn are much scarier than raises on the flop.

While just calling isn't a bad play, and will pay off if the big blind bets the turn and the loose lady calls before you raise, I prefer to raise now. On the actual hand, the hero raised the flop and both players called. Blanks came on the turn and river, and the big blind called all the way. When the hero showed the winner, the big blind showed A-J.

2. TOUGH TO PLAY? STAY AWAY

This exercise involves your ability to count your outs and determine the pot odds. A middle player limps and the button raises. You call in the big blind with A♠ 10♥ along with the limper (6.5 bets, three players). The flop comes 5♥ 4♣ 2♦. You check, the limper checks, and the opener bets (7.5 big bets).

THE CASE FOR CALLING

- With these pot odds, you need 5.5 outs to call.
- If the villain has a bigger ace, you have five outs. Four threes give you half the pot, and three tens win the whole pot. That's a fold.
- If the villain has a smaller ace, you are a big favorite.

- If the villain has a pair bigger than your 10, you have seven outs.
- If the villain has a pair smaller than your 10, you have 10 outs.
- Otherwise, unless he flopped a straight, you are ahead or have 10 outs.

THE CASE FOR FOLDING

A great player in my discussion group plays in the largest limit hold'em games and he argued for folding. In his view, the correct play depends on the kind of opponents in the game. In a passive game, calling is fine, but in an aggressive game you have a lot of ways to get into trouble. The big problems are:

- You have bad position.
- You could be facing a check-raise.
- You don't know where you stand.

Let's start with position. In aggressive games, you generally want to avoid playing marginal hands when you are out position, particularly when you find yourself sandwiched between a bettor and a potential raiser. You have no idea how much it will cost you to see the next card.

Note that if you get check-raised, you are likely priced in to see the turn, but the price of seeing one more card just got higher. Then there is the issue of not knowing where you stand. Does an ace help you or hurt you? You have no real way of knowing. A 3 is a good card, but you could easily be splitting the pot with another ace (or two). On your really bad days, someone has a 6, you hit your straight, and lose. And if your straight is best, you aren't going to get paid off, so the implied odds when a 3 hits are terrible. If an ace hits and the action heats up, are you prepared to fold? It doesn't make too much sense to draw to a hand, if you might have to fold it when you hit it.

WHAT SHOULD YOU DO?

Calling isn't terrible, but your life will be a lot simpler if you avoid hard decisions out of position. On the actual hand, the hero folded.

DISCUSSION

This is a hand where you almost certainly have quite a few outs, but you don't know which cards are outs and which are losers. This puts you at a big disadvantage when playing the later streets. (You have negative implied odds.) You'll have a hard time out-playing anyone if you don't know when your hand is good. This is likely going to cost you money on the later streets when you are beaten.

A normal out is a pretty sure winner. When you draw to a straight or flush, you know that when you hit one of those outs, most of the time you will win. This is not true of these outs. Second, when you're up against two villains, you need to discount your outs even more. And when you could easily be dominated, your outs can be worse than worthless—they can be deadly.

I would still usually call here, but the case for folding is also pretty good since you are out of position, another live player is yet to act on the flop, and you're not sure which of your outs is good. The more aggressive the game, the more you should lean toward folding. If you call, you want to proceed cautiously.

> Your life at the poker table will be a lot simpler if you avoid needing to make hard decisions out of position.

3. THE THREE-BET FREE CARD

This is a routine play in the arsenal of most strong players. Understanding it will help you to use it to your advantage, and to counter against it. Here is a classic example: You raise from middle position with Q♠ 10♠, and only the big blind calls (5.5 bets and two players). The flop comes 9♣ 8♥ 5♦. He checks, you bet, and he raises (8.5 bets).

WHAT SHOULD YOU DO?

This is an almost automatic reraise. You have 10 outs, so you are going to the river, no matter what. Suppose you reraise and then don't improve on the turn. The big blind probably will check to you, and you can check behind him and take a free card. You have cut the cost of seeing two more cards in half. You spend an extra small bet on the flop to save a big bet on the turn. And if you hit one of your outs on the turn, you have the opportunity to win a bigger pot.

FROM ANOTHER VIEWPOINT

It's important to remember that in hands like the one in this example, the auto three-bet should not be your default line when you miss the flop in position, but have overcards and a backdoor draw. As the games get higher in stakes and the players get better, a good opponent will quickly recognize if you're three-betting too often in these situations and will four-bet you with reckless abandon, then lead the turn putting you in a bad spot when you don't improve.

If you are going to three-bet every flop that you either (a) flop a big hand, or (b) miss the flop and hope to get a free card on the turn by three-betting, you need to remember that there will be many more cases of "b" than "a". Your smart opponent knows that too and will therefore raise you back (four-bet), or at a minimum, lead lots of turns. Therefore, it's imperative to keep your game in balance against good opponents. You do that by mixing up your calling and raising in these types of hands. I think, in fact, you need to weight your play more heavily towards calling to stay in balance. Obviously, the worse your opponents are the more you can play out of balance; that is, play exploitatively.

FROM MY VIEWPOINT

I think a lot depends on the villain. Basically, I will raise here until I see a particular player push back. I have a pretty tight image, so most players respect my raises. Even if they see me check behind the turn, they are afraid that the next time I will have a big hand. Only a few players in my games understand what I am doing and are capable of countering it. As my friend said, "The worse your opponents are, the more you can play out of balance."

In addition, this play does not put me out of balance. I am three-betting with quite a few other hands other than overcards and backdoor draws. I am also not three-betting every time I get check-raised There are situations where I fold or call. However, I know some very good players who play a check-raise on the flop as a fold or raise situation. When they get check-raised by a blind, they will either raise or fold. I am not recommending this, but it seems to work pretty well for them.

A similar (and related) situation is playing as the big blind against an opener. I think this is often a check-raise or check-fold situation. I almost never check-call. The only exception is when the board is ugly, and there is a good chance I will get raised again. Then I will sometimes check call. I often don't check-raise when there is an ace on the board.

ANOTHER EXAMPLE

Everyone folds to you on the button and you raise with A♠ K♣. Only the small blind calls (5 bets, two players). The flop comes J♣ 9♣ 2♠. The small blind checks, you bet, and he raises (8 bets, two players).

WHAT SHOULD YOU DO?

You are calling anyway with 8.5 outs (2 outs for the backdoor flush, and 0.5 outs for Q-10 to a straight). For the price of one small bet, you will usually get two shots at making your hand. Let's assume that you are beaten right now and your outs are all good. (Of course, this isn't true if he has a hand such as A-9.) If you just call, you will need to fold unless you improve on the turn, as there will be 5.5 bets in the pot and you will have six outs.

With a free card, you will see the river. That gives you a 33 percent chance of winning instead of 19 percent. A 33 percent chance of winning nine bets is an expectation of three bets. A 19 percent chance of winning eight bets is an expectation of 1.5 bets. So for the cost of one small bet, you win an average of an extra 1.5 bets. This is a good investment.

Now suppose the 9♣ were the 9♦ instead. You have only 6.5 outs. The raise is still worthwhile, earning you around 1.27 small bets for the cost of one small bet. This analysis supposes three things: (1) all your outs are live; (2) you will not get reraised again on the flop; and (3) the villain will give you a free card on the turn. These suppositions will not always be true, of course.

Some players make this play 100 percent of the time. When a blind check-raises the flop, they reraise every time. When this happens, if I am the big blind, I will frequently bet into them on the turn. I think you need to mix it up a bit. Also, when I three-bet the flop, if I have taken the free card on the turn once or twice before, I will sometimes bet the turn instead of taking the free card. Observant players who expect me to check will figure me for a strong hand, and I might be able to take the pot right there with a bet.

On the actual hand, the hero raised and was called. He took the free card when the turn was the 4♥. The river was the A♦ and the villain called a bet on the river. The villain had J♦ 7♦.

4. AN "EASY CALL" ISN'T ALL THAT EASY

An early player opens. A middle player calls. I three-bet from the small blind with J♠ J♦. The big blind calls, as does everyone else (12 bets, four players). The flop comes Q♠ J♣ 9♥. I have a set on a dangerous board. I am going to play it fast. I bet, the big blind raises, the early player calls, and the middle player folds. I reraise, and the big blind caps it. The early player calls as well. There are now 12 big bets in the pot and three players. The turn card is the 8♦, putting four straight cards on the board. I pass, the big blind bets, and the early player raises.

It's decision time! I'm pretty sure that at least one of my opponents has a straight, and they might both have one, so I almost certainly need to improve to win the pot. There are 15 big bets in the pot, and it costs me two bets to call, so the pot is laying me 7.5 to 1. There are 10 cards that make me a full house or better—and with 10 outs, I need only 4 to 1 odds to call. It's an easy call, right?

Not so fast! I could be facing two more raises. Then the turn would cost me four bets to win 20 bets, which is only 5 to 1. All of a sudden it is a close decision. What about the chance that I make my hand and lose? Seems pretty unlikely, but someone could have a set of queens. This is a closer decision that it might seem at first, but it is still a call. Also, if I improve I am likely to get a crying call or two on the river.

I call. It's hard to lay down a set. Sure enough, the big blind raises. The surprise is that he is all in—I hadn't noticed that. The early player raises, and now it costs me four bets to win 19, which is a little worse than I had thought. It also hurts my implied odds, since there is only one player who might pay me off on the river. But "in for a penny, in for a pound," so I call again. The river is a blank. I check. The early player bets, and I fold. The big blind shows a straight. Surprisingly, the early player mucks his hand. He announces that he had a set of queens, so I put in four bets on the turn with exactly one out, the last jack.

WHAT SHOULD I HAVE DONE?

Did I play this hand badly? Should I have figured the early player for a set of queens? Not really. Look at it from his perspective. On the turn, he should figure he is up against a straight, so he is raising while behind. With only three of us in the pot, he is getting 2 to 1 on every raise. He puts in a bet and two other players put in a bet, but he only has a 25 percent chance of improving when he needs 3 to 1. He is playing badly by raising. The only raise of his that is correct is the last one, when the big blind is all in. Now his raise is on the side, and he can be pretty confident that his hand is best.

Since he is an experienced player, I should not expect him to have the hand he had. It was more a fluke that I was drawing to one out rather than something I should anticipate. So, my play is correct overall, even if my decision on the turn was closer than I had thought in the heat of battle.

If you find yourself in a similar situation, remember that a set is not a guaranteed winner. With a very ugly board, there are rare occasions where it is right to lay it down. When you are figuring your pot odds after a bet and a raise, you have to give serious consideration to the chance that you will have to call two more raises, and that could reduce your pot odds. Against a likely straight, it is not correct to raise with a set in a three-way pot. It is marginal in a four-way pot, and it is not a good play in a five-way pot, though you won't see that happen very often. Further, always pay serious attention to players' stacks, as that might affect a close decision. You want to know if someone is about to go all-in.

5. LIMP, RERAISE: AN EXERCISE IN HAND READING

A new player to the table limps in under the gun. Everyone folds to me in the small blind, where I raise with 10♠ 10♦. The big blind folds and the limper makes it three bets. I call (7 bets, two players). The flop is A♥ Q♦ 2♦. I check and the limper checks. The turn is the 5♠. I bet and he calls. The river is the 4♥. I bet and he calls.

WHAT DOES HE HAVE?

On the flop, I should have a pretty good idea what he has, if I just stop to think a moment. First, with what hands do players limp and then reraise? In a multiway pot, they could have a wide range of hands. A player could have a big pair, or a hand such as K♥ Q♥ or K♠ J♠ that plays well in a volume pot.

However, when playing heads up, they are far more likely to have A-A or K-K. When he checks the flop, it means one of two things: Either he is slowplaying A-A or is afraid to bet K-K with an ace on the board. The K-K is more likely. In either case, I am way behind. There aren't a lot of other big hands he could have where I am the favorite. Any hand with an ace or queen has me drawing to two outs. There is no hand he can have that I can beat, unless he plays a very unusual way.

WHAT SHOULD I HAVE DONE?

With his betting pattern and that board, my 10-10 is really a small pair. I had hoped to flop a set and I didn't. I cannot figure out a hand that matches his betting that I can beat. I should tend to slow down, particularly on the river. What did he have? K-K. When you don't know how someone plays, usually assume they play straightforward poker. Most players do, so you are making a good assumption. When an early limper three-bets in heads-up action, he usually has A-A or K-K. And when an early limper three-bets in a multiway pot, he can have a big pair, but he can also have strong suited cards.

6. BIG PAIR VS. ACE ON THE TURN

A solid aggressive player raises from early position. You reraise from the button with K♠ K♣. Only the opener calls (7.5 bets and two players). The flop is 7♥ 2♠ 2♦. She checks, you bet and she calls (4.8 big bets). The turn is the A♦. She checks again. After you get done cursing about how an ace always comes down when you have pocket kings, what do you do?

WHAT SHOULD YOU DO?

This situation occurs pretty frequently, and there is a good way to play it. The situation is:

- It is the turn.
- There was a raise before the flop.
- There is an ace on the board.
- You are last to act.
- You probably have the best hand if the villain does not have an ace, but you will lose if he has an ace.
- If you are ahead, there are not a lot of cards that will beat you on the river.

Your strategy should be:

- Check the turn.
- If the villain bets the river, call.
- If the villain checks the river, bet.

Here's why this strategy works: If the villain has an ace, you will lose the minimum and will get to a showdown for one bet. If the villain does not have an ace, you are going to get one more bet at best. Your reraise before the flop suggests a big pair or A-K. The ace is scary to a player who doesn't have one, and the villain is likely to fold to a turn bet. By checking, you accomplish two things: (1) you encourage a bluff on the river; and (2) you are more likely to get a call on the river with this stop and go play.

In the actual hand, the river was the 7♣. This might seem like a scary card, but the villain raised from early position and is unlikely to have a 7 or 2. The villain checked the river and called a bet with 6♥ 6♣.

Here's a slightly different example. You raise from early position with K♥ K♣. Only the small blind calls. The flop is A♠ J♣ 4♥. He passes, you bet, and he calls. The turn is the 10♦. You should check. On the actual hand, the hero checked. The river was the 5♥. The villain bet and the hero called. The villain had 8♠ 8♣.

Now let's look at an example where you should bet. Two middle players limp. You call on the button with J♣ 10♣. The small blind folds and the big blind checks (4.8 bets, four players). The flop comes J♦ 7♥ 2♠. The big blind checks, the first middle player bets, the second middle player folds, and you raise. Only the early player calls (4.4 big bets, two players). The turn is the A♦. The middle player checks. This time, you should bet.

Why?

It was not raised before the flop. Since he limped before the flop, it is less likely that he has an ace. And he has less reason to fear an ace in your hand. Also there are a lot of cards that could come on the river that could beat you. You don't want to give him a free card to hit a king, queen, a possible gutshot straight, or a runner-runner flush.

TWO MORE EXAMPLES

You can apply this concept to hands where the overcard to your pair is not an ace. The next two examples illustrate this play.

HAND A

You raise from the cutoff with Q♠ Q♣, and only the small blind calls (5 bets, two players). The flop is K♠ 4♦ 2♣. He checks, you bet the flop, and the villain calls (3.5 big bets, two players). The turn is the 6♣. He checks. This is a good time to check behind him. Giving a free card is not terrible here because he is not very likely to have a strong draw. Remember that he called from the small blind, not the big blind. Most players don't do this with a bunch of small cards.

Could you be costing yourself a bet? Perhaps. If he doesn't have a king, he probably didn't pair the board. He might have a pocket pair, in which case he would probably call. Since he didn't reraise you preflop, his pocket pair will likely be small. Could you be saving yourself a bet? If he has a king or his small pocket pair has turned into a set, you will be saving a bet by checking the turn. This play is not automatic. Against a very passive player, you want to keep betting, but against most players you can afford to show weakness here and check. This is particularly true because the pot is small. In small pots you should be more likely to make the deceptive play.

In the actual hand, the hero checked. The river was the 8♥. The villain bet, the hero called and won when the villain showed J♦ 9♠. It's hard to comprehend why the villain called on the flop, but it is pretty likely that he would have folded to a turn bet. Checking definitely won a bet here.

In the previous example, let's make the flop K♠ 4♦ 2♠. Now there is a possible flush draw and the danger of giving a free card goes up. However, your opponent is also more likely to bet a missed draw on the river; and if he makes a flush on the river, you have just saved a bet.

HAND B

A middle player limps, the cutoff raises, and you reraise from the button with 7♠ 7♣. Only the cutoff calls (8.5 bets, two players). The flop is A♣ 8♣ 6♣. The cutoff checks, you bet, and he calls (5.25 big bets, two players). The turn is the Q♥. He checks. What should you do now?

You should also check. There are now three overcards to your pair on the board. You are either way ahead or way behind—and if you are behind, you have a draw to a flush that might be the best hand. It is not very likely that he will fold on the turn with this board after calling the flop, and it is extremely unlikely that he will fold a stronger hand than yours. After showing weakness on the turn, you probably need to call on the river, except against extremely passive players.

In the actual hand, the villain checked the turn. The river was the K♠. Both players checked and the villain showed J♦ J♣. An important point to remember is not to check if the top card on the board isn't very high. For example, suppose you have 7-7 and the board is 10-8-3. Many people will call on the flop with two overcards to the board. Typically they will fold the turn if they don't make a pair or pick up a good draw. If the turn card is a 5, you don't want to give a K-Q or an A-J a free chance to draw out on you if there is any chance they will fold to a bet.

7. GIVING UP A FREE CARD

Most players seem to view giving up a free card to someone who is on a draw as an unmitigated disaster. Is this really true? Are there times where you are better off giving up a free card to someone on a draw? Let's return to a hand from the previous section. You raise from the cutoff with Q♠ Q♣, and only the small blind calls (5 bets, two players). The flop is K♠ 4♦ 2♠. He checks, you bet the flop and the villain calls (3.5 big bets, two players). The turn is the 6♣. He checks. Suppose you are pretty sure he has a flush draw.

WHAT SHOULD YOU DO?

It can still be correct to check. The key is this: If the villain will be more likely to bet a missed draw when you check the turn, you are better off checking.

Assume that if you bet:

He will call.

When he makes his flush, you will lose one more bet on the river. Either you will bet and get raised and fold, or he will bet and you will call.

When he misses his flush, he will fold to your bet.

OUTCOME	PROBABILITY	AMOUNT WON/LOST	EXPECTATION
He makes it	20%	-2	-0.4
He misses it	80%	1	0.8

Overall, you will gain around 0.4 bets if you bet. If you check, assume he will bet whether he makes or misses.

OUTCOME	PROBABILITY	AMOUNT WON/LOST	EXPECTATION
He makes it	20%	-1	-0.2
He misses it	80%	1	0.8

You gain 0.6 bets by checking. That is better than betting. Notice that we assumed he always has a flush draw. If he has a king in his hand, you gain even more by checking.

Of course this analysis makes quite a few assumptions about how the villain will play. Against very aggressive players who are likely to bet their missed draw no matter what the action is on the turn, you are better off betting. Against very passive players who will not bet a missed draw, you are better off betting. You are looking for a moderately aggressive player before you give a free card here.

8. THE "NATURAL" PLAY

A semi-maniac raises under the gun and the cutoff raises all in for three bets. You cap the betting on the button with Q♣ Q♠, and the small blind and early player call (12 bets, four players, one of whom is all in). The flop is 9♦ 7♣ 3♦. The small blind checks and the early player bets (13 small bets).

WHAT SHOULD YOU DO?

A number of players would say you should just call on the flop. Their reasoning is that if the small blind has overcards, he isn't going to fold if you raise. Your raise will put 15 bets in the pot and he will only need to put in two bets to call. With six outs and 7.5 to 1 pot odds, he is getting the right price to call. Actually, given the two diamonds on the board, he might have fewer than six outs, but most players will call with two overcards in a pot this big.

If he has A-K, the theory goes, your primary goal should be to get him out, rather than get the most money in the pot. Since a raise on the flop won't do it, you should call on the flop, hope the maniac bets the turn, and then raise. Then the small blind won't have the pot odds to call. If all goes according to plan, he will only be getting around 5 to 1 pot odds to call your turn raise, and he should fold A-K.

Let's analyze this more carefully. Let's assume the small blind has A-K, and will fold if we check-raise the turn.

SITUATION #1: WE RAISE ON THE FLOP

Suppose we raise on the flop, and both players call. A blank comes on the turn, and we bet. They both call. If a blank comes on the river (87 percent), we win a pot of 20 small bets. We put in four small bets on the turn and river. We lose 13 percent of the time. Our expectation is 13.9 small bets.

SITUATION #2: WE RAISE ON THE TURN

Instead, we call on the flop along with the small blind. The early player bets, we raise, the small blind folds, and the early player calls. We win 18 small bets 100 percent of the time at a cost of five small bets, for an expectation of 13 small bets. Based on this analysis, even if everything goes exactly as the advocates of calling want it to, our expectation is higher by raising the flop. The strategy of getting out the small blind at all costs is a loser. But it is much worse!

All of this assumes the conditions are perfect:

- The small blind has A-K
- The small blind will not fold to a flop raise.
- The small blind will fold to a turn raise.
- The other two players do not have an ace or king.
- The early player will bet the turn.

It is ridiculous to make these assumptions. There is no reason to assume the small blind has A-K, as there are a number of other hands he might have. If he has A-J, we are thrilled to have him keep calling, since he only has three outs. Adopting a special strategy based on the assumption that he has A-K is dumb. And even if he does have A-K and we drive him out, one of the other two players could have an ace or king. If they do, driving out the small blind may not save the pot for us.

These fancy plays to drive out players are fashionable among some authors and message board gurus. However, they are usually bad plays. In almost every situation, the straightforward play is the right one.

9. LET'S DISCUSS IT

You open-raise from the cutoff with A♣ 8♥. A loose and very aggressive player in the big blind calls (4.5 bets). The flop is 9♠ 5♥ 3♦. The big blind checks, you bet, and he calls (3.3 big bets). The turn is the K♣. He checks again.

WHAT SHOULD YOU DO?

Check. Since your opponent is very aggressive, there is a good chance he will bluff on the river. Also, because your opponent is loose, he could have called the flop bet with a wide range of hands, including overcards and inside straight draws. This actually increases the probability that he will bluff the river, since he will hold more hands with which he knows he cannot win at the showdown.

Even though your opponent may have six outs to beat you, the pot is not that large, so it is less important to bet to protect your hand. But if you bet, a very aggressive opponent may bluff check-raise the turn, which may force you to fold the best hand. Finally, your opponent may have already made a pair, and checking the turn allows you to take a free card those times when you are behind.

THE DEBATE

I had an online discussion with a friend who is a very good player. He disagreed with me and was in favor of betting in this scenario. First, what would the loose aggressive player (a "**LAG**") have called with on the flop?

Let's consider a few possibilities.

A pocket pair? This is unlikely. A LAG will raise before the flop against a button opener. He flopped a pair? This is again unlikely. Most players, including a LAG, will regard a pair of nines or lower as a vulnerable hand. There are many overcards to their hand and they will try to protect it by playing fast on the flop. A draw? This is a very dry board; there are no draws except for a few unlikely gutshots.

Bigger overcards? This is unlikely. A LAG will raise with a good ace before the flop against a button opener. He might even raise with any ace. A big hand or a pair of kings? He might slowplay this and go for a check-raise on the turn. If he does, the recommended line of checking the turn and calling the river cost you less than betting the turn, unless you are going to fold to the check-raise.

Two overcards? Bingo! That's about the only hand that makes sense with this action.

Of course, there is no guarantee that he has two overcards to the flop. People play in strange ways, but that is his most likely holding and you should adopt a strategy that maximizes your profit against his most likely hand.

BET OR CHECK?

What is the best strategy against two overcards? Since the king hit on the turn, the player no longer has two overcards. He will probably fold or bluff raise if we bet. Here is my friend's analysis: "I agree that his range is most likely not a better ace or a pair, but primarily overcards. That's exactly why I like barreling the turn, because I don't think it's likely that we get bluff-raised here very often. So the question becomes: Do we make more (one extra big bet) by letting him bluff the river than we lose (the whole pot) when we give him the free card and he hits one of his 6-outs on the river?

"If we assume he always and only has two overcards worse than ours, and he always acts as we say below, then when we bet the turn and he folds, we always win 6.5 small bets. When we check the turn and check-call the river, we win 8.5 small bets 87 percent of the time, which equals 7.4 small bets. We lose two small bets 13 percent of the time, which equals minus three small bets. The net result is that we win 7.1 small bets.

"However, this calculation assumes he always folds the turn to our bet and will always bet the river when he misses. We need to adjust these EV (expected value) calculations to adjust for how often he deviates from that, and also for the chance that he has something other than two over cards. I think that when we do, it gets really close, maybe even flips.

"Here's a key point: Against a passive player, who won't bluff the river, a bet is clearly the right choice. You don't gain a bet on the river when he misses, but you can lose the whole pot if you give a free card."

CONCLUSIONS

In a situation like this in which you have position and some showdown value, check when:

- The pot is small.
- You think your opponent might bluff raise the turn.

- There are many draws on the board.
- Your opponent is likely to bluff if you will check.

You should bet more often when:

- The pot is large.
- Your opponent is unlikely to bluff-raise the turn.
- There are few draws on the board.
- Your opponent is not too likely to bluff the river.

You might think that you should bet more with a draw-rich board; however, a draw-rich board makes it more likely that your opponent is on a draw and doesn't have overcards. While you don't like to give a free card, you will need to call a check-raise from an aggressive player who may like to check-raise with a draw. Most of the time, the villain will miss his draw. By checking, you save money when he hits and usually gain a bet when the aggressive villain misses his draw.

10. HOW IMPORTANT ARE EXPOSED CARDS?

The dealer mistakenly turns over the Q♠. A tight player under the gun opens with a raise. Everyone folds to me in the big blind. While folding, one player exposes the K♦. I look down to see K♣ Q♦. (I would have had pocket queens if the dealer hadn't messed up!) As any good stud player will tell you, whether your cards are live is very important, and one of my hole cards have already shown up. However, the pot is offering me 3.5 to 1.

WHAT SHOULD I DO?

For an answer, let's turn to PokerStove. Here's how the exposed cards affect us for different ranges for the villain's hand. For example, if he plays the top 10 percent of his hands in this situation, we normally win 39 percent of the time with K-Q, but with the two exposed cards, we only win around 32.6 percent of the time.

HIS RANGE	WE WIN – NO EXPOSED CARDS	WE WIN – EXPOSED CARDS
Top 5%	31.5%	27.6%
Top 10%	39.0%	32.6%
Top 15%	46.2%	39.2%
Top 20%	48.8%	41.8%
Top 25%	49.9%	42.6%

With 3.5 bets in the pot, you only need to win around 22 percent of the time to break even. Even against extremely tight players, it seems like I should call. In every case, I am getting the right price, even out of position.

You might wonder if the win percent from Poker Stove is all that accurate. In order to win a showdown at the river, you first have to get to the river. How often are you going to flop a hand you can continue with? It turns out that you will call more than 22 percent of the time on the flop. You will flop a pair, even with the two cards removed, 23.4 percent of the time. You will flop a straight around 1 percent of the time. In addition, you will play on if you flop J-10-x, J-9-x, or 10-9-x. With two overcards and a straight draw, you are getting the right price to play on, even if your overcards only have four outs. In fact, you can play any connected cards, even if two of your outs are exposed. In some ways, 7-6 is better than K-Q, since you are less likely to be dominated.

In the actual hand, I folded and the opener showed A-K. It looks like I dodged a bullet, but even in this case I win almost 20 percent of the time. It looks as though I almost had a playable hand; however, if a king flops, I am going to lose some serious money after the flop. I did indeed dodge a bullet!

11. FOLD A STRAIGHT DRAW WITH A SUITED FLOP?

Let's look at a common situation where many experts would recommend that you fold. A middle player raises and the cutoff calls. You call from the big blind with 8♠ 7♠ (6.7 bets and three players). The flop comes K♦ 6♦ 5♦. You check, the cutoff bets, and the button calls (8.7 small bets).

WHAT SHOULD YOU DO?

My first instinct is to fold. You could be drawing dead and even when you make your straight, sometimes a diamond will come on the river and kill your hand. But this situation will happen often enough so that it is worth further analysis.

First, there is a greater than a 1 percent chance that someone has flopped a flush. When you have two suited cards, you will flop a flush one time in 118; however, most flops will not have three cards of the same suit. This flop contains three suited cards, so the chances someone has flopped a flush go way up. With four suits, your chances of the board hitting your suit are around 14 percent. There are two players in the hand, but they might not both be suited. Your chances of being against a flopped flush are probably around 15 percent to 20 percent. Throw in the fact that there is a bet and call on this board and it is probably closer to 20 percent than 15 percent Even though the opener's bet looks like a standard continuation bet, not everyone will routinely make a bet with this board.

Here are my assumptions:

- One person has a diamond.
- Any time a diamond comes, you will fold.
- There will be a bet and two calls on turn, unless you fold.

Here is what can happen:

OUTCOME	PROBABILITY	WIN / LOSS
Diamond on Turn	19.1%	-1
Straight on Turn, Diamond on River	2.5%	-3
Straight on Turn, No Diamond on River	10.3%	11.7
Blank on Turn, Straight on River	11.8%	11.7
Blank, Blank	56.2%	-3

Whether you should call depends on how likely it is that someone has flopped a flush.

FLOPPED FLUSH	EXPECTATION (2 BETS ON THE TURN)	EXPECTATION (1 BET ON THE TURN)
0%	0.85	0.41
5%	0.66	0.24
10%	0.46	0.06
15%	0.26	-.11
20%	-0.07	-0.28

The key here is: How likely is it that someone has flopped a flush? If you agree that it is around 20 percent, then you should fold. Calling isn't terrible, but it seems like a losing play, unless you expect to get a lot of action if you make your straight.

I have heard a few good players recommend raising in this type of situation. This is an interesting idea. You could win the pot if the early player is putting in a continuation bet and doesn't have anything, and the cutoff has just a medium diamond in his hand. I probably wouldn't do it, just because I am a little afraid of getting reraised by a made flush or a hand such as A♦ J♠. And if the opener reraises and the cutoff folds, that messes up the odds for your 6-outer. But you only have to win this bet around 10 percent of the time, and you have outs if you get called.

But that evaluation is too rosy. If you are going to get reraised 20 percent of the time or more, you have to win quite a bit more often than 10 percent of the time to compensate for the risk you are taking. If you want to bluff raise in a situation like this, I would prefer to do it with a hand that has the A♦ in it. This hand has several advantages over the straight draw:

- You are drawing to the nuts.
- You cannot be drawing dead.
- You have 9 outs instead of 6.

Since no one else has the A♦, you are more likely to win the bluff, and you are less likely to get reraised.

Put all these things together, and I think that hands with the A♦ are much better candidates for a semibluff raise than this kind of straight draw. Does that make continuing with the straight draw a bad play? Not necessarily, but it's not one I am likely to make. In this situation, you can make a good case for raising, calling or folding—there is no "right" answer. But if the pot were smaller, I would almost certainly fold against two opponents; and heads up against an opener, I would raise.

12. A "SIMPLE" CALLING DECISION

You raise from middle position with A♦ Q♠ and only an unknown player in the big blind calls (4.5 bets, two players). The flop is K♦ 8♥ 8♦. The big blind checks, you bet and he raises (7.5 bets).

WHAT SHOULD YOU DO?

This is going to involve quite a bit of math. Although none of it is complex, if you are only interested in the answers, skip to the conclusions. The answer depends on what hands you put him on. Let's analyze this one in depth. His possible holdings are:

- An 8
- A king
- A flush draw
- A pocket pair
- Air (nothing)

To evaluate these holdings, first calculate the number of his hand combinations. We raised preflop raise from middle position, and he's in the big blind. Here's a likely calling range: 2-2, A-2, A-2s, K-7, K-2s, Q-8, Q-2s, J-8, J-3s, 10-7, 10-3s, 9-6, 9-3s, 8-6, 8-3s, 7-5, 7-3s, 6-5, 6-2s, 5-4, 5-2s, 4-2s, and 3-2s.

So, he has the following number of hand combinations from that range:

An 8	70 hands
A king	93 hands
A pocket pair	70 hands
A flush draw	51 hands
Air	479 hands

Now we have to weight them to account for the fact that our opponent check-raised us on the flop. Here are estimates of how often he will check-raise us with each hand:

An 8	50%
A king	35%
A pocket pair	40%
A flush draw	60%
Air	10%

Therefore, if we weight his hands, we come up with:

Hands with an 8:	70 x 50% = 35
Hands with a K:	93 x 35% = 33
Pocket pairs:	70 x 40% = 28
Flush draws:	51 x 60% = 31
Air:	479 x 10% = 48

Finally, let's look at how likely you are to be ahead after one more card with each holding. If he has an 8, you have no one-card outs, although you could make a runner-runner straight, which is worth half an out. We won't count this since you aren't too likely to call a big bet on the turn to draw to a gutshot. If he has a king, you have three outs. If he has a pocket pair, you usually have six outs. If he has a flush draw you have 37 outs (the non-diamonds). If he has air, you have 41 outs (everything except the six cards that give him a pair.)

HAND	OCCURS	OUTS	WEIGHTED OUTS
An 8	20%	0	0.0
A king	19%	3	0.6
Pocket pair	16%	6	1.0
Flush draw	17%	37	6.6
Air	27%	41	11.2

If you add these, it comes out to over 19 outs. With 4.5 bets in the pot, this turns out to be an easy call. But what if he never check-raises without at least a pair or flush draw? Let's make the "air" category zero. Then you have:

HAND	OCCURS	OUTS	WEIGHTED OUTS
An 8	28%	0	0.0
A king	26%	3	0.8
Pocket pair	22%	6	1.3
Flush draw	24%	37	9.0
Air	0%	41	0.0

That's 11.1 outs, which is still a clear call. So even if the check-raiser always has a hand, you should still call. Now, suppose he will only check-raise with a flush draw 40 percent of the time instead of 60 percent.

HAND	OCCURS	OUTS	WEIGHTED OUTS
An 8	30%	0	0.0
A king	28%	3	0.9
Pocket pair	24%	6	1.4
Flush draw	18%	37	6.5
Air	0%	41	0.0

That's 8.8 outs—a clear fold.

CONCLUSIONS

- If he will *ever* check-raise as a pure bluff, call.
- If he will never check-raise as a bluff:
  a. If he will check-raise with a flush draw more than half the time, call.
  b. Otherwise, fold.

Here is another way to put it:

1. Against aggressive or tricky players, call; and
2. Against passive, predictable players, fold. This might seem obvious, but it's nice to know that the math supports it.

9 HOW TO PLAY AGAINST DIFFERENT TYPES OF OPPONENTS

To improve your game in your pursuit of playing mistake-free limit hold'em, you must adjust your play to competently deal with a wider variety of situations than you did as a beginner. In particular, you must learn how to play against several special types of opponents. This chapter gives you important pointers on how to adapt your play against the five most common types of players—solid, tight, loose, passive and aggressive.

To this discussion of "the usual list of suspects," I have added one particularly annoying archetype that you're sure to encounter—the super-aggressor who tries to steal your blind every time he's in a pot with you. Since this type of player is such a troublemaker, I have placed him first and go into quite a bit of detail in discussing how to best play against him.

PLAYING THE BLIND AGAINST AN AGGRESSIVE VILLAIN

In describing this type of aggressive villain, I am thinking of a particular player I've played with frequently. I hate playing with him because he raises my big blind frequently and then seems to outplay me the rest of the way. When I try to play back at him, he is always more aggressive than I am, and I always seem to take the worst of it. Sound familiar? He is not some mindless maniac—he's a highly successful player who adopts a tight-aggressive style from early position and a loose-aggressive style from late position. He is fearless and reads people well. I have tried to match his aggression, but being out of position and less familiar with that style of play, it hasn't worked out well for me.

Here's one example. The villain opens from middle position. I call in the big blind with Q♥ 9♦ (4.5 bets, two players). The flop is J♣ 9♠ 3♦. I check, he bets, I raise, and he reraises. I expect him to reraise here 100 percent of the time. I call (5.25 big bets, two players). The turn is the 5♦. I don't want to give a free card, so I bet. He raises. I know he will raise here with a draw or with air, so I call (9.25 bets).

The river is the A♦. I check and he bets. With the ace coming down, there are now a lot of hands he could have opened with that beat me, but there are now 10.25 bets in the pot, so I call. He shows J♥ 10♠ and wins a big pot. Notice how I built a big pot with middle pair, which is only an okay hand, and I also was out of position. After losing five big bets in this hand, I realized that I needed another approach that suits my style and is simpler.

A SIMPLE STRATEGY

I chose the passive approach. This should at least be an option in your arsenal, if not your normal approach to playing this type of player. The strategy is to check and call the whole way, keeping the pot small. Let's look at the math of this approach:

Suppose he will try to use his position to his advantage:

- When he hits the flop (or a later street), he will bet every street.
- When he misses, he will bet the flop and turn, but check the river.

My strategy will be:

- When I totally miss the flop, I will fold on the flop.
- When I flop any pair or have a pocket pair, I will call all the way.

Although this does not figure into these calculations, I obviously will call the flop and turn with two overcards, a good draw, and with a gutshot straight draw.

OUTCOME	MY INVESTMENT	POT SIZE (SMALL BETS)	MY WIN/LOSS (SMALL BETS)
He misses it	4	11.25	7.25
He makes it	6	15.25	-6.0

However, around two-thirds of the time I will miss the flop when I call as the small blind. That will cost me around two-thirds of a small bet. Using the win percent of his distribution of hands, we can calculate the expectation of playing various hands. First, assume we start with a pocket pair. Here is how we do:

EXPECTATION OF PLAYING POCKET PAIRS FROM THE BLIND AGAINST AN AGGRESSIVE VILLAIN					
START WITH	10%	15%	20%	30%	50%
2-2	-0.82	-0.34	-0.20	0.00	0.27
3-3	-0.74	-0.26	-0.13	0.13	0.47
4-4	-0.67	-0.18	-0.04	0.24	0.72
5-5	-0.61	-0.12	0.07	0.42	0.98
6-6	-0.57	-0.07	0.23	0.69	1.26
7-7	-0.42	0.07	0.49	0.93	1.61
8-8	0.01	0.42	0.78	1.27	2.04
9-9	0.45	0.80	1.16	1.76	2.51
10-10	1.04	1.39	1.85	2.45	3.00
J-J	1.70	2.17	2.60	3.03	3.44
Q-Q	2.65	3.01	3.35	3.62	3.92
K-K	3.73	4.01	4.13	4.25	4.49
A-A	5.16	5.24	5.21	5.72	5.25

Therefore, if he will raise with the top 10 percent of his hands, we need at least 8-8 to show a profit. If he raises with the top 20 percent, we need 5-5 or better to make a profit. Now, let's assume that we draw to two unpaired cards and make a pair. The following chart lists the results that we can expect.

EXPECTATION OF PLAYING UNPAIRED CARDS FROM THE BLIND AGAINST AN AGGRESSIVE VILLAIN					
MAKE A PAIR	10%	15%	20%	30%	50%
2-2	-0.94	-0.78	-0.73	-0.67	-0.57
3-3	-0.91	-0.75	-0.71	-0.62	-0.51
4-4	-0.89	-0.73	-0.68	-0.59	-0.43
5-5	-0.87	-0.71	-0.64	-0.54	-0.36
6-6	-0.86	-0.70	-0.59	-0.45	-0.26
7-7	-0.81	-0.65	-0.50	-0.37	-0.15
8-8	-0.57	-0.54	-0.41	-0.26	-0.01
9-9	-0.53	-0.42	-0.28	-0.10	0.14
10-10	-0.34	-0.22	-0.05	0.12	0.30
J-J	-0.10	0..03	0.20	0.31	0.44
Q-Q	0.22	0.30	0.45	0.50	0.60
K-K	0.58	0.63	0.71	0.70	0.78
A-A	1.05	1.03	1.07	1.02	1.03

I used the following ranges of hands that the aggressive villain might have to calculate these percentages:

AN AGGRESSIVE PLAYER'S RANGE OF HANDS	
HIS RANGE	POSSIBLE HANDS
10%	8-8, A-9s, K-10, Q-10s, A-J, K-Q
15%	7-7, A-7s, K-9s, Q-10s, J-10s, A-10, K-10, Q-J
20%	6-6, A-4s, K-8s, Q-9s, J-9s, 10-9s, A-9, K-10, Q-10, J-10
30%	5-5, A-2s, K-5s, Q-7s, J-8s,10-8s, 9-8s, A-7, A-5, K-9, Q-9, J-9,10-9
50%	3-3, A-2s, K-2s, Q-2s, J-4s, 10-6s, 9-6s, 8-6s, 7-6s, 6-5s, A-2, K-5, Q-7, J-7, 10-8, 9-8

Now let's put all these numbers to work. Suppose he opens under the gun. If he is very tight early (which is possible but unlikely), he might open with the top 10 percent of his hands. Opening with the top 15 percent is more likely. If he opens with his top 15 percent, you see from the first table that you can profitably call preflop with 7-7 or better If you don't have a pair, you can also call with any A-2, K-8, Q-10 or better.

Why do I include K-8? Flopping a pair of kings gives us an expectation of 0.63 bets. Flopping a pair of eights will give us an expectation of -0.54 bets. Since we will flop each pair equally often, our average expectation is positive. Note that although the overall expectation of flopping a pair of eights is negative, once we flop it, we have already invested one bet, and the expectation for calling the rest of the way is positive.

As for suited hands, I would call with A-2s, K-7s, Q-9s, and J-10s. Here are the hands I would play against each of his ranges:

HANDS TO PLAY AGAINST EACH OF AN AGGRESSIVE PLAYER'S RANGES

HIS RANGE	HIS POSITION	HANDS TO CALL WITH IN THE BIG BLIND
10%	Tight Early	8-8, A-2, K-8, K-7s, Q-10, Q-9s, J-10s
15%	Early	7-7, A-2, K-8, K-7s, Q-10, Q-9s, J-10s.
20%	Middle	5-5, A-2, K-4, K-2s, Q-8, Q-7s, J-10, J-9s
30%	Cutoff	3-3, A-2, K-2, Q-6,Q-5s, J-8, J-7s, 10-9, 10-8s
50%	Button or Small Blind	2-2, A-2, K-2, Q-2, J-4, J-3s, 10-6, 10-5s, 9-8, 9-7s

This paragraph is only for those who are interested in the math. Some people may think it is better to determine the expectation of a hand like K-2, by seeing how often K-2 wins against his range instead of seeing how often a pair of kings wins and how often a pair of deuces wins. The problem with the method is that it includes the times you win with a king-high hand. With our approach, you will never call on the flop without a pair, so you will never win with a king-high hand. So, the win percent of K-2 against his range is too high.

What about calling him down with an ace? Without going through the math, against a 20-percent villain, you can profitably call down with A-K through A-J. Against a 50-percent villain, I would call with hands as weak as A-8. Weaker aces are slightly profitable, but they are very marginal calling hands. Caution: This does not mean you should use this as your default strategy against everyone. If you are going to adopt this strategy against very aggressive players, play your normal game against the other players at the table.

What if the aggressive villain adapts? Suppose he sees how you are playing and starts checking behind you on the turn? You have a couple of choices. You can bet into him on the river (risking a raise if he was slowplaying or decides to bluff), or you can check the river to try to induce a bluff. This strategy does not provide all the answers.

Can you raise from the big blind with your big pairs? It doesn't hurt you on other hands. Normally you would need to mix up your play, but knowing you don't have a big pair doesn't help him exploit your other hands. If they have a positive expectation, the villain has no way to exploit you if you just check and call. However, if you use this strategy I recommend that you don't raise with big pairs. The whole point is to use the villain's aggressiveness against him. Let him keep firing into you. If you don't usually raise him, suddenly raising may make it too easy for him to get off his hand.

> Use the villain's aggressiveness against him—let him keep firing into you.

Now let's move along to playing against other types of special players. We'll start by discussing ways you can mix up your play to confuse your opponents.

MIXING IT UP TO CONFUSE YOUR OPPONENTS

When you are playing against good players, they will eventually notice how you play and adjust to your style. For example, if you never bluff check-raise on the turn, they will start folding to your check-raises. Most experts recommend that you mix it up to make yourself harder to read. They will tell you to not always play the same hand the same way. There is merit in this advice, but before you start mixing up how you play a hand, you need a "normal" or default method of playing it. Then you can occasionally play it differently to make life harder on the villains.

When I recommend a play in this book, the play I suggest is usually the normal way to play a hand. Occasionally you will want to vary your play, but not too often. In fact, some factors should make you vary your play less often.

VARY YOUR PLAY LESS OFTEN WHEN:

- Your opponents are weak.
- The pot is big.
- There are lots of players in the hand.
- You rarely play with this group of players.

In these situations, make the play that usually wins the most or loses the least. Don't worry about some meta-game consideration of trying to set them up for a bigger win on some future hand. You may not get the opportunity. Also, in some situations, you don't want to mix up your play. For example, suppose a lot of limpers are in the pot and the flop comes 8-5-2.

You have A-8 and the player on your right bets. Raise. Raise 100 percent of the time! You probably have the best hand, and you don't want players sticking around with overcards because there are too many overcards to your pair of eights.

PATTERNS TO WATCH FOR

There are patterns you need to watch out for. Some players love to bet their weak hands and check their strong ones. Others like to bet the flop and check the turn, but they will usually fold the river against a bet. You cannot afford to be so predictable. Good players will figure this out. Even without mixing it up, there are things you should be doing to make yourself harder to read. Play the same way with lots of different hands. Consider a common situation: A player opens with a raise and you call from the big blind. I will check-raise with many hands ranging from a flopped full house to a flush draw to an overcard and a gutshot straight draw. That makes the check-raise hard to read.

When you have a playable hand, there are three ways to play it: bet, check-raise, or check-call. Many players decide to mix it up by using each strategy part of the time. They will bet a flush draw, check-raise with top pair, and check-call with other pairs. However, by mixing it up, they become more predictable.

Game theory says that you should generally bet your best hands—and a few of your worst hands. I do some of this, but I also expand my mix of hands by betting and raising with marginal hands. I gamble a bit more with my mediocre hands. As a result, I rarely run pure bluffs with hopeless hands. Purists will argue that this is the wrong way to play, but it is an effective way to make it harder for your opponents to put you on a strong hand when you bet or raise with a strong holding.

> Make the play that usually wins the most or loses the least.

Of course, we don't always have good opponents. We usually play at tables where a few of our opponents are good, solid players, while some play loose and stay in pots with seemingly hopeless hands; others are tight and rigorous in their hand selections; some are timid and passive even with good hands; and a few are very aggressive and never seem to slow down.

Let's look at 16 hands where I adjusted my play against different types of players. Analyzing them will show you the lessons you can learn from my mistakes.

16 GAME SCENARIOS

1. PLAYING AGAINST A PASSIVE PLAYER

A new player comes into the game and posts his blind in the hijack seat (two seats off the button) so that he can receive a hand without waiting. I am in the cutoff seat just to his left with A♠ J♣. Everyone folds to the new player, who checks. I raise. A very loose, passive player on the button calls for two bets. The blinds fold and the hijack calls (7.5 bets, three players). The flop is A♥ 7♥ 3♦. The hijack checks to me, I bet, and both the button and the hijack call. The turn is the 6♥, putting three hearts on the board. Again, the hijack checks, I bet, and the button calls. The hijack folds.

The river is the J♠, giving me top two pair. The board is A♥ 7♥ 3♦ 6♥ J♠. While I am getting ready to bet, the passive player on the button surprises me by betting out of turn. I have top two pair, so I raise. He calls. We will see his hand in a moment.

WHAT'S WRONG WITH MY PLAY?

Against a normal player, raising with top two pair is clearly indicated here. But this is not a normal player. He is very passive—so why is he suddenly betting on the river? Here was my analysis. I have to figure that he liked the jack, but how could it have helped him? He is passive, so he isn't betting a pair of jacks with an ace on the board. He must have a better hand. There are two likely hands, a set of jacks or two pair.

His play fits with pocket jacks. Being a passive player, he would not reraise before the flop with a pair of jacks. He certainly is not going to raise with his jacks when there is an ace on the board. And if he spiked a jack on the river, he is going to bet. What about jacks up? Would he play J-7s, J-6s, or J-3s? He is very loose, so it's certainly possible. He would call to the river with his pair and then bet when he makes his two pair. While this involves some horrible play on his part, he is capable of it. There are many more ways for him to have made jacks up than trip jacks, so there is really nothing wrong with my play. Raising is fine. I would expect to be ahead most of the time.

So what did he have? He showed 5♠ 4♥ for a straight. He cold-called two bets before the flop with 5-4 offsuit! Then he called the flop with only a gutshot straight draw. When he caught his perfect card, he didn't raise the turn. And when I raised him on the river, he was clearly afraid of a flush, so reraising was out of the question for him.

So what did I do wrong? I tried to figure out the play of a very loose, very passive player. I never considered the straight—I couldn't see how he could have played 6-5 suited for two bets, let alone 6-5 offsuit.

THE LESSON

- Don't over analyze the play of horrible players. Just assume they can have anything. When a player who has been checking and calling all the way suddenly bets out, he usually has either a very good hand or a weak one. In either case, you shouldn't raise when it is a close decision. They will probably only call the raise when you are beaten.

2. WHAT ELSE COULD HE BE BETTING?

Two early players limp. The game has been very loose, and I don't think a raise will knock many players out, so I just call with 9♥ 9♦. Three more players call, including both blinds (6 bets, six players). The flop is 8♠ 8♥ 4♦. Both blinds check, and the first limper, who is a loose-passive player, bets. The next limper folds, I call, and everyone else folds (4 big bets, two players). The turn is the Q♣. The limper bets and I call (6 bets). The river is the 10♦. The limper bets and I call again. The limper shows 10♦ 8♦ for a full house.

WHAT'S WRONG WITH THIS PLAY?

When a passive player bets into five other players with this board, he has something. Some players might try to steal here, but passive players don't try to steal from five people, so he has a hand. What can it be? An 8 sure seems likely. He could even have pocket fours. Whatever it is, he almost certainly has a better hand than I do. The pot isn't huge, so I am not getting a good price to draw to two outs. Also, there are still four more active players behind me on the flop. If he doesn't have me beat, there are a lot of other players who might.

Finally, when the queen comes on the turn and he doesn't slow down, it is really time to give it up. He doesn't know for sure that I don't have an 8 when I call on the very dry flop. However, he seems unfazed. Just because he is passive doesn't mean he isn't worried about what I have—in fact, passive players are usually the most fearful.

THE LESSON

- When a passive player leads into a big field, beware! A passive player will be afraid that you have a big hand, so he will have an above average hand when he bets.

> The biggest mistakes weak players make are playing too many hands, chasing, and being too passive.

3. CALLING AGAINST A BLUFF CATCHER

A tight, solid player raises under the gun (**UTG**). A loose player calls. I three-bet from the button with 9♥ 9♦. They both call. The flop is J♥ 7♥ 7♠. They both pass, I bet, the tight UTG raises, the loose player goes out, and I call. The turn is a blank. I pass, he bets, and I call. The river is another blank. I pass, he bets, and I call. He shows J-J for a set of jacks.

WHAT'S WRONG WITH MY PLAY?

My opponent is a tight player who opened UTG and I have three-bet him—yet he still raises me on the flop. I have told him I have a strong hand. He isn't impressed. And I don't have more than he should be expecting. (To put it another way, I am at the bottom of my range.) What can he have that I can beat? I am behind to a jack, a 7, or any bigger pair. His most likely holding is A-J. I am dead to two outs except for a backdoor flush draw, assuming he doesn't have a bigger heart.

The only hand I can beat is a flush draw. Is he going to raise me with a draw? Probably not this guy, unless he has a couple of overcards as well. If this is his hand, he is probably the favorite. But I still call him three times to get to a showdown, where all I can beat is a bluff. This was a perfect chance to get out early: If I had folded when he raised, I would have saved five small bets.

THE LESSON

- When you have already revealed the strength of your hand and your opponent bets or raises, you are probably beaten, particularly if he is tight. At this point, you basically can only beat a bluff. When you can only beat a bluff, consider your opponent. If he is tricky, you will need to call him down most of the time. If he isn't, get out quickly.

4. A POINTLESS BET

A hyper-aggressive yet decent player opens with a raise from middle position. He plays too many hands, but he plays pretty well after the flop though very aggressively. I three-bet from the button with A♣ 10♣. The flop comes 9-9-7 rainbow. He bets. I call, planning to call him down with my ace high. The turn is a king, and he checks. I decide to bet because he had shown weakness—he check-raises.

WHAT'S WRONG WITH MY PLAY?

There is no particular point to my bet. Is it for value? What weaker hands will he call with? Is it a bluff? What stronger hands will he fold? In reality, when the table bully suddenly checks the turn, red flags should go up. Why is Mr. Aggressive suddenly checking? If I check the turn, I can find out for one bet on the river. If he is ahead, it only costs me one bet; if he is behind, he is likely to bluff.

THE LESSON

- Don't bet hands with showdown value just because someone shows weakness. Against very aggressive players, be more suspicious of a check than a bet. Against very aggressive players, try to induce a bluff on the end.

5. ANOTHER POINTLESS BET

Here is a hand the villain played badly. He raises from the cutoff with A♠ 10♥. I reraise from the small blind, and I have a pretty tight image. He calls (two players, 7 bets). The flop is

7♠ 4♣ 2♥. I bet, he raises, and I call (5.5 big bets). The turn is the Q♣. I check, he bets, and I call (7.5 bets). The river is the 9♠. I check, he bets, and I call. I show A♦ K♥ and take the pot.

MY HAND   **VILLAIN'S HAND**

THE BOARD

WHAT'S WRONG WITH HIS PLAY?

Aggression is good, but it needs to be tempered with some thought. What do I have to three-bet before the flop? Most likely are a big ace, K-Qs, or a medium to big pair. While it is possible I might fold a hand like A-J on the turn, by the time I get to the river there are extremely few hands I can have where I will not call a river bet. If he bets, there will be 8.5 big bets in the pot.

While his play might make some sense if I had not three-bet before the flop (I could have a busted club draw), it makes almost no sense as the action went. As in the previous hand, you should have a reason to bet. You either want to make a worse-hand call (value bet) or a better-hand fold (bluff). It is hard to know which he has in mind here. Is it for value? What weaker hands will I call with? A-9? Not likely. Is it a bluff?

What stronger hands will I fold? A-J or maybe 2-2? Normally when you have a hand with some showdown value on the river (such as an unpaired ace or a small pair) and your opponent checks to you, the best play is to check behind him.

THE LESSON

- If your hand has some showdown value on the river, check when you close the action. If you are not sure whether you are betting for value or as a bluff, you usually should not bet.

6. THE LUNATIC WILL BET IT FOR YOU

A couple of players limp and I call on the button with 10♥ 9♥ and both blinds call. The flop is a miraculous K♥ Q♥ J♥ giving me a straight flush. The table maniac, who bets on anything and everything, fires out from the big blind. Everyone folds to me. I call. The small blind goes out, so I am heads up with the maniac. The turn comes another heart. He fires again. I pray he has the A♥ and raise. He folds.

MY HAND

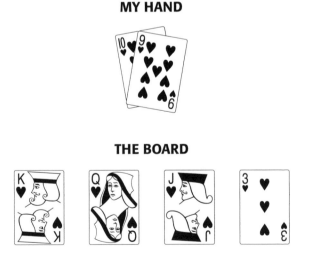

THE BOARD

WHAT'S WRONG WITH MY PLAY?

Why is it a bad play? He is a maniac. He will bet the river. I am sure to get another big bet. And if I am lucky enough to run into the ace of hearts, he will still have it on the river. Basically, I have just told him I have a flush. There is no other hand I can raise with. That will scare even a maniac. If he bets the river, I can always raise at that point. If, by any miracle, he checks the river, I can still bet the river and I will probably get a call. Betting the river after he checks is a lot less scary than raising on the turn. There is almost no scenario where I make more money by raising the turn.

THE LESSON

- Against a maniac, let him bet for you, especially if the board is scary. Give him lots of chances to bluff at it. Don't try to take the initiative away from the maniac, when you have position. Let him hang himself. You don't need to be in a hurry to pull the trigger when you have position. Only raise earlier if:
  - **a.** Giving up a free card is dangerous, or
  - **b.** You might lose your customers if a scare card comes on the river.
- An example of a possible scare card is when there are three suited cards on the turn. A fourth card of the same suit might scare off anyone without the ace of the flush suit.

> Let the maniac bet it for you!

7. IN A HURRY TO RAISE THE MANIAC? DON'T BE

I am dealt A♣ K♣ in middle position. I raise and a maniac in the cutoff calls, as well as the big blind. The flop is 6♠ K♠ 6♦. The big blind checks, I bet, and the maniac raises.

The big blind goes out and I just call. The turn is the 2♠. I check-raise the maniac, and he makes it three bets. I call. The river is the 9♦. I check, he bets, and I call. He shows J♠ 8♠ for a flush.

MY HAND   **VILLAIN'S HAND**

THE BOARD

WHAT'S WRONG WITH MY PLAY?

When the spade comes on the turn, I am either way ahead or way behind. If he has the flush or a 6 (not impossible for a guy who calls two bets before the flop with J-8s), I am drawing dead. Otherwise, I'm in great shape, probably way ahead. However, raising on the turn presents some problems. If I am way ahead, I make it easy for him to get off the hand. A check-raise on the turn is a powerful move, and as it turns out, when I am way behind, it costs me two more bets. There is little profit in raising the turn.

Against less of a maniac it would probably make sense to three-bet the flop and bet the turn, because that is more likely to get a call on the turn from a weaker hand. But with the maniac, I am better off to let him take the lead. Let him bluff off his chips.

How about check-calling the turn and check-raising the river? That is probably better. It is not clear what hand he will call with on the river that I can beat. But he is a maniac. This line loses the same amount as the line I took, but usually wins more when he doesn't have much. Some people might say you should raise the turn to charge him more if he has a single spade in his hand. There is a bit of merit to this, but he isn't going anywhere with a spade in his hand, and if a fourth spade comes down and he makes his flush on the river, just calling will cost you less money.

THE LESSON

- Don't be in a hurry to raise the maniac. If you are pretty sure he will keep betting, wait until the river. If you are going to have to call a reraise because you have a pretty good hand and your opponent will bluff raise, tend to bet or raise a little less often. Basically, play more conservatively against tricky opponents and maniacs. Don't try to match the aggressiveness of a very aggressive player.

> Don't try to get aggressive with a maniac. Let him keep betting.

8. KEEP IT SMALL, STUPID!

A tight but hyper-aggressive player opens under the gun. He doesn't play a lot of hands, but when he does play one, he is extremely aggressive. I three-bet with 7♦ 7♣. The small blind and the opener call (10 small bets). The flop is 10♥ 8♠ 3♥. The small blind checks and the opener bets. I decide to try to get the small blind out. The worst of all worlds happens: The small blind calls and the hyper guy reraises! I call and the small blind calls (20 small bets). I figure the small blind has hearts.

The turn is the 2♦. The small blind checks, the opener bets and we both call (13 big bets). The river is the 5♦. The small blind checks, the opener bets, I call, and the small blind folds. The hyper guy shows K♥ K♠.

WHAT'S WRONG WITH MY PLAY?

I should probably fold preflop. This guy is very tight and he opened under the gun. My 7-7 is the worst hand I will three-bet with against an UTG opener. I could easily muck the hand preflop and save 10 small bets. When the small blind calls two bets cold on the flop, he is most likely on a draw. I thought about him slowplaying a big hand like top set, but with two hearts on the board, most good players aren't going to miss a chance to make other players pay to draw.

THE LESSON

- When playing a tight, very aggressive player, don't play a marginal hand.

9. WAY AHEAD OR WAY BEHIND?

A loose player limps under the gun and everyone else folds to me in the cutoff, where I have A♦ 10♥. I have raised this loose player quite often when he has limped, so I decide to mix it up and just call. The button raises behind me, the blinds fold, and we both call (7.5 small bets, three players). The flop is A♣ 7♥ 3♠. The limper comes out with a bet. I am worried that the opener on the button may have a bigger ace than mine, so I just call instead of raising. The button folds.

The turn is the 6♣. My opponent bets. I decide I have not shown the strength of my hand yet and I raise. The limper reraises. I call (10.75 big bets). The river is the 5♠. He bets. I call. He shows A♠ 7♣ for top two pair.

WHAT'S WRONG WITH MY PLAY?

First, I don't like my play preflop. Why let the blinds in when I can isolate against a weak player? There are times to mix up my play; however, the advantage of having dead money in the pot far outweighs the benefit of mixing up my play. And why worry about being deceptive against a weak player? They aren't usually paying attention anyway.

When the limper bets on the flop with an ace out there and a preflop raiser, it means one of two things: (1) Either he is such a weak player that he doesn't respect the ace, or (2) he has a strong enough hand that he doesn't care about the ace. I am either way ahead or way behind. I could raise to find out, but the preflop raiser is still to act behind me and he could have a bigger ace. Would he fold a bigger ace if I raise? We'll never know.

My worst play came on the turn. When he bets out, he is indicating that he really doesn't care about the ace on the board. I may not have shown the strength of my hand, but he still bet into the preflop raiser with an ace on the board, and he kept firing after I called the flop. In other words, he should suspect that someone is strong.

I am either way ahead or way behind. That is usually a bad situation for raising—that's calling time. This is particularly true when I have position. If the player slows down, I can always bet the river. When he three-bets the turn, I am toast and I probably should muck it. It is extremely rare that someone makes it three bets on the turn without a very big hand. If I am up against a set, I am drawing dead. Against two pair, I have either five outs or (as it stands) three outs. The outside chance that he is bluffing or that I might overtake him makes my call on the turn a mistake, even with a pot that big. The pot is nine big bets, but it will cost me two big bets to get to a showdown, so the pot odds aren't all that great. Once I call the turn, calling the river seems mandatory

THE LESSON

- Don't mix up your play preflop when you have a chance to isolate against a weak player and drive out the blinds. Dead money is your friend. When there is an ace on the flop and someone bets into a preflop raiser, this is a classic case of being either very strong or very weak. You may want to raise while it is cheap to see where you stand. When a player three-bets on the turn, he usually has a big hand, so unless you have a strong reason for thinking otherwise, one pair won't win.

> If you start with better hands than the other players at the table, you will win. Everything else determines how much you will win.

10. MAKING A THIN VALUE BET AGAINST A TRICKY PLAYER

I raise from the button with A♥ 8♦. Only the very loose and aggressive big blind calls (4.5 bets, two players). He has shown that he will make very aggressive moves. The flop is 5♠ 3♥ 2♣. I bet and he raises. With two overcards and a straight draw, I have an easy call (4.25 big bets, two players). He is quite capable of raising with just about anything, so my ace could be the best card. The turn is the A♦. He bets and since I have position, I want him to keep bluffing. Of course, if he has a 4, I am badly beat but I can't be sure of that. I call (6.25 bets).

The river is the 2♠. He checks. I figure his check shows weakness and my aces are the best hand, so I bet. He raises. He is tricky, and there are 9.25 bets in the pot. I feel I have to call, and he shows 7♠ 4♠ for a wheel straight.

PLAY AGAINST DIFFERENT TYPES OF OPPONENTS

WHAT'S WRONG WITH MY PLAY?

I made several mistakes. On the flop, I should three-bet to take the free card. However the big mistakes take place on the river. He is a tricky player. For some players, the check on the river shows weakness or that they have given up, but this is not that kind of player. With four to a straight on the board, this is not a great place to value bet one pair. My best play is to check. Should I call his raise? Since he is a tricky player, probably yes, although even tricky players don't usually bluff raise on the river. With 9.25 bets in the pot, you only need to win around 10 percent of the time to make calling a good play.

THE LESSON

- This hand demonstrates a key point about value betting the river. If you don't think you can fold to a raise, you should be less likely to make a thin value bet. When you make a thin value bet, you don't expect to win most of the time when someone calls. If you are risking two bets, your value bet probably isn't profitable since you will call a raise.

- Don't make marginal bets into tricky players on the river. Save them for more predictable players, where you can comfortably fold to a raise. Don't usually make thin value bets into boards where four to a straight or four to a flush are out there. When you get check-raised on the river, the villain almost always has a legitimate hand. Players who are hyper-aggressive before the flop are not always hyper-aggressive on the later streets, particularly on the river.

11. BET A GOOD HAND INTO A SCARY BOARD?

I raise from early position with K♠ Q♠. A very aggressive player reraises from middle position. The small blind calls, but the big blind folds (10 bets, three players). The flop is K♣ Q♦ 9♣. I check, and everyone checks behind (5 big bets).

The turn is the 3♦. I bet, the aggressive player calls and the small blind folds (7 bets).

The river is the J♦. I bet, and the aggressive player raises. I curse under my breath and call. He shows Q♣ J♥. My two pair is bigger than his and I take the pot.

WHAT'S WRONG WITH MY PLAY?

Although it worked out well in this case, my river bet is a bad idea. With that board, two pair is almost reduced to a bluff catcher. Any 10 makes a straight, and almost any big pocket pair makes a set. And while it is less likely, my opponent could have made a backdoor flush; in fact, if he was on a draw, there is a very good chance he made it. And all the things that make the board scary for you should make it scary for him. It is going to be hard to get a call from a weaker hand: If he has any kind of legitimate hand for his preflop three-bet, he is likely to either fold or raise, neither of which is something you want to see.

THE LESSON

- Don't bet good but not great hands into scary boards. You are likely to have to call a better hand if you get raised. When you make a thin value bet into a scary board, the board makes it hard for players to call with hands that you can beat. With a good but not great hand, tend to check to very aggressive players on the river. Give them a chance to bluff at you. Although most players rarely bluff-raise on the river, they may be raising with a strong hand that you can beat. You have to call for one more bet with a strong hand.

12. DON'T BUILD A POT YOU CAN'T WIN

Everyone folds to an aggressive player in the small blind, who raises. I reraise from the big blind with Q♥ J♥. He calls (7 bets, two players). The flop is 10♠ 10♦ 7♦. He checks, I bet and he raises. He could be raising on anything, and I want to keep the initiative, so I reraise. He makes it four bets and I call (7.5 big bets, two players). The turn is the 2♠. He bets and I call hoping for a miracle on the river. The river is the K♦. He bets and I fold. I lost four big bets on the hand with nothing!

WHAT'S WRONG WITH MY PLAY?

I got carried away by the fact that he is aggressive. Even though I had a hand that looked pretty before the flop, once the flop comes I have absolutely nothing. I should give it up when I get check-raised on the flop. Sure, it is possible he is on a stone-cold bluff, but sometimes you don't have the hand to defend against this. However, to win this pot I will need to go to war with a hand with no showdown value. That means building a very big pot.

Sometimes you will win the pot by answering aggression with aggression, but it makes more sense to do so with some decent outs or decent showdown value. Two weak overcards isn't a good hand with a pair and a flush draw on the board. With an ace or a small pair, it makes sense to call down an aggressive player here, but then you don't want to get aggressive and slow him down. If he is on a bluff, you want him to keep betting. If he isn't, you don't want to put any more in the pot than you have to.

THE LESSON

- Don't build a big pot with a hand that has no showdown value. If you don't have an ace, a pair or a decent draw, you should usually fold and wait for a better place to go to war.

13. WHAT COULD HE BE CALLING WITH?

An early player limps, and a very tight player on the button raises. I am in the small blind with A♥ Q♦. Normally, I would reraise here, but this guy is very tight so I decide to just call. The big blind folds, and the limper calls (7 bets, three players). The flop is A♣ 8♥ 3♥. I pass along with the limper. The button bets. I raise, the limper folds and the button calls (5.5 big bets). The turn is the J♠. I bet and he calls (7.5 bets). The river is the 10♦. I bet, and he calls. He shows A♠ Q♠ and we split the pot.

WHAT'S WRONG WITH MY PLAY?

As it turns out, betting the river didn't cost me anything, but I should not make this bet. What can he have? He is tight, so it is unlikely he raised before the flop with a hand like J-10s. His most likely hands are a big ace or a big pair.

Once I check-raise the flop, he is pretty likely to have a big ace. His only other possible hands are K-K, Q-Q, J-J, 10-10, or 9-9. It is possible, but not likely that he has big hearts, as well. Plenty of aggressive players could have a wider range, but a tight player isn't going to raise before the flop and then call the check-raise, without a very strong hand.

The turn doesn't change things much although he is less likely to have 10-10 or 9-9. Tight players aren't going to call with two overcards on the board, when you act this strong. Many of them would have folded K-K or Q-Q by now. On the river, we should look at what he will call me with. He isn't calling with a busted flush. He is calling with big aces. Will he call with K-K or Q-Q? Perhaps he will. Let's give him a 50 percent chance of calling. So here are his possible hands:

HAND	WAYS	WIN / LOSE	PROBABILITY
A-A	1	L	100%
K-K	6	W	50%
Q-Q	3	W	50%
J-J	6	L	50%
10-10	6	L	50%
9-9	6	W	25%
A-K	8	L	100%
A-Q	6	Tie	100%
A-J	8	L	100%
A-10	8	L	100%

If we don't weight the possibilities, there are 37 possible hands that I lose to. There are only 15 wins and six ties. Those are not good odds. If you weight the possible hands, based on the action, for the chance that he actually holds those hands it gets even worse: 31 losses and only six wins. None of this even takes into account that he will raise the river with many of the hands I lose to. I will have a hard choice if I get raised. As it turns out, I had perhaps the best outcome, getting a push. Checking the river would have made more sense.

Someone may argue he might have a hand like K♥ J♥, and he will give you a crying call on the river with his pair of jacks. However, a rock isn't going to raise a limper before the flop with this hand. He will limp along if he is going to play it.

THE LESSON
- Don't shift into automatic gear just because you have a good hand like top pair, big kicker. When a rock keeps calling you, you need to give him credit for a hand. Unless you have a big hand, slow down. When there are lots of big cards on the board, you need to be more cautious.

> When a rock continues to call, he has a hand.

14. WHEN A WOLF ACTS LIKE A SHEEP

Everyone folds to an aggressive player in the small blind, who limps. I check in the big blind with 5♥ 3♠ (2 bets, two players). The flop is 10♠ 4♠ 4♦. He checks, and I bet. He calls (2 big bets, two players.) The turn is the 5♦. He bets and I call (4 big bets, two players). The river is the K♣. He bets, I call, and he shows me A♠ A♣.

WHAT'S WRONG WITH MY PLAY?
Aggressive players don't limp from the small blind. Aggressive players don't check the flop when heads up against

161

a big blind who has never voluntarily put a chip in. When an aggressive player suddenly turns into a pussycat, my big hand detector should be going off like crazy.

It is probably not worth it even trying to steal this pot with a bet on the flop. Then when he calls, even more alarm bells should be going off. He didn't raise like an aggressive player making a move. He just calls. Nothing about his play makes sense—unless he has a monster hand. This is a tiny pot, so the smart thing is to give up on it.

THE LESSON
- When an aggressive player starts acting completely out of character, be afraid. Be very afraid!

15. CALLING A ROCK WILL PUT YOU IN A HARD PLACE

A tight and aggressive player (**TAG**) raises under the gun. I reraise from the cutoff with A♦ K♠, and the tight-aggressive player caps it (9.4 bets and two players). The flop is K♣ 5♣ 2♠. The villain bets and I call (5.7 big bets). The turn is the 3♥. The villain bets, and with position I decide to just call (7.7 bets). The river is the Q♠. The villain bets and I raise. I get reraised and call.

WHAT'S WRONG WITH MY PLAY?

Before revealing the villain's hand, let's think about what the villain could have. When a tight player caps they usually have a strong hand. It could be as limited a range as A-A, K-K and A-K. Some players will do it with hands like Q-Q, J-J, and 10-10. Some maniacs will cap it with almost anything, but this is a tight player. And keep in mind that she opened under the gun. She isn't doing that with junk.

If she is extremely tight, we are in deep trouble. This chart shows the number of combinations for each hand. For example, with an ace in our hand, there are three ways to make A-A.

HAND	WINS	TIES	LOSSES
A-A	0	0	3
K-K	0	0	3
A-K	0	9	0

The best I can hope for is a tie. Raising is crazy against this range. Now, let's add a few more hands:

HAND	WINS	TIES	LOSSES
A-A	0	0	3
K-K	0	0	3
AK	0	9	0
Q-Q	0	0	3
J-J	6	0	0
10-10	6	0	0

We now have six wins and nine losses, hardly a good situation to raise. And given that we are guessing at her range, she is more likely to have capped with Q-Q than with 10-10. That might not even be in her range. You can add more hands to her range. She might have K-Q, A-Q, A-Js, and A-10s.

HAND	WINS	TIES	LOSSES
A-A	0	0	3
K-K	0	0	3
AK	0	9	0
Q-Q	0	0	3
J-J	6	0	0
10-10	6	0	0
K-Q	0	0	9
A-Q	9	0	0
A-Js	3	0	0
A-10s	3	0	0

We now have 27 wins and 18 losses. But that's still not a good raise. She isn't calling a raise with A-Js or A-10s, so you can throw out six wins. When deciding whether to raise, you have to consider the hands the villain might have when she calls. That leaves us with 21 wins and 18 losses. That's still not a very good raise because of the reraise danger.

Further, while our tight player may have raised under the gun with A-Q, would she have capped preflop and bet the turn with it? You cannot be too sure this hand is in her distribution, so raising the river was a bad play. Also, calling a reraise on the river was a bad play. Big laydowns on the river are usually a bad idea, but this isn't a big laydown. You have advertised a big hand and a tight player isn't intimidated in the least. Very, very few players will try a three-bet bluff on the river. She isn't one of them: She isn't putting in another raise unless she has a big hand.

She had one! She showed Q♦ Q♣. This is another example of being "way ahead or way behind," which is a bad time to raise. And here, the "way ahead" isn't all that strong.

THE LESSON
- When a tight player opens early and caps it, proceed with extreme caution. With only a pair and a lot of big cards on the board, play a bit slower, even if your pair is a big one. Three bets on the river, you should quiver. Quiver with fear. Don't call without a very good hand against most players.

16. A ROCK IS A ROCK IS A ROCK

A middle player limps and I raise from the button with A♥ J♠. A tight, very passive player calls from the big blind, along with the limper (6.5 bets, three players). The flop is A♠ Q♦ 4♣, and both players check to me. I bet, the big blind raises, the limper folds, and I call (7 big bets, three players).

The turn and river are blanks and I call both streets. The big blind shows A♣ Q♥. I was drawing almost dead on the flop.

WHAT'S WRONG WITH THIS PLAY?

I called five small bets for a chance to win 13.5 bets. For that to be profitable, I need to win more than 27 percent of the time. Against an aggressive player, it makes sense to call all the way, however this is a very passive player. She saw me raise before the flop and probably figures me for an ace. Passive players don't try to make moves against a raiser when an ace flops. Her raise says she can beat my ace. What hands could she have that would beat my ace? With such a dry board, she must have two pair or a set. Unless her two pair is exactly A-4, I only have runner-runner outs. (She wouldn't call in the big blind with Q-4, even suited.) It's possible I would be folding the best hand here. She could be raising with A-10. However, this won't be the case enough of the time to make calling profitable.

Some players might argue that you should call one more bet, and see what develops since there's so much money in the pot. However, this only really makes sense if you can figure what might happen on the turn that you would like. There are so many situations where you are drawing close to dead that seeing another card will only get you into trouble.

THE LESSON

- If you raise with an ace and an absolute rock raises you when an ace comes on the flop, you are almost certainly beaten. Top pair, good kicker is a good hand, but it is not always a hand you should take to the river.

> Passive players don't make moves against a raiser when an ace flops.

10 HOW TO CORRECT MISTAKES IN JUDGMENT

My goal has always been to play mistake-free poker, but when I first began playing hold'em, I played a lot of hands badly—and I paid the price for my mistakes. I'd like to save you some time and money by describing them in detail to help you avoid making the same mistakes. During each session, I documented these hands and then reviewed them. I also discussed them with my e-mail group of poker friends to get their insights on how to improve my game.

Some of these hands involve making a bad call against a special type of opponent—they might have been good calls against a different player, but not for the particular one I was up against in the hand. For example, most players in medium-limit games will not bluff check-raise on the turn or bluff-raise on the river. However, some strong players and some reckless players will make these plays—so, making a "bad" call when you're playing against them may be the right play.

As you read along, you be the judge. Do you see the mistake? Before I analyze it, try to figure it out for yourself and then devise a better strategy for playing the hand.

31 GAME SCENARIOS

1. KEEP IT SIMPLE

In a loose game, I open for a raise early with K♥ J♥. A very loose player calls, as do both blinds. The flop is Q♣ J♠ J♦, so I have trips with a good kicker. I bet. The loose player calls, and both blinds fold. The turn is the lovely K♠. I bet and the loose player thinks a while and then raises. I decide to go for the check-raise on the river, so I just call.

At this point he could have a straight (A-10 or 10-9) as well as the case jack. He could also have a big draw like A♠ J♠ or Q♠ 10♠. He is unlikely to have K-K or Q-Q, since he didn't three-bet preflop, but it is not impossible that he flat called with those hands. The river is the 9♠, making the board Q♣ J♠ J♦ K♠ 9♠. I check, hoping to check-raise. He checks behind me and announces that he has a straight.

MY HAND

THE BOARD

WHAT'S WRONG WITH MY PLAY?

First, I take a risk for no gain. If he will bet the river and call my check-raise, then he will call on the turn and call on the river. I still win two more bets without taking the risk of winning no further bets. Second, when the third flush card and the possible straight hit on the river, I must bet. If he has three jacks, he is going to be frightened to bet. With the possible flush, he might check a straight, just as he did. Third, if he happens to be raising on a big draw (unlikely for this guy), I will lose him if he misses. At most, he will bet the river and fold to a raise. And if he makes his hand I might do even better, winning an extra bet on the turn and two more bets on the river if he raises.

THE LESSON

- When you make a big hand out of position, play the straightforward way. Keep betting and raising. Don't try for the check-raise, unless you are against a very aggressive player; and even then, you could just keep betting. When the board gets scary, you are going to have to bet your own hand more often.

> When the board gets scary, bet your own hand more often.

2. PLAYING SCARED IN THE FACE OF WEAKNESS

I open in middle position with 8-8. A fairly solid player three-bets on the button. A loose, aggressive player calls in the big blind and so do I (9.5 bets, three players). The flop is K-6-4 rainbow. The action goes pass, pass, pass. The turn is a deuce. The big blind checks and I go into the tank. I was surprised when the original raiser checked the flop. I have seen players do this when they flopped a monster, and I'm afraid that he flopped a set of kings. However, there are almost five big bets in the pot, so isn't it worth one big bet to see where I stand? My bet might even pick up the pot, but I wimp out and check.

So does the raiser. The river is a queen. The big blind fires out. Knowing he will bluff a lot, I call. The button instantly overcalls and the big blind mucks. I show my hand and the button shows his A-Q to take the pot.

WHAT'S WRONG WITH MY PLAY?

On the turn there are a lot of possible hands for the button. He could have a pair bigger than my 8-8, he could have the set of kings, or he could have a hand like A-Q, A-Js, or A-10s (although the latter is a bit unlikely for this solid player.) If he has the ace hands, he isn't too likely to call the turn. Once he checks the flop, he is less likely to have the pocket pairs. If he has J-J, he doesn't want to give a free card to two opponents.

The button wasn't a particularly aggressive or tricky player. While I should consider the possibility that he was slowplaying a monster, I shouldn't consider it the most likely scenario. The more likely scenario is the obvious one: He checked because he missed the flop. There is at least the 17 percent chance of winning the pot on the turn, which is enough to make betting profitable, and there is also a significant chance I have the best hand—so giving a free card is horrible.

But, this is not the only time I wimp out: I should raise on the river. When we get to the river, there is a decent chance the button has A-Q. Given the way he played, it is his most likely hand. There is a good chance the button won't call a raise. Let's look at the option of raising in more detail. There are 5.25 big bets in the pot. If I raise, I am risking two bets to win 5.25. Calling only risks one bet. Without going through all the math, you need around a 16 percent chance of winning to call and around a 28 percent chance of winning to raise. For raising to be justified, there needs to be around a 12 percent chance that he has A-Q or K-Q.

What hands would he three-bet preflop and then check? He isn't the kind of player that will three-bet with K-Q very often, so let's rule it out. Since he checked twice, he probably doesn't have a pair, so he might have raised with A-K, A-Q, A-Qs, or A-Js. He might have A-10s. Since he hasn't bet the flop or turn, we can rule out A-K. In fact, his most likely hand is A-Qs, the exact hand he had. There is more than a 12 percent chance that he has a queen.

It is a little more complicated than that. For a raise to be correct, there has to be at least a 12 percent chance that:

- The bettor has a weaker hand than mine or a hand he will fold to a raise.
- The button has a better hand than mine.
- The button will fold when I raise.

There are many situations where all three won't be true; however, in this one, there is a really good chance they all are. This should be a clear raise. You actually don't need a 12 percent chance of everything working to justify a raise. If you end up losing two bets, people will notice that you raised with a relatively weak hand on the river. They are more likely to pay off your raises when you have a big hand, so there are benefits to making this play even if it doesn't work this time.

THE LESSON

- If the flop is checked, you must bet medium-strength hands on the turn. If you get raised, you can always fold if you are pretty sure you are beat, but don't be in too big a hurry if the raiser is a tricky player. Don't assume that non-tricky players are making tricky plays—they probably have exactly what they are representing.
- When the preflop raiser checks the flop and there are more than two people in the pot, he is more likely to be weak. Checking a monster on the flop is more common when heads-up on the flop. When a frequent bluffer makes a play that reeks of bluff, consider raising to shut

out overcalls. Even if you are wrong, it will help your image.

3. WHAT ELSE CAN HE HAVE?

I have K♠ 5♦ in the big blind. An early player gypsies and everyone folds. I take the free look at the flop. (2.5 bets, two players) The flop is A♥ K♦ 6♥. I check, and he bets. Since he didn't raise preflop, I don' think he is too likely to have an ace. I raise. He calls (3.25 big bets). The turn is the A♣. I bet, and he calls (5.25 bets). The river is the 9♠. I bet, and he calls. He shows K♣ J♦.

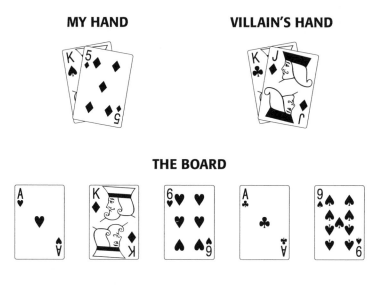

MY HAND	VILLAIN'S HAND

THE BOARD

WHAT'S WRONG WITH MY PLAY?

My bet on the river is a bad idea. What hand is he calling me with on every street? The most likely hand is one with a king. Players don't gypsy from early position with a weaker king than mine. And he isn't folding a king after calling this far, so betting into a king is a loser.

Could he have a draw? Absolutely, but he isn't calling me with a busted draw; however, he might bet it if I check so betting earns me nothing against a draw. Could he have a small pocket pair? If so, he will call my bet but check behind me. It's possible, but how likely is he to call a flop raise with just a pocket pair with an ace and king on the board? When I bet and get called, I am unlikely to win, so why bet?

Some players subscribe to the theory that when you are planning to call, you should always bet. There is merit to this if you drop the word "always." This is one of those exceptions. If you check, two good things can happen: (1) he could check his king behind you (good players won't do this, but good players don't limp in early with K-J); or (2) he could also bluff. In either case, you are better off checking.

Another argument for betting is that when you bet a good (but not great) hand on the flop and turn and don't get raised, you should bet the river. Usually with a stronger hand, he will raise before the river. That argument doesn't apply here. I didn't just bet the flop: I raised. And there is an ace on the board. He isn't going to raise me with a weak ace or a strong king. He has to be afraid of my holding an ace. With this board and my raise, his turn call shows a fair amount of strength. His lack of a raise doesn't indicate weakness, and it certainly shouldn't make me feel confident that I have the best hand.

THE LESSON

- Be cautious about betting second pair, weak kicker on the river if the top card is an ace. If you are going to call on the river, you shouldn't always bet. Consider checking if there is a chance your opponent will bet a missed draw. If you have raised, don't take an opponent's not reraising as a sign of weakness.

4. TURN ACTION MEANS MORE THAN FLOP ACTION

I have 10-10 in the big blind. An aggressive player in first position opens for a raise. A late player makes it three bets, and I call. The flop is jack-rag-rag. I pass, the opener passes, and the late player bets. I raise, the UTG player folds, and the late player reraises. Now I am starting to worry that he has a bigger pair than my tens. I call. The turn is a queen. I pass. He passes. The river is a blank. I pass. He passes behind me. When I show my tens, he mucks.

WHAT'S WRONG WITH MY PLAY?

There is nothing wrong with suspecting a big pair on the flop. But when he checks on the turn I have to reassess his hand. Is he really going to check the turn with a big pair? Is he going to give me a free card with Q-J on the board? Lots of aggressive players will three-bet on the flop with very little. They might want to keep the lead or get a free card. When he checks I have to put him on a smaller pair than mine. There were no draws on the flop, so I should have bet the river. I will get paid off with a lot of hands, including possibly A-K.

THE LESSON

- You have to reassess your opponent's likely hand after the turn action. You cannot get too fixated on your view based on the flop, as raises on the flop often don't mean a lot. When a player acts strong on the flop and weak on the turn, he is probably weak. You need to make thin value bets on the river when you are first to act. The only exception is that you should give a very aggressive opponent the chance to bluff.

5. IF IN DOUBT, VALUE BET STRONG HANDS

I have K♠ 8♠ on the button. A very loose player limps from the hijack seat. I raise because I want to isolate against this loose player, who usually will fold to a continuation bet. I am not thrilled when the small blind insta-calls, and I am puzzled about what he might have. The flop is K♥ 8♣ 6♠, giving me two pair. It is checked to me, and I bet. The small blind calls, and the loose player sticks with his form and folds to a flop bet. At this point I am not sure about the small blind, but I suspect a medium pair, though a set isn't impossible.

The turn is the Q♠, giving me a flush draw to go with my two pair. He checks, I bet, and he calls. Since he didn't check-raise, a set seems less likely. The river is the 9♦. To my surprise, the small blind comes out betting. In my experience, this usually happens when the player makes a big hand on the river and is afraid of my checking behind. With a big hand earlier, they usually check-raise the flop or turn. Without a ton of analyzing, I decide to just call, because his bet worries me. He turns over pocket aces.

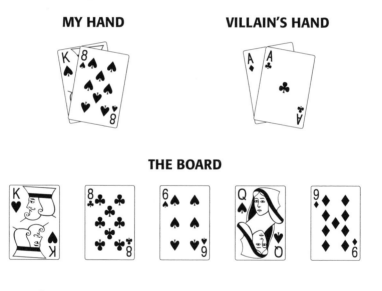

MY HAND

VILLAIN'S HAND

THE BOARD

WHAT'S WRONG WITH MY PLAY?

I missed a raise on the river. There are a lot more hands I can beat than hands I lose to. If the river card made two pair for him, I almost certainly have the better two pair. Could a draw have gotten there? There are three possible straights draws: 7-5, 10-7, and J-10. While it's possible he called preflop with 7-5s or 10-7s, this isn't very likely. And would he have called all the way to the river with J-10? It is hard for me to figure out a hand he would play this way. He picked a very odd way to play A-A, and that definitely confused me. However, two pair is just too strong a hand to not raise with simply because of my uncertainty.

THE LESSON

- When an opponent's action doesn't make sense, you should slow down a little, but don't stop entirely. When the board is not very coordinated, you should bet and raise more freely.

6. DISGUISING YOUR HAND BY NOT BETTING?

A tight player opens under the gun. It is folded around to me in the big blind with J♦ J♥. I like to disguise strong hands in the big blind to protect all the weak hands I play, so I just call. The flop is 10♣ 8♠ 5♣. I check, he bets, I check-raise, and he reraises. Since I check-raise a lot of hands in the big blind, I decided to disguise my hand and just call. Also, since this guy seems very tight, I don't see him routinely reraising on the flop.

The turn is the Q♦. I decide to check-raise the turn, but he checks behind me. Now I am considering that he might have raised the flop on a flush draw to get a free card. The river is the 6♣. Now I am worried he got there with a flush draw, and I check. He checks, and when I show the jacks, he mucks.

WHAT'S WRONG WITH MY PLAY?

For the cost of a raise on the flop, my opponent got free cards on the turn and river. If he had A-K, he had two chances at six outs—and I got little value for a premium hand with a favorable flop.

Many openers routinely reraise on the flop after a blind check-raises. This occurs a lot on a board with mostly smaller cards. Some players in the blind will always raise an opener when rags flop, figuring the flop likely missed the opener. The opener reraises for three reasons: (1) to keep the initiative; (2) to try for a free card; and (3) in the hope that the blind will fold a shaky check-raise. I tend to check-raise from the blinds a lot with overcards, draws and pairs. Since most of the time I don't have a hand where I want to make it four bets, I don't usually four-bet with my strong hands—but this is a mistake. I need to punish the routine three-bet. If I don't four-bet, I still need to bet out a lot on the turn. My pocket J-J is a very vulnerable hand, and this is a terrible situation to give out a free card. Sometimes the three-bet by the opener means something, but with J-J, I have one of the better hands I will be check-raising with and I need to get value from the hand.

THE LESSON

- With an overpair to the board, where a fair number of overcards are possible, don't slowplay on the flop. Many openers routinely three-bet on the flop when you check-raise from the blinds. If they do this, you need to reraise on the flop or bet the turn. If you are not sure, don't give a three-bettor on the flop too much credit. When out of position, tend to keep the lead with your strong hands.

7. MAKE A PLAY

I open under the gun with A♠ Q♥. Everyone folds to the button, who makes it three bets. I call. The button had just sat down and this was his second hand. I had never played with him before, but the table talk indicated he was an animal. (An **animal** is a very aggressive player who tries to run over the table.) The flop is J♣ 7♦ 5♥. I check. He bets. There are 8.5 bets in the pot. I have six outs to pair one of my two cards, and he might be making a move with a worse ace or even a weaker hand, so I call.

The turn is the 10♦ giving me a gutshot to go with my overcards. I check and he bets. There are now 5.75 bets in the pot and I have a gutshot to add to my two overcards. That's

10 outs. I call. The river is the 4♠. I check. He bets. At this point, I am likely to be beat, but for 7.75 bets I will make the call. I only need to win 11 percent of the time to make this play profitable. He turns over 3-3 and is surprised when it holds up.

MY HAND

VILLAIN'S HAND

THE BOARD

WHAT'S WRONG WITH MY PLAY?

Calling is fine on every street. It turns out all my outs were live, but I really need to discount them quite a bit. First, even an animal can wake up with a big hand. My opponent could have a big pair or A-K. If he has A-J, an ace is not an out, but a trap, and the same goes for A-10. However, if he really has a very wide range for his three-bet, I am getting the odds to call on each street.

The real question is whether I should just call or take the lead. With a pocket pair or a flopped pair, it might make sense to call him down, as I am either solidly ahead or solidly behind. If I am ahead, I can let him keep betting it. If I am behind, I am going to the river cheaply. However, with just two big cards, it makes more sense to make a play for the pot. There are many ways to do this:

177

- Check-raise the flop and bet the turn.
- Check-raise the turn.
- Check-raise the river.
- Bet the flop.
- Bet the turn.
- Bet the river.

I like the first two options, though option one is a bit cheaper. Option two, check-raising the turn, is a bit scarier to the other player, and it also lets you see what comes on the turn before making a choice. Option two also gives you the choice to check the river. If he calls your raise, check folding the river isn't a bad option. That means that check-raising the turn costs exactly the same amount as the line I took, but gives me a significantly greater chance to win the pot. Waiting until the turn gives me more flexibility: If a total blank comes and I just have an ace high, I can just check and fold. Option one costs less and also gives me a better chance to win than just calling down the whole way.

Keep in mind that animals tend to call a lot. They have to. They are making moves with a lot of weak hands, so people will play back at them a lot. So even a strong move like a check-raise on the turn may not get him to fold a hand like 3-3.

THE LESSON

- When you are considering calling a player down with a weak hand, consider making a raise instead. Be more inclined to raise with an ace-high type hand than a pair. With the pair, be more inclined to just call all the way. With 10 or more outs on the turn, betting or check-raising is better than calling.

8. CAN YOU RAISE THE SIDE POT?

I have Q-Q in the big blind. Five players limp into the pot, I raise, and only the small blind folds (11 small bets, six players).

The flop is 10-6-4 with two diamonds. I bet and get three callers (7.5 big bets). The turn is a king. I bet. Two players call and the last player raises all in for 70 percent of a big bet. I call and the other two players call. The river is a blank. I bet and both players with chips fold. The all-in player shows K-6 for two pair.

WHAT'S WRONG WITH MY PLAY?

When I get raised on the turn, there is a good chance I am beat, but it's far from a sure thing. Sometimes a player who is about to go all in will put the rest of his chips in with a weaker hand. He might be on a draw and raise, figuring he is getting 3 to 1 on his money. Also, when there is no danger that you can be raised again, you can bet or raise with a somewhat weaker hand. Even if I am beat, there are over 12 big bets in the pot. There will be more bets in since the other two players are calling. I am almost getting good enough pot odds to call with two outs. Note that if I am beat, I know at least seven of the outstanding cards. I see my two cards and four cards on the board. And if I am beat, the raiser has at least a king. So two out of the remaining 45 cards (not 46) cards will make three queens.

Calling is a close decision. It depends on how sure I am that the raiser has me beat.

But there is a much easier decision: I must raise. If either or both of the remaining players calls, I am ahead for the side pot. Why not try to get an extra bet from the guys who are chasing? Clearly the time to raise is on the turn. If either guy has a flush draw, I won't get any extra money out of him if he misses on the river. Raising also can provide my hand some protection if either player with chips has an ace and I can get him to fold.

THE LESSON

- When a player raises all in and you are pretty sure you are beat, you can still raise to create a side pot. If you can create a side pot where you are favored, it doesn't matter if you are going to lose the main pot.

> An all-in raise is often weaker than a raise made by a player with more chips.

9. TAKING ONE OFF WITH OVERCARDS

This kind of situation happens frequently. I raise from early or middle position with A-J. The button makes it three bets and I call. The flop comes with three small cards. I check. He bets. I don't want to look weak and I might hit one of my six outs, so I call.

WHAT'S WRONG WITH MY PLAY?

There are 8.5 bets in the pot when he bets. I have six outs. That gives me a 13.3 percent chance of hitting one of them. I need a 10.5 percent chance of winning to call, so it's an easy call, right?

Not so fast.

Do I really have six outs? What if the three-bettor has a hand like A-Qs? Now I am drawing to three outs. What if he has Q-Q? Again, I have three outs. And if I hit a jack, it is likely to cost me quite a bit of more money. Suppose there is an 80 percent chance that I have six outs. I now have only a 10.2 percent chance of making the winning hand, so it is a slightly losing play. And depending on the raiser, I could have quite a bit less than an 80 percent chance of making the winning hand.

What about implied odds? Can I make more money if I hit my hand? Perhaps. However, if an ace comes, many players will give up with a small pair. If a jack hits and the jack gives me the best hand, then I will make some money. However, there are also reverse implied odds. If I catch one of my cards and I am still behind, it will cost me quite a bit of money.

There is one other critical factor here—I am out of position, so I will need to act first whether I make or miss. When out of position, you generally don't want to make a marginal call. This is a pretty close decision, as some players three-bet a lot though they never or rarely call an opening raise; that is, they will either raise or fold. If the reraiser is very aggressive and three-bets a lot, I should take a card off. But if the reraiser is pretty tight and won't three-bet very often, I should fold.

This all assumes the three-bettor is not one of the blinds. If he is, there is less money in the pot, but I have position. Those two factors probably cancel each other out, and I should play the same way. However, if I have anything in addition to the two overcards, I should call. Even a backdoor flush draw or good backdoor straight draw would be enough. A gutshot straight draw with two overcards is an easy call. You can consider a check-raise, if you think the three-bettor might fold.

THE LESSON

- When someone three-bets before the flop and you flop two overcards, fold to most players. Call only the more aggressive players, if you have any extra outs, including a backdoor draw.

10. WHEN YOUR HAND DOESN'T DESERVE RESPECT

Two players limp preflop, and a solid, straightforward player raises on the button. I call with K♦ 4♦ in the big blind. Everyone calls (8.5 bets, four players). The flop is K-rag-rag, with no diamonds. Everyone passes to the button, who bets. I raise. The other two players fold to the button, who reraises. I call. The turn is a blank. I check, he bets, I call. The river is another blank. I check, he bets, I call. He turns over K-K for a set of kings. I was drawing almost dead on the flop and totally dead on the turn.

WHAT'S WRONG WITH MY PLAY?

When I raise on the flop, it is pretty likely that I have a king, but that doesn't slow the button down. Against some players, this wouldn't be a big deal because some players routinely three-bet in this situation to get a free card on the turn. However, this is not a tricky player. He figures me for a king and keeps betting—he almost certainly can beat my king with no kicker. Against a tough player, I need to call down with top pair, even with no kicker, but against this player, I should not.

THE LESSON

- If you have raised with a weak raising hand and it doesn't faze your opponent, consider that you are beat. Consider who you're playing against: Don't call down straightforward players with marginal holdings.

11. CALL TWO BETS FOR A CHANCE AT HALF THE POT?

The preflop action is passed to the player in the cutoff seat, who raises. I have A-9 in the small blind and I reraise. Both the big blind and the cutoff call (9.5 bets, three players). The flop comes Q-Q-10. I bet, the big blind folds, and the cutoff calls (5.75 big bets, two players). The turn is another 10. I bet and the cutoff raises (8.75 big bets). I figure he might be making a move with an ace, so I call. The river is a 4. I check and call his bet. He shows K-Q for the full house.

WHAT'S WRONG WITH MY PLAY?

People will make moves with an ace on a two-pair board, but this isn't a typical case. I am making this play on the turn, but a more common move is betting or raising the river. There are 8.75 bets in the pot, so it might seem that I only need a 10 percent chance of winning to call, but there are two problems with this analysis. First, I am hoping to win half the pot, not the whole pot, so the pot is offering 4.25 to 1 when I need to have a 20 percent chance of winning.

It's even worse than that: The cutoff is likely to bet the river as well. I will need to put in two bets to win half of 9.75. The pot is offering me less than 5 to 2 or 2.5 to 1. Is he really making a move with an ace here one-third of the time? This is an unlikely move. He has to be pretty sure I don't have a queen or 10 (or K-K) to justify it. It is far more likely I am beat, so I should save the two big bets.

THE LESSON

- A raise on the turn is likely to be a legitimate hand. Try to pick off bluffs less often if you may only win half the pot if you are right; and try to pick off a bluff less frequently if you may have to call twice.

12. FOUR BETS PREFLOP

I have been card dead, so I've only played a few hands for the last couple of hours. A player raises under the gun. He is neither too aggressive or passive, nor too tight or loose. I three-bet from the cutoff with K♥ K♣. The blinds fold, and he caps it (9.5 bets, two players). The flop is J♥ 5♦ 3♣. He bets. I call. The turn is the 3♦. He bets and I call. The river is the Q♦. He bets. I figure I can only be beaten by aces and I am unlikely to get reraised since the third diamond hit the board, so I raise. He calls and shows A♦ A♣.

MY HAND   **VILLAIN'S HAND**

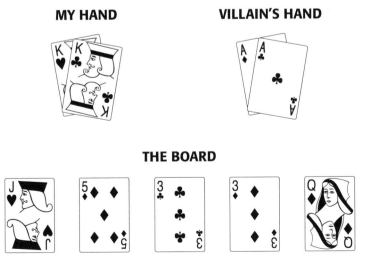

THE BOARD

WHAT'S WRONG WITH MY PLAY?

First, it is not true that I am only beaten by aces. If he has Q-Q, which is quite possible, the river killed me. Let's consider what he might four-bet with. He is a solid player. Here are some of his possible ranges. Remember that I have a tight image, so he isn't likely to think I three-bet light, especially against an under-the-gun raiser.

HIS RANGE	MY WIN PERCENT ON THE FLOP	MY WIN PERCENT ON THE RIVER
A-A, K-K	14.3%	7.14%
A-A, K-K, Q-Q, A-K	62.8%	41.7%
A-A, K-K Q-Q, J-J, A-K, A-Qs	59.7%	43.7%
A-A, K-K, Q-Q, J-J, 10-10, A-K, A-Q, A-Js	70.7%	65.5%

Unless I think he is four-betting pretty aggressively, raising on the river is a mistake. Not only am I the underdog against most of his likely ranges on the river, but if you take into account that I am calling all the way, he might not bet some of his worst hands on the river. Would he bet A-K on the river after I call the flop and turn? Probably not, so my win percentage when he bets the river is probably lower than that indicated above. I cannot fold here, but a raise is a bad idea.

Only aggressive players will four-bet with weaker hands. When a player has not shown that kind of aggressiveness, I should not be assuming he is making the unusual play. I should assume he has the kind of hand he is representing. How about raising the flop? That looks like it would have been a better play. Unless he is extremely tight, I am going to be the favorite. Looser players will often cap with modest holdings like suited connectors preflop in a big multiway pot. They seem to assume that since they are going to call anyway, they might as well play for a big pot. Some folks just like to gamble, but this is a very different situation: This is a tight player heads up.

THE LESSON

- Unless you have a specific reason to think otherwise, you should assume that someone who four-bets preflop has a big hand, particularly heads up. Capping the action preflop in a multiway pot can mean a much weaker hand than in a heads-up pot, particularly if it is an aggressive player. The corollary is that capping in a heads-up pot by a less aggressive player should make you slow down a lot.

13. FOUR BETS PREFLOP REVISITED

It's a middle-limit online game. A middle player raises, and I reraise from the cutoff with J♠ J♦. A solid player on the button caps it. The opener calls and I call. (13.5 bets, three players). The flop comes 9♠ 6♥ 5♣. The middle player and I check to the button, he bets, and we both call. I figure the original opener has overcards (8.25 big bets, three players). The turn is the 5♠. We check to the button, he bets, the middle player folds, and I call (10.25 bets). The river is the A♦. I check to the button, and he bets. I figure I am beat, but the pot is big, and I call. He shows Q♦ Q♥.

MY HAND   **VILLAIN'S HAND**

THE BOARD

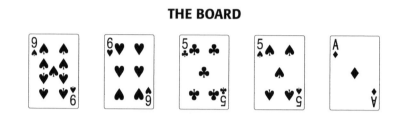

WHAT'S WRONG WITH MY PLAY?

One can argue that four bets means a big pair, particularly after an opener and a raiser. The key point is that the four-bettor had no money invested in the pot before betting. He has already seen two players show strength, so this is not the most likely place to make a move. At this point I have no reason to suppose he is a maniac. I put the third player on a big pair or most combinations of two cards 10 or higher. Let's compare this hand to the previous hand:

HIS RANGE	MY WIN PERCENT ON THE FLOP	MY WIN PERCENT ON THE RIVER
A-A, K-K	7.9%	0.0%
A-A, K-K, Q-Q, A-K	32.7%	0.0%
A-A, K-K Q-Q, J-J, A-K, A-Qs	35.3%	1.6%
A-A, K-K, Q-Q, J-J, 10-10, A-K, A-Q, A-Js	44.1%	13.5%

Jacks are much weaker than kings, but with this board and 15.5 bets in the pot, calling on the flop is pretty easy unless the button is extremely tight. However, I need to keep in mind that the button came in cold with four bets. He wasn't an opener who was reraising after putting in two bets already. He has seen a raise and reraise in front of him, so he is more likely to have the stronger ranges than the weaker ones.

What about the call on the river? If he had A-K, he got there. There is no legitimate hand left that doesn't beat me. However, the pot is very big (around 11.25 big bets) and I only need an 8 percent chance of winning to justify a call. Without the ace on the river, it is an easy call; with the ace, it becomes a real crying call where you expect to lose. Based on the number above, it looks like I have a chance to make a big laydown, though I don't think calling is a big mistake.

However, if I am going to call, there may be a better play than calling on the river. If I am planning to call anyway, I should bet the river. Either way, it costs me one bet. (If I get raised, I am not calling.) The ace could be a scare card for my opponent if he has K-K or Q-Q, so there is a small chance he will fold the river. That's worth a shot in a big pot.

THE LESSON

- An opener who puts in the fourth bet is less likely to have a big hand than a player who hasn't put any money into the pot yet. It is usually correct to call down with a pretty big pair in a four-bet pot, but don't do it if the raiser is particularly tight, and if too many overcards to your pair are on the board.

14. GIVE UP THE INITIATIVE? WHY?

A semi-maniac raises under the gun. A total maniac in middle position calls. I reraise from the button with A♦ A♣. A very loose player calls in the big blind, and the maniacs also call. The flop is 9♠ 9♦ 5♠. I don't like the pair on the board or the spade draw. The big blind bets. Both maniacs call. I am trying to figure out what everyone could be playing. The big blind has some kind of pair based on his past play. Does he have the 9 or a 5? There aren't that many hands that everyone can call with. I have position, so I decide to just call and see how things develop on the turn. I have no read on anyone; perhaps the turn will give me some insight.

The turn is the 4♥. The big blind bets, the semi-maniac folds, and the maniac raises. Now I am really worried about a 9, and it is two big bets to me. They could even both have nines and I could be going for a ride. I decide to fold. The big blind calls. The river is the 7♣. The big blind checks, the maniac bets, and the big blind calls. The maniac shows K♥ J♦ and the big blind wins with 5♦ 4♦. At least it was suited when he called two raises as the big blind!

MY HAND	MANIAC	BIG BLIND

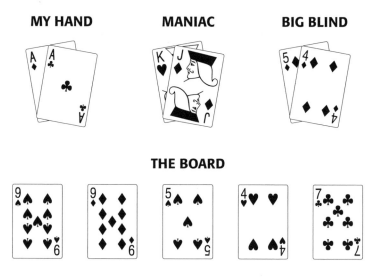

THE BOARD

WHAT'S WRONG WITH MY PLAY?

First, I cannot get scared just because there is a pair on the board. Even with three opponents, it is not that likely that one of them has a 9. Here are some probabilities:

PLAYERS	PROBABILITY OF SOMEONE HAVING A 9	ODDS
5	43%	1 in 2.4
4	34%	1 in 3
3	26%	1 in 4
2	17%	1 in 5.8

With three players, there is only a 26 percent chance that one of them flopped trips. Even with this action, I shouldn't be too frightened about it, so I am very likely to have the best hand on the flop. I need to raise, which would accomplish a lot of things. First, it charges people who are hanging around with overcards. Second, it helps me to clarify where I stand. If someone other than the maniac raises, I have to slow down; however, I am getting a better idea of how strong everyone else is on the cheap street. Third, I keep the initiative. If I raise the flop, it is unlikely that it will get bet and raised to me on the turn, so I won't have to face a difficult decision for two big bets.

Once I check the flop, I probably need to call the turn. I have shown a lot of weakness. I three-bet before the flop and then just called on the flop, so they have to figure me for A-K. The maniac's play even makes some sense. If I have A-K and she can get me out, she now has two more outs if a king comes. (Of course, if I have A-K, she only has five outs, not six since a king is gone and she may have no outs at all if the big blind has a 9. But then, she is a maniac.) So once I play my hand that weak, I probably need to call on the turn. There are 11.25 big bets in the pot and I am getting 5.5 to 1 pots odds. I only need to have the best hand 15 percent of the time to break even. With these crazy players, I should take my chances.

Finally, assuming the big blind has a pair, there are three fives out and only two nines. He is more likely to have the 5. With most sane players, you would expect that when he bets bottom pair on the flop and gets called in three places, he might slow down, but no one has indicated they have a better hand.

THE LESSON

- If you don't know where you stand and you have a good hand, stay aggressive on the flop, as you will learn more on the cheap streets. Don't assume that someone made trips when a pair comes on the board. They probably didn't. Don't assume that crazy players play at all like you do. If you have not revealed the strength of your hand, and someone bets into you, you need to call quite a bit more often.

15. CALLING THE FLOP WITH OVERCARDS

A middle player opens with a raise. He is a pretty straightforward player. I reraise from the button with A-K. The blinds fold, he calls, and the two of us go to the flop. The flop is 10-X-X rainbow. He checks, I bet, and he check-raises. I call.

WHAT'S WRONG WITH MY PLAY?

There are 7.5 bets in the pot when I am faced with calling his raise. The overcards give me six outs. That means I need around 7 to 1 to call. Sounds like I am getting the odds; however, there are a few things to consider. First, I need to remember that I three-bet before the flop, so he probably expects me to have a strong hand. He isn't going to check-raise me without something, unless he is very aggressive.

What if he has A-10 or K-10? I cannot really count on six clean outs, so I need to discount them. If I only have five outs, then calling with the overcards is a losing play. Of course, you cannot routinely three-bet before the flop and fold to a check-raise. If you do this, strong players will start making moves.

THE LESSON

- Calling with just overcards on the flop should be done only if the pot is large. You usually need more than 8 to 1. If the other players look strong or the board is coordinated, you need significantly more.

16. TAKE THE MONEY

An early player and a middle player limp. The button raises. I have K♦ Q♥ in the big blind, and I call along with the limpers (8.5 small bets, four players). The flop is K♣ 8♥ 3♣. I want to narrow the field, and the button is pretty aggressive. I am pretty sure he will bet if everyone checks to him, and I will be the next to act. My raise is likely to drive out the two limpers. But my plan goes awry: I check, the first limper bets and both players call. I realize that a raise will not drive anyone out, so I decide to just call and wait to bet the turn (6.25 big bets).

The turn is the J♦. I bet, the early limper calls, the second limper folds, and now the button raises (11.25 big bets). I think for a while. Two players have shown a lot of strength, and the early bettor is still to act so I fold. The early limper calls the button's raise. The river is the 2♣. The limper checks, the button bets, and the limper calls. The button shows A♣ 10♣ for a flush. The limper says he had K-J.

MY HAND	LIMPER	BUTTON

THE BOARD

WHAT'S WRONG WITH MY PLAY?

My play on the flop is terrible. Checking for a check-raise isn't bad, since I am so confident the button will bet, but when it gets back to me, I must raise. It may not fit in with my plan to drive players out, but I probably have the best hand. Raising will get three more bets into the pot with the best hand and that is too much money to pass up. Sure, it's important to try to eliminate players, but that is not the primary purpose of betting and raising. The primary purpose is to get people with weaker hands to pay you off, and this is an ideal situation for that.

Even worse is my fold on the turn. What does the button raiser have? A-K or a set? If so, he probably raises on the flop. However, he could also have a big draw or a pair and a flush draw. There are too many hands I can beat to throw away my hand with over 11 bets in the pot, and unless the limper is going to fold for one more bet, there will be over 12 bets in the pot.

The reality is that I don't have any idea of what the raiser has. In retrospect, a big draw that improved on the turn fits his play pretty well. However, when you can't know what a player has, you need to fall back on who the player is. This guy is capable of a bluff raise, and there is no particular strong hand that easily fits his betting pattern. When you cannot figure out what someone might have, fold in a small pot and call in a bigger one. What made my play even worse is that the particular player seems very fond of semibluff raises. I have seen him do it before. With all the draws on the turn, I need to give this serious consideration.

As it turned out, I saved money by folding—but that doesn't make it the right play. I was ahead when I folded. With the size of the pot, folding was the wrong play. The fact that the raiser hit his flush on the river doesn't change that.

THE LESSON
- When you think you have the best hand and there are several players in the pot, bet or raise, even if it won't drive people out. Don't fold top pair to a raise if there are possible draws, and you have seen the player raise on a draw before. If you cannot figure out a plausible hand for someone who bets or raises, be more inclined to call. Don't get wed to your plan: Even if your goal was to eliminate people, when that doesn't work out, consider changing your plan completely.

17. WHEN YOU GET OUTPLAYED

An early and middle player limp into the pot, and I raise on the button with A♦ 10♦. The big blind calls, as well as the two limpers (8.6 bets, four players). The second limper, an old regular who plays too loose and calls too much, is pretty aggressive and will occasionally make a move.

The flop is A♠ 6♣ 6♠.

Everyone checks to me. I bet, the big blind calls, the first limper folds, and the second limper raises (12.6 small bets). I figure he is likely to put me on an ace as the preflop raiser. He says he can beat an ace. It is early in the hand, and it will cost me a lot of bets to find where I stand. Also, there is the big blind, who could have a 6. So, I fold. The big blind calls. The turn is the Q♣. The big blind checks, the limper bets, and the big blind calls. The river is the 10♣. The big blind checks, the limper bets, and the big blind calls. The limper turns over 2♠ 2♣. The big blind shows and wins the pot with a pair of tens.

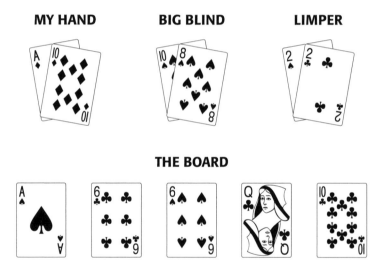

MY HAND	BIG BLIND	LIMPER

THE BOARD

WHAT'S WRONG WITH MY PLAY?

My play is probably correct, but it is an interesting hand anyway. What could the limper have? A better ace? Unlikely. With a good ace, he is probably raising before the flop. A weaker ace? Is he really check-raising a preflop raise with A-9 or weaker? He could think he might have the best hand and wants to find out on the cheap streets. He could easily call a gypsy preflop with a hand like A-5s.

Could he have a 6? There are a few hands he would call a gypsy with preflop, including 7-6s, 6-5s, and 6-6. Would he wait until the turn to raise with a 6? He is out of position (with regard to me), so he could easily decide to raise on the flop. I probably would. How about a flush draw? Would he check-raise with a flush draw? It's possible. He cannot have a big draw. He cannot have overcards or a straight draw or a pair with a flush draw on this board. Is he on a total bluff? Possible, but unlikely. There is a very good chance I have an ace for my preflop raise and bet.

When he raises, there are 12.6 small bets in the pot. Assuming he will keep betting, it will cost me five small bets to win 16.6. If the big blind sticks around, the pot would be larger; though if the big blind does stick around, I am probably in trouble. So the pot is basically offering me 3.3 to 1. If it were just me and the limper, I still don't have an obvious call. There is a chance he is raising with a weaker ace or a flush draw. I only need a 23 percent chance of winning. One problem is that if he is raising on a flush draw, he will get there one-third of the time. With a weaker ace, I could still end up with only half the pot, therefore, even if he is not ahead, there are possible problems.

A further problem is the big blind. He could easily be sitting there with a 6, as his play fits perfectly. He could also have a flush draw. I don't see him calling with a weak ace, but it's possible. With both of them in there, I don't think I can call.

The limper's play is not as crazy as I had originally thought. If I am raising on a hand without an ace, I am still going to bet the flop. He has the chance to take the pot away with a raise. If the big blind doesn't spike a 10 on the river, the limper wins a big pot. I need to change my evaluation of the limper's play a bit. He is probably better than I give him credit for.

THE LESSON

- Consider bluff raising a tight preflop raiser when an ace flops. This is probably best if he raises from late position. If he doesn't have an ace, you could steal the pot for two small bets. When you get caught, you will get paid off more often on your legitimate raises. Always be prepared to change your evaluation of a player—don't assume that every unusual play is a bad one. Of course, you will sometimes fold the best hand.

18. IF YOU PAY FOR INFORMATION, USE IT

I raise from early position with Q♠ Q♥. Everyone folds to an unknown player in the big blind, who makes it three bets. I decide to just call. The flop is A♠ J♥ 7♣. He bets. I decide to raise because: (1) I might have the best hand; (2) he might fear an ace and fold, which wouldn't be a bad outcome; and (3) I can find out if he has an ace. He reraises, and I call. The turn is the 7♦. He bets and I call. The river is the 7♥. He bets and I call. He shows pocket jacks.

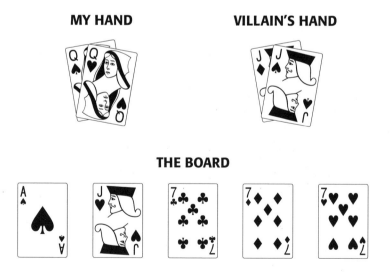

MY HAND   **VILLAIN'S HAND**

THE BOARD

WHAT'S WRONG WITH MY PLAY?

There is nothing wrong with not reraising before the flop. I think my raise on the flop is much better than a call or fold. If I call, I never know where I stand, and he can have too many hands I can beat to warrant a fold. However, his reraise on the flop tells me a lot. Based on my preflop and flop raises, he has to figure me for an ace, even a good ace, but this doesn't slow him down. Most players won't be three-betting the flop with K-K or 10-10, so he is acting like he has a good ace. I should fold.

THE LESSON

- When you raise for information and get a bad answer, take advantage of the info you paid for and fold. When you represent an ace and still get raised, most opponents are telling you that they can beat an ace. If you don't know anything about an opponent, assume he plays an ordinary game, not that he is extremely tricky or aggressive.

19. NOT RAISING WITH THE NUTS?

The under-the-gun player limps and a semi-maniac calls from middle position. I check from the big blind with A♠ 6♦. The flop is A♥ A♣ 4♥. With the semi-maniac behind me and a small pot, I decide to check. They both check behind me. The turn is the lovely 6♣. With a second flush draw, I bet, praying for action. I get it when the opener folds but the semi-maniac raises. I reraise, and he calls.

The river is the 6♥. I like the fact that it completes a flush, but with two pair on the board, a flush isn't going to give me much action, and anyone with an ace now has the same full house as I do. I bet, not expecting much action, and the button raises. I figure we are splitting the pot and just call. He has Q♥ 10♦, a total bluff! I guess he has graduated from semi-maniac to maniac.

WHAT'S WRONG WITH MY PLAY?

I have the stone cold nuts. He cannot have quads or a bigger full house, and there is no straight flush on the board. He can only tie me. Where he cannot beat me, there is absolutely no reason to not keep on raising: I can't get hurt by the play. As it turns out, I am not going to make any more money on the hand (unless he is crazy enough to try another bluff raise); however, I could have. I needed to give him the chance to make a mistake.

THE LESSON

- Just because you are pretty sure you are splitting the pot doesn't mean you cannot raise with the nuts.

20. NOT RAISING WITH THE NUTS—AGAIN?

I have been card dead for two hours and have barely played a hand. Two players limp and the button raises. I reraise from the small blind with A♦ K♦. The big blind folds, but the limpers and button call (13 bets, four players). The flop comes Q♥ 10♠ 5♣. I bet, the limpers call, and the button raises. I call the raise, one limper folds, and the other calls (10 big bets, three players).

The turn is the J♥. I check, the limper checks, and the button bets (11 bets). The limper is a calling station. I get greedy. I finally have a hand, and I want to win a huge pot. I figure a bet will lose the calling station. I am also afraid that a raise (combined with my three-bet preflop) will tell everyone the nature of my hand, as everything about my action would indicate A-K, and everyone may fold. I decide to just call and trap everyone. The calling station also calls.

The river is the 10♣. I bet, and only the calling station calls. As I get ready to take the pot, the calling station turns over J-10 for a full house. When the table asks why she didn't raise, she said she was afraid I might have Q-Q for a bigger full house. I silently thank the poker gods for timid players.

HOW TO CORRECT MISTAKES IN JUDGMENT

MY HAND   **VILLAIN'S HAND**

THE BOARD

WHAT'S WRONG WITH MY PLAY?

As the hand played out, I lost the least amount I could have lost on this hand. However I still played it wrong. First, it is a bad idea to slowplay a straight here. People could be drawing to beat me or split the pot with me, and there is a flush draw on the board on the turn. Anyone with an ace or king could make the same straight I have if the wrong card comes on the river. Also, there are 11 bets in the pot. With a big pot, you rarely want to slowplay. In this case, not raising probably didn't cost me the pot. A calling station isn't going to fold two pair, even for two big bets.

Should she have folded? If she knows my hand, she has four outs. She is getting 6.5 to 1, which is far from a good enough price. However, she doesn't know my hand, and she may figure there is a chance she has the best hand. She only needs a 5 percent chance of winning without improving to show a profit with a call. So if I raise, she is likely to make a mistake and call, but by checking, I don't even give her the chance to make the mistake.

THE LESSON

- Don't slowplay in a big pot. Don't slowplay a straight with a potential flush out there. If you haven't won a pot for a long time, you will be tempted to get away from the normal way to play to make something big happen. Don't do it!

21. SLOWPLAYING A FLUSH ON THE FLOP

I raise from early position with Q♦ 10♦. Only a middle player calls. The flop is J♦ 6♦ 3♦. On the flop, I bet, he raises, and I just call, figuring that three bets will scare him off and I can check-raise the turn (4.7 big bets). The turn is the A♠. I check and he checks. (4.7 big bets). The river is the 8♦. I figure that he might have raised on the flop with a big diamond, and he is unlikely to call with a hand that I can beat so I check. He checks behind me with 10♥ 10♣.

WHAT'S WRONG WITH MY PLAY?

I flop a monster and go to the river to win a tiny pot. To start with, I must three-bet the flop. If he is drawing to a big diamond, I need to make him pay. If another diamond comes on the turn, I am either going to lose or get no action. The flop is my chance to make money, and I need to take it. I don't need to be afraid that putting in a lot of action on the flop gives my hand away. Many people will slowplay a made flush on the flop, so raising with the flush is somewhat deceptive. Once the turn comes, the ace is a scare card for most of his hands, making it less likely that he will bet. I should probably bet the turn.

THE LESSON

- When you flop a flush, play it fast. Another card of the flush suit will kill your hand or your action. With a big hand out of position, tend to play it fast. The only time you might slowplay is when you have a monster.

22. WHEN YOUR WORST FEARS COME TRUE

The first three players limp. I have 9♦ 9♣ in middle position. I figure I am not too likely to win the pot without improving, so I decide to just call and play the hand like a small pair. If I don't flop a set, I am probably done with it. The button and small blind call, and the big blind checks (7 bets, seven players).

The flop is 8♥ 6♠ 2♠. Everyone checks to me. With this flop, the game plan changes. I bet, the button raises, and the small blind reraises. The small blind is a very aggressive player who could have a small pair—or absolutely nothing. Since the button could have a hand like A-8 or a flush draw, I call. The button calls (8 big bets, three players). The turn is the 8♠. The small blind bets and we both call. The river is the J♦. The small blind bets and we both call. The small blind has 8♣ 3♠ for trip eights and the big blind has Q♠ 5♠ for the winning flush.

WHAT'S WRONG WITH MY PLAY?

When I called on the flop I was hoping that the other two players had a pair of eights and a flush draw. Those were the most likely hands for these two players. The turn card helps both of these hands, so the hands that I could have beaten have now turned into hands that beat me.

Maybe one player is fooling around. The odds that they both are fooling around are extremely slim. If I call two more big bets to get to a showdown, the pot is offering me 12 to 2 (or 6 to 1) to call. I have to win one out of every seven times to break even—and that is the best-case scenario. I am not closing out the betting and a player who raised on the flop is yet to act behind me, so I could be going on a multi-bet ride.

To win, it must be true that:

- I was ahead on the flop.
- Neither of my opponents has an 8
- Neither of my opponents has two spades.

- Neither of my opponents has a jack.
- No spade comes on the river or neither has one spade.

It's just too big a parlay to play!

THE LESSON

- When you are hoping your opponent has particular hands and the turn card turns those hands into hands that beat you, you usually want to fold. This is particularly true if there is more than one opponent in the hand and you are not closing out the action.

23. LONGSHOTS COME IN

The under-the-gun player is new to the table and posts a blind instead of waiting one more hand for the big blind. Weird, but it happens. He checks and everyone folds to me on the button. I raise with A♦ 2♣. Both blinds call and the blind-poster reraises. I now officially hate my hand, since I could easily be dominated by a big ace—namely, any ace—but I call anyway (12 bets, four players).

Four of us see the flop of 8♥ 6♣ 2♥. The small blind bets, and everyone else calls. I mess up my count of the pot. I only count the preflop action as nine bets, not 12. Based on this, I need around four outs to call. I have five outs, but they need to be discounted a bit because of the flush draw. It seems like marginal decision and I am still influenced by "hating my hand," so I decide to fold. The turn is the A♣ there is a lot of action the rest of the way and the blind-poster wins a large pot with A♦ Q♦. If I call one small bet on the flop, I win that large pot!

WHAT'S WRONG WITH MY PLAY?

Of course, miscounting the pot is a clear mistake. With 15 bets in the pot, I only need three outs to call, so it's a clear call. With my miscount, there are 12 bets in the pot after the action on the flop. With five outs, I only need eight bets to call. When making a close decision about calling, you should consider factors like, "Am I going to close out the betting for this round, or can someone raise me?" and "Will I have good position?" This is a perfect situation. I am closing out the flop betting, and I am on the button.

What about the implied odds? They mostly favor me. If the A♥ comes down, I could lose some money to a flush, but in most cases, I am likely to make more money on the later rounds when I hit. My hand is well disguised, and I do get to act last.

However the real problem wasn't the math: It was my attitude. Once I decided I hated my hand, I was looking for any excuse to muck it. I had good reason to hate my hand, as it turns out that my A-2 was dominated by A-Q until the flop came down. Once the deuce hits the flop, everything changes. Anyone with a big ace now goes from a big favorite to a big dog. The deuce by itself isn't all that exciting: A pair of deuces isn't likely to win this pot, but it gives me outs to a very good hand.

THE LESSON

- When making a close decision about calling, be more likely to call if you are closing out the action and you will be the last to act on later rounds. You should be more likely to play a well-disguised hand. Don't underestimate bottom pair with a good kicker in a big pot. You only need 8 to 1 pot odds to play it. In hold'em, everything can change on the turn of a card. You need to be flexible enough to adapt when that happens.

24. ONLY ONE HAND CAN BEAT YOU

We are playing shorthanded with only seven players at the table. The hijack and cutoff are new and both post blinds to be dealt a hand. The first two players fold, the two posters check, and I raise from the button with A♠ Q♣. Both blinds and both posters call (10 bets, five players). The flop is A♦ Q♥ 2♥. On the flop, everyone checks to me and I bet. The small blind raises and everyone else folds to me. Since I have position, I just call (7 big bet bets). The turn is the 5♦. He bets, I raise, and he calls (11 bets). The river is the 7♠. He checks, I bet, and he check-raises. I just call and he shows A♣ 7♣.

MY HAND   **VILLAIN'S HAND**

THE BOARD

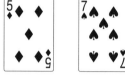

WHAT'S WRONG WITH MY PLAY?

I should raise. There are absolutely no straights or flushes, so he either has a set or two pair. If he has two pair, I have a better two pair. It is extremely unlikely he has A-A or Q-Q since he didn't raise preflop. He isn't likely to raise on the flop with 5-5 or 7-7, I have raised preflop and there is an ace on the board.

Could he have 2-2? Perhaps, but out of position and with some draws out there, he is more likely to keep raising on the turn. Two pair is his most likely hand. It is really hard to go through this entire analysis while at the table, but there are a couple of good indicators:

- An absence of flush and straight possibilities
- No pair on the board
- Few likely sets on the flop when he raised

THE LESSON

- With top two pair, you need to take a lot more time to consider whether to raise on the river. If there are no draws and few likely sets, you should put in the extra raise.

25. A BIG HAND IS NOT A LICENSE TO BET

The game is very passive, with a lot of limping and few preflop raises. An early player limps, and I decide to limp from the button with 8♣ 7♣. Both blinds play (4 bets, four players). The flop is 10♠ 7♠ 7♥. Both blinds check to the limper, who bets. I raise. The small blind calls and everyone else folds. At this point I figure that the small blind has a flush draw, since that is the most common hand with which to cold call a bet and a raise on the flop (4.5 big bets, two players.)

The turn is the 2♠. He checks. I am so excited about having trips that I decide to ignore my previous read and bet. Naturally, he raises. I kick myself a few times and I call (7.5 bets). The river is the lovely 10♣. He checks, I bet, and he grudgingly calls. I show my full house, and he mucks.

WHAT'S WRONG WITH MY PLAY?

Every now and then, I am mystified by my own play. I put him on a flush draw, his flush got there, and I still bet. Why, I am not sure. My best guess is that I hadn't had many big hands for a long time, and I was reluctant not to bet when I had one. However, that is bad poker. The whole point in reading your opponents is to use that information, not play on automatic. As it turns out, I made more money on the hand, but it was still a bad play.

Let's look at a couple of other aspects of this hand: Should he have called the flop? It costs him two bets to call with 3.5 bets in the pot, and he needs around 11 outs to call. If all he has is a flush draw, he is not getting the right price with his nine outs to a flush. Even worse, he could make his flush and lose, which will happen around 25 percent of the time. What if he has overcards as well as a flush draw? That looks like 15 outs, but with my raise, there is a very real chance that I have a 7. You need to discount his outs heavily. You might argue that I am unlikely to have a 7—wouldn't I slowplay a big hand like that? No, not with a flush draw on the board and three opponents. Should I have called the turn raise? There are 6.5 bets in the pot, meaning I need 6 to 7 outs. I have 10 cards that make me a full house; so, yes, I should call.

THE LESSON

- Don't bet just because you have a good hand. If you make a read on a player, trust it. It is true that later actions can change your read, but don't just ignore it. Calling a bet and a raise with just a flush draw isn't always right. You need to consider the size of the pot.

26. ISOLATE AGAINST THE STEAMER

A decent player has suffered several bad beats in a short time and is clearly steaming. He opens from the hijack for 10 chips and you notice he only has one chip left. It is folded to me in small blind with K♣ J♥, and I am already in for three chips. Since he cannot hurt me much after the flop, I decide to call. The big blind calls. The flop is 9♣ 6♦ 3♠. Acting out of turn, the all-in player bets his last chip. We ignore the order of action, and we both call one chip.

The turn is the K♥. I bet and the big blind raises. The big blind is not a particularly tricky player and this seems like a really odd spot for a bluff raise, with only a small side pot. After some thought, I fold. The big blind shows 9-6 and beats the all-in player's K-10. I had the all-in player dominated.

WHAT'S WRONG WITH MY PLAY?

There is absolutely no reason to let the big blind play in this hand. Playing K-10 offsuit in the small blind is a marginal hand. But if I can play it heads up against a steaming opener who could have almost anything, I am getting the right price to play. Add in the fact that I cannot get hurt much after the flop if he has a real hand like A-K, and this is a great situation. However, by letting the big blind play, I am now out of position the rest of the way with a so-so hand.

Raising is far better here than calling. Actually, I would have had the opener dominated and the big blind almost certainly folds. Here is the math of the situation. Assume that:

- We have a 50 percent chance of beating the steamer.
- We have a 60 percent chance of beating the big blind if he plays.
- If we raise the big blind folds.

If we raise, we have a 50 percent chance of winning 27 chips or an EV of 13.5 chips (after we invest 11 chips). If we call, we have a 30 percent chance of winning 33 chips or an EV of 9.9 chips. Calling costs an average of 3.6 chips.

THE LESSON

- If you can isolate against a steaming player, always raise rather than call. If an all-in player (or close to it) is the only player in the hand and you are going to play, virtually always raise instead of calling, unless you have a really big hand. Dead money is our friend. Getting the big blind out is almost always a good thing.

27. WITH THE RIGHT POT ODDS, ANY TWO CARDS CAN BE PLAYED

I observed this hand. The blinds are $15 and $25. A middle player raised all-in for $40. Everyone folded including the small blind. The big blind folded. Surprised, I asked the big blind what she had. She said she had 7-2 offsuit.

WHAT'S WRONG WITH THIS PLAY?

This one is probably pretty obvious to most no-limit players, but limit players get this wrong all the time. The big blind would have had to risk $15 to win $74. She would have needed to win 16.8 percent of the time to breakeven. Against any reasonable range, she would win more than this. If the middle player would raise with 50 percent of his hands, she wins $11.37. Here is how the big blind would fare depending on what percent of his hands the middle player would go all-in with.

PERCENT OF HANDS	BIG BLIND WINS
50%	$11.37
40%	$10.97
30%	$10.36
20%	$9.65
10%	$7.20
5%	$2.39

Calling is only a losing play if you are certain that the opener has a pocket pair bigger than sevens. Important: 7-2 is *not* playable if the other player is not all-in. In that case, you could lose a lot more money on the later rounds if you flop second best.

THE LESSON
- When the pot odds are big enough, any two cards are playable.

28. STRONG HAND & BAD POSITION? PLAY FAST

An early player and a middle player limp. I call in the small blind with 9♥ 7♦, and the big blind checks (4 bets, four players). The flop is the lovely 9♦ 9♣ 7♣. With a monster hand and tiny pot, this seems like the perfect spot to slowplay. I check, the big blind checks, the early player bets, the middle player calls, and I just call. The big blind folds. The turn is the K♦. I check and it gets checked around. The river is the 7♥. I bet, the early player folds, the middle player raises, and I call. The middle player shows A♥ 7♠, and I take the pot.

MY HAND	VILLAIN'S HAND

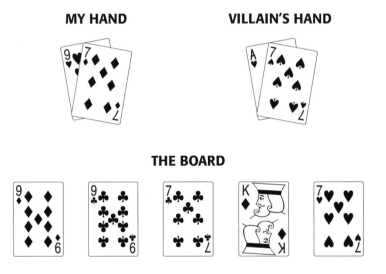

THE BOARD

WHAT'S WRONG WITH THIS PLAY?

Talk about butchering a hand! First, I should bet the flop. Check-raising the flop is announcing that I have a 9 in my hand, so betting is much less threatening. In fact, so many people will slowplay with a 9 in their hand that betting this big hand is deceptive. Then I need to bet the turn. I can represent a king and still get action from a 9 or a flush draw. Finally, I must reraise the river. The only hand that can beat me is K-K, and it is almost impossible that the villain limped in with K-K.

THE LESSON

- When out of position, you must play your big hands aggressively. On the flop, you can often disguise a big hand more by betting than by check-raising.

29. WHAT DOES A TELL REALLY TELL YOU?

An aggressive player raises from the button. I have A♠ A♦ in the big blind and I decide to use his aggressiveness against him and just call. The flop is 8♣ 6♥ 3♦. I check, he bets, and he seems to throw his chips out with an unusual amount of force. I take this as a sign of weakness. I was planning on check-raising, but I am afraid he will fold, so I just call.

The turn is the K♦. I check, he bets. At this point I am kind of stuck. If I just call, I am out of position and he might check the river behind me. I could just call and lead out on the river, but I figure he might have a king or a flush draw, so I check-raise. He thinks for a moment and folds.

WHAT'S WRONG WITH THIS PLAY?

The villain is a friend of mine and later we talked about this hand over dinner. He told me he had pocket jacks. Apparently, he bet with extra force, not because his hand was weak, but because he felt vulnerable. He wasn't too excited about my calling with overcards.

He also told me that I took the only line that would have gotten him to fold. If I had three-bet the flop and kept betting, he would have called me all the way. If I had stuck with my original plan and check-raised the flop, he would have called me all the way. The combination of the king on the turn and my suddenly going from acting weak to acting strong convinced him I had a king and got him to fold. The line I took was the least profitable way to play my hand.

THE LESSON

- It is hard to understand the significance of most tells, unless you have a very clear read. Usually stick with the most straightforward way of playing your hand. Many players mix up their play too often, particularly when they are out of position. If you want to get a call, check-raising the turn is usually the worst way to get it.

30. SECOND PAIR? KEEP BETTING!

I am new to the game, and I post a blind between the small blind and the button. The button raises, and I call with 10♥ 4♥. Both blinds call (8 bets, four players). The flop is Q♣ 10♠ 6♦. Everyone checks to the button, who is a fairly good player, and he bets. I raise, and only the button calls (6 big bets, two players). The turn is the 5♣. I bet and the button calls (8 bets). The river is the 5♠. I decide I don't like my weak kicker and I check. He checks behind me, and mucks when I show my hand.

WHAT'S WRONG WITH THIS PLAY?

First of all, I completely misread my hand on the river. I don't have a weak kicker (my 4 doesn't play), I have two pair with a queen kicker. Also, I have little reason to be afraid that he has a better hand. If he had a queen, a decent player would have raised earlier. I am losing to a few hands such as J-J, A-10 and K-10, but there are a lot more hands in his range I am beating.

There is a chance that he is waiting to raise on the river with a big hand, but with flush and straight draws out there, he usually isn't going to be that patient. I don't know if he would have paid off a river bet, but with a hand like 5-5, A-6, or even A-K, he might. One of the two or three biggest mistakes weak players make is to not bet the river for value. While this is not as glaring a mistake as many weak players make, I have no reason to slow down here.

THE LESSON

- If you have been betting second pair for value all the way, bet again on the river unless a scare card comes.

31. BIG HAND? YOU DON'T HAVE TO RAISE

I am new to the game, and I post a blind between the small blind and the button. This is a fairly high-stakes game ($25/$50). Everyone folds to me and I raise with K♥ 8♥. The small blind folds and the big blind reraises (I have never played with him before). I call (6.6 bets, two players). The flop is Q♥ J♠ 9♠. I check, the big blind bets and with an overcard, the backdoor flush, and the gutshot straight draw, I decide to peel a card. I call (4.3 big bets, two players).

The turn is the 10♦. He bets, I raise, and he reraises. I hope he just has a king and not A-K, so I call (10.3 bets). The river is the 9♦. He bets and I call, praying he just has another king and not A-K. He shows me A-K for the higher straight.

WHAT'S WRONG WITH THIS PLAY?

The four cards to a straight on the turn is pretty obvious. If I have a king or 8 I have a straight. I raised before the flop making it more likely that I have big cards, yet he still bets into me. Unless he is a complete fool, he has to know of the danger. Raising is a mistake here for two reasons: (1) he three-bet preflop, so A-K is a real possibility and the risk of losing two extra big bets is real; (2) there are few hands he can call a raise with that I can beat. With two pair or even a set, most good players would seriously consider check-calling the turn, instead of betting.

It is possible he might bet a set and call my raise. Let's assume he will bet A-K, K-K, Q-Q, J-J and 10-10 on the turn and call a raise. There are 12 combinations of A-K and 21 possible sets, so 21 times I win an extra bet by raising and 12 times I lose two bets. Overall I am losing money when I raise. However, the situation is worse than that. If he has the set, he will improve 23 percent of the time, and I will lose at least one more bet on the river. I don't always win an extra bet by raising when he has a set. Also, if he has a set, he might not bet such a scary board. This weights his distribution when he bets more toward having A-K.

Some people might argue he could also bet and call a raise on the turn with weaker hands such as a flush draw and a pair There aren't a lot of hands he can have, however. About the only hands most players would three-bet with before the flop are A♠ Q♠ and A♠ J♠, and he might check with those. Since we don't have the K♥, it is also possible he has the same king-high straight as I do with a redraw. If he has K♠ Q♠ or K♠ J♠, I will win half the pot at best.

If I assume he is competent, and unless I know he is hyper-aggressive, I should assume he is aware of the straight danger when he bets and that should slow him down with all except the best hands. I should not assume he is a fool or maniac since I have no history with him.

THE LESSON

- Always assume that an unknown player is competent until you see evidence that he or she is not. Be cautious about marginal raises on the later streets, as you are often risking two bets to win one extra bet. This is particularly true if raising makes it very obvious what you have. And be cautious about making marginal raises against unknown players, as you will usually not be able to fold to a reraise.

Now let's turn our attention to some techniques you can use to pull yourself out of the hole when you're running bad.

11 HOW TO PLAY WHEN YOU'RE RUNNING BAD

You've probably lost to a four-outer on the river, and may think that you suffered the worst beat possible. You're not even close! Just about every improbable way of losing will happen at the poker table over time. This one happened to me.

With pocket 7♥ 7♦, the flop comes down J♠ 7♣ 3♥. The villain calls my flop bet with Q♣ 6♥. He has no pair and no draw. Perhaps he was hoping for a queen? His only possible way to win was if a 4 and a 5 were the next two cards. In other words, he had one-half an out. He only wins this pot 1.6 percent of the time. With a 98.4 percent chance of winning, I lost!

ONE BEAT WORSE THAN THE NEXT

LOSING WITH FOUR ACES?

How about the famous hand from the 2008 WSOP where Motoyuki "Moto" Mabuch had A♠ A♥ on a board of A♣ Q♦ 9♠ 10♦ A♦ lost with quad aces to a royal flush? While it was incredibly dramatic, and losing in the Main Event like that has to be horribly traumatic, that isn't really that horrible a beat. On the flop, the aces are only an 84 to 16 favorite.

THE WORST BEAT!

Here is the worst beat I can conceive of: You are dealt A♠ A♥ and the flop comes A♣ A♦ 9♠. If the next two cards are Q-10 and you lose to a royal flush (or you lose to any straight flush), you take the title. Your hand had a 99.9 percent chance of winning on the flop and you lost to a hand with 0.1 percent chance of winning. You can proudly claim the worst beat possible! Until this happens, try to keep a little perspective on your bad beats. Almost certainly someone has taken a worse beat than yours—and everyone thinks his beats are worse than yours.

> When you're winning, you feel like you'll never lose again. When you're losing, you feel like you'll never win again. Feelings lie!

CHANGE YOUR SELF-TALK

When you are running bad, you can do things to make it worse or make it better. If you handle the bad streaks well, you will lose less in them and come back faster. This can have a significant effect on your overall win rate. If you are like many players, when you are running bad you will start mentally documenting how bad you are running. You want to come home and tell your spouse or your poker buddy how terrible your session was to get some sympathy. Since all poker players have bad streaks, you won't get much sympathy from an ordinary bad streak. It has to be memorable. You want to tell them exactly how many times you lost with aces, or how many time you flopped two pair and lost to sets or flushes.

There is a serious problem with this. You are spending a lot of your emotional energy convincing yourself how badly you are losing. You relive the loss over and over in your mind. This will affect your play. The more you talk yourself into feeling like a loser, the worse you will play and the better your opponents will play against you.

Self-talk, what you say to yourself in reaction to events, has a very powerful effect on your mental attitude and behavior. Negative self-talk will make you play worse. You may stop raising when you should, because you have convinced yourself you will just lose anyway. For example, if you have a couple of bad beats, you can think to yourself, "I just can't win. No matter what I do, I lose." Or you can think to yourself, "I got my money in with the best hand. If I keep doing that I have to win eventually." Which self-talk do you think will help you to play better?

> Control your self talk and you will control your emotions.

Saying negative things out loud also has an effect on the others at the table. When they start to see you as vulnerable, they will start to try to exploit you, too. They will start raising you more and taking more shots at you. And it's not just talk. Suppose you have just lost with pocket aces when some fool called three bets to play J-5 suited and caught a 5 on the turn and a jack on the river. Quietly muck your aces. Don't show the table your losing hand. Don't go for their sympathy. Remind yourself that the fool is going to lose all his money and you will probably get some of it.

Don't do anything to enforce a loser image. Don't spend your time remembering exactly how bad you are running. No one cares that you only won two of the last 24 flops you took. It doesn't matter that you haven't won a pot in three hours. The more you keep track of things like this, the more tempted you will be to start chasing or playing badly.

You will be tempted to make bad calls when you're on a losing streak because you are so desperate to try to win a pot. Resisting that temptation will earn you money. You will not make it back by trying to make something happen when the cards don't cooperate. You need to wait for the cards. This requires practice. The more you work at staying positive after a series of losses the better you will get at it. When you're running bad, you must do your best to put it all behind you and try to play the next hand as well as possible. If you played correctly, mentally praise yourself for playing correctly. You cannot control the outcome, only how you play. If you play well, you will win in the long run.

CREATE YOUR OWN
VERSION OF THIS BOOK

Sometimes, especially when you're running bad, you will misplay a hand. If you beat yourself up about it, you will probably play worse. If you are really upset about a bad play, take a break. Walk around a bit. Fresh air often helps. And do your best to not dwell on the bad play during your break.

If you seriously want to improve, I recommend you take one more step. Start your own version of *Hold'em Hands I Played Badly*. When you realize you have made a bad play, write it down. Do it right at the table while it is fresh in your mind. When you get home, write it in a notebook or on your computer. Spend some time thinking about it. Look for clues that will help you recognized the situation in the heat of battle at the table. Then review all your errors on a regular basis. Reinforce the learning—you will be surprised how much your game improves.

This process could have another big benefit. When I play a hand badly, it tends to haunt me. I go over the hand in my mind time after time. It's a little depressing to be so focused on my failure. However, once I write the hand down, I can let it go. It frees up my mind so that I can get back to the game and the rest of my life. Perhaps my subconscious is now satisfied that I understand the lesson I have learned from my play.

> When you're losing, you cannot catch up by playing more hands.

10 THINGS TO DO WHEN YOU'RE RUNNING BAD

#1

It's time to get up when:

- You are tired
- The game is bad
- You are upset

#2

Many people play longer when they are behind and get up earlier when they are ahead. This is probably the opposite of the right way to play. When you are behind you are often either in a bad game, playing badly, or both. That's the worst time to play a long session.

#3

Losing tires you out. If you are running bad, you should tend to quit a bit earlier.

#4

It is not the bad beat that costs you the most—you cannot control losing that money. Far more important is how you play the hands right after you've suffered the bad beat.

#5

Don't base any decision on whether you are ahead or behind.

#6

When you are losing, you will be tempted to play more actively to have a chance to get even. Don't do it! Losing less when you are losing is just as important as winning a lot when you win.

#7

Resist these four temptations when you're running bad, and you will win a lot more money over the long run:

- Don't play more hands
- Don't call more often
- Don't bet more with mediocre hands like middle or bottom pair
- Don't try to make a move

#8

When you are losing, you might feel that people are picking on you. It will seem like every time you bet, someone raises you. This may or may not be true, but don't get too wild in trying to stop it.

#9

Remind yourself about these three things:

- You are not in the middle of the worst losing streak in the history of poker.
- You are not in the middle of the worst session in the history of poker.
- The last bad beat you took is not the worst beat anyone has ever had.

#10

Don't tell everyone how bad you are running. You don't want to convince people that you are a pathetic loser. You want to convince them that you are an invincible winner to be feared.

Next up on our agenda is a special chapter with pointers on how to play the very popular kill games that many casinos spread.

12 PLAYING KILL-POT HOLD'EM GAMES

Many smaller limit hold'em games are played with a **kill**, which means that if you win two pots in a row, you must post a blind that is larger than the big blind, and the limits go up for that hand. If you win a third pot, you must kill again and keep killing until you lose.

There are two types of kill games: full kill and half kill.

In a **full-kill game**, the limits double. If you are playing $8/$16 with a full kill, after you win two hands in a row you must post a $16 blind (twice the normal $8 big blind), and the limits go up to $16/$32 for as long as the kill is in effect.

With a **half-kill** you post 150 percent of the big blind and the limits go up 50 percent. In $8/$16 games, the extra blind is $12, and the limits go to $12/$24.

If you are the **killer** and you were going to have to post a blind anyway, you still only need to post the amount of the kill. For example, if you were going to post an $8 big blind and you must post $12 for a half kill, you only post the $12. This is sometimes called a **cheap kill**. How the kill affects the order of play varies from casino to casino. In some casinos the killer acts in the same order as he would have acted without the kill. In others, the killer gets to act last on his first action, and then the order goes back to normal.

WHEN YOU HAVE A LEG UP

When you win a pot, you are said to have a **leg up**, and the dealer will usually put a special button in front of you. This special button indicates that you've won the first pot of a potential two-consecutive-pots win that would lead to the next pot becoming a kill pot. If you regularly play in a game with a kill, or even occasionally play in one while waiting to get a seat in your normal game, you need to understand the importance of killing and having a leg up because they affect your play.

Lots of players love to kill the pot, since it leads to bigger action. They will go out of their way to play with a leg up just so they can get the chance to kill. Others want to ride their rush. They think that since they won the last pot or two, they are on a rush and should play looser as long as the streak lasts. This can be a big mistake.

Poker hands are independent events. The outcome of the last hand has no effect on the probability of winning the next hand unless other players at the table believe that you are "hot." In that case, they might be more likely to fold decent hands against you. The more superstitious your opponents are, the more likely you should be to ride a rush. However, you generally don't want to change your play after winning a pot or two unless you are in a game with a kill.

THE COST OF A BLIND

Posting a blind costs around one-half the amount of the blind. Posting a $20 blind will cost you an average of around $10. Normally, you cannot avoid this cost since posting blinds is the price of being dealt a round of cards. However, you have a choice about posting a kill.

For this discussion, let's assume that you are in an $8/$16 game with a kill. Suppose you have a leg up. You are second to act, and the first player folds. Perhaps the weakest hand you might normally raise with in this position is A-9, and you are dealt A♦ 9♠. You should fold. The problem is that winning the pot costs you some money.

With a half-kill, you will need to post a $12 kill and that costs you $6, which is almost a small bet. In many live games, this is the same amount as the rake. It is as though you are playing to win a pot that will be raked twice. With a full-kill, it is even worse. You will post a $16 kill and that will cost you $8, which is more than the rake. Therefore, when you have a leg up, you should play just a bit tighter because you are getting a worse price for the cost of entering the pot.

LEG-UP EXCEPTIONS

Here are a couple of other factors to consider when you have a leg up. If you are under the gun, you don't need to tighten up much with a leg up, particularly in a half-kill game. Since you are going to post the big blind for the next hand anyway, the kill doesn't cost you as much. If you will post a $12 kill if you win and an $8 big blind if you don't, killing only costs you $2 (half of the extra $4 you add to the blind).

Also consider your position. If you are in the small blind with a leg up, you will be on the button in the next hand. Killing with good position doesn't cost you as much as killing with bad position. Finally, if the big blind rarely defends, you don't need to adjust as much. When you get a walk with a leg up, you don't need to kill. If the big blind rarely defends his blind, your chances of getting a walk increase greatly.

WHEN YOU ARE THE KILLER

When playing as the killer, your first instinct might be to call a raise just as frequently as you would call a raise in the big blind. You are getting the same pot odds, and you often have better position. However, you generally want to play a little tighter. If you win, you will be forced to post another kill and that will cost you money over the long run.

All the exceptions for adjusting for a leg up apply here. If you are going to be the big blind next hand or will have great position, take that into account. Also, a big blind who rarely defends will defend even less in a kill pot, since he has to call a much larger raise, so you can steal a bit more as the killer. Some good players will raise with almost any two cards when they are the killer and have good position.

SOME OTHER ADVICE

If it is your turn to post the big blind in a kill pot, consider skipping a round unless you are in a game with a lot of limping. Normally, posting an $8 big blind costs you around $4, but it will cost you more in a kill pot. You will not be able to play as many hands, so your blind will turn into dead money. With a full kill, a raise to $32 will not give you good pot odds to play a lot of hands from the big blind, as you will have to throw away many hands you would normally play.

Here are the pot odds with a full kill.

BIG BLIND'S POT ODDS WITH A FULL KILL	
No kill, 1 raiser	3.5 to 1
Full kill, killer raises	1.3 to 1
Full kill, other raiser, killer folds	2.5 to 1

You get significantly worse pot odds to defend your blind. This also explains why you can try to steal a lot more often as the killer. A decent player in the blinds will defend quite a bit less and you should successfully steal more often.

With a half kill this is not as bad.

BIG BLIND'S POT ODDS WITH A HALF KILL	
No kill, 1 raiser	3.5 to 1
Half kill, killer raises	2.25 to 1
Half kill, other raiser, killer folds	3.25 to 1

Against an aggressive killer, you should still consider taking a break. If you are the killer with a half kill, you should probably only try to steal a little looser.

Finally, weak players love to kill and defend their kill. When a weak player in the big blind has a leg up or is the killer, you should try to steal less often. On the other hand, better players may understand the consequences of killing, and may play tighter with a leg up or when killing the pot. You can try to steal from them more often.

Hopefully, these suggestions on how to play kill pots will lead you to more success in both half-kill and full-kill games. Now let's move on to discussing some techniques you can use to optimize your profits when you're playing multiple tables online.

13 MULTI-TABLING ONLINE

A number of people make good money playing a lot of tables online at the same time. Finding sites where you can play 16, 20, or more tables isn't that hard. If you are a winning player it can increase your hourly rate. You might not win as much in each game, but you can still earn more per hour.

Here are some possible numbers for a $5/$10 game.

TABLES	WIN PER TABLE	TOTAL WIN PER HOUR
2	$7.5	$15
4	$5	$20
6	$4	$24

If increasing from two tables to six cuts your hourly rate on each table in half, you still make significantly more money per hour.

9 TIPS FOR PLAYING MULTIPLE TABLES ONLINE

1. **Play tighter.** The fewer hands you play, the less often you will be playing several hands at the same time. This reduces stress and mistakes. The better you play after the flop, the more hands you

can play. When you play a lot of tables, your play isn't as good. Marginal hands are less likely to be profitable. You will have fewer and less accurate reads on your opponents.

2. **Don't get tricky as often.** Stick to the obvious play.

3. **Don't try to pick off a lot of bluffs.** When you haven't been paying as much attention to players, your guesses won't be as accurate. This doesn't mean you should never try to pick off bluffs, just don't do it too often.

4. **Stay calm.** Even if you are playing several hands, you have plenty of time to make good decisions on them all. Even if the site's software is beeping at you, take your time.

5. **If you are playing a hand and you get a marginal hand at a second table, don't play it.** It's not worth taking your attention away from the hand you are already playing.

6. **Take breaks.** It seems like a bigger effort to sit out from several tables, but you need breaks more when you multi-table. Taking a meal break will mean leaving all the tables. You may hate to do it, since it takes a while to get back on those tables. Do it anyway. You will play better without the distraction of hunger and with some time to clear your head. There will always be more games.

7. **Don't spend all your time multi-tabling.** Playing lots of hands helps you improve, but so does playing hands with a lot of thought. I like to mix up live play, which is much slower with online multi-table play.

8. **Don't expect to play as long.** You will tire more quickly.

9. **Be sure you are signed up for rake back.** You will generate a lot of hours and this will be a significant factor in your profits.

THREE GAME SCENARIOS

1. THE BEST-LAID PLANS

I am playing several tables online. A tight player opens under the gun. I raise from the cutoff with A♣ K♣ and only the opener calls (7.5 bets, two players). The flop is Q♥ 9♥ 9♦. He checks, I bet, and he calls. I am a bit concerned, since tight players usually fold here unless they have something. If he has something, it is a very good hand given this flop. The turn is the 2♣. He checks. I consider checking, but decide I want a free showdown, and he hasn't shown much strength yet. I bet and he calls (6.75 big bets). The river is the Q♠. He checks. I bet earlier for a free showdown and I got the opportunity, so I check. He shows A♥ 10♥, and we split the pot.

WHAT'S WRONG WITH MY PLAY?

First, when I think about his hand after he calls on the flop, I miss one obvious candidate, the heart draw. Being a tight, under-the-gun raiser, he probably doesn't have a 9 in his hand. He might have A-Q. That is not too likely, since most players will raise with it on the flop, but it is still possible. He might have another A-K. Or he could have hearts. I should definitely have that in my calculations. When it gets to the river, I need to reevaluate. He probably doesn't have a queen or 9. He hasn't made an aggressive move yet. If he has a heart draw, he probably has an ace, so I am looking at splitting the pot. I need to bet the river. It is basically a free roll. If he folds, I win more than three big bets.

What if he is slowplaying a big hand? What if he has a hand like 10-10 or J-J, and is afraid to raise because of the queen on the board? Then it depends on how often he will fold. If he will fold 25 percent of the time, that is worth (on average) 0.8 big bets. If you will lose a big bet, 25 percent of the time (which seems high), that costs you 0.25 big bets. This is clearly profitable.

Throw in the meta-game consideration. If he calls you and splits the pot, everyone will see your aggressive play on the river. It could easily win you some calls on future hands. This is a case where playing multiple tables online probably cost me. First, I misread his hand. Second, I decided on a plan (bet for a free showdown) and didn't change the plan when the situation changed.

THE LESSON

- Don't let a pair on the board blind you to a flush draw. It is more likely that someone has the flush draw than trips. Just because you have decided on a plan of action on an earlier round, doesn't mean you need to stick to it when circumstances change. If you are pretty sure you are splitting the pot, bet.

2. THERE'S NO RULE AGAINST BETTING WITH THE NUTS

I am playing multi-table online. I raise from early position with A♥ 8♥. A middle player calls along with both blinds (8 bets, four players). The flop is Q♥ 5♣ 4♥, and both blinds check. I bet, the middle player raises, and the small blind calls. The big blind folds (7 big bets, three players). The turn is the 7♥. The small blind checks to me, I check, and the middle player checks.

The river is the 2♥. The small blind checks, I bet, the middle player folds, and the small blind calls. The small blind has 10♥ 9♥, for a made flush on the turn. A bet on the turn would have earned me two or three more big bets.

WHAT'S WRONG WITH THIS PLAY?

Here is the danger of playing multiple tables online. When the small blind cold-calls two bets on the flop, his most likely holding is a flush draw. If that is his hand, a bet on the turn becomes an obvious play. I had some bad luck with another heart falling on the river, but a bet on the turn is still the right play.

While it might have been possible to miss the likely flush when playing multiple tables, another key principle comes into play here. With a made flush on the turn, a fourth card of the flush suit will kill the action on the river. You need to be aggressive, particularly in a multiway pot.

THE LESSON

- When a player cold calls two bets on the flop and there are suited cards on the board, a likely holding is a flush draw. If there is no flush draw and two connected cards, consider a straight draw, likely with two overcards. When a scare card hits the board, don't expect the previous aggressor to keep betting, particularly in a multiway pot. With a made flush on the turn, tend to bet and raise since another card of the flush suit can kill your hand or your action.

3. ONLINE BIGAMY

The first player limps and I raise from early position with A♠ Q♠. The next early player calls, the small blind raises, the limper folds and I call. Now the other player caps it and we all call. Three of us see the flop and there are 14.5 bets in the pot. The flop is Q♣ 9♦ 5♥. The small blind bets, I raise, the other early player calls, the small blind reraises, and we both call (11.8 big bets).

The turn is the 10♠. The small blind bets, I call, the other player raises, and I go along for four bets (23.8 big bets). The river is the J♠. Everyone checks. The small blind shows A♥ A♣ and the other early player shows 9♥ 9♣ for a winning set.

WHAT'S WRONG WITH MY PLAY?

First, it is not clear I should raise the flop, but when I do, I get a lot of information. One player cold-called two bets and the small blind isn't slowed down at all by my raise. They are both showing a lot of strength. I should be very worried. But because I am playing two tables at once and not paying enough attention, I ignore the information.

> There's no point in raising to see where you stand if you don't pay attention to the answer.

At some point I have to realize that top pair, top kicker isn't any good. The pot may be huge, but these guys can't keep raising with nothing. The best time to realize my hand is good is probably after the second raise on the turn. The pot may be huge, but I am drawing dead. Even if no one has a set, I have three outs. A pair of aces and a set should be no surprise. There is a reason the pot is huge. They have huge hands. And the third bet on the turn or river usually means the nuts or something close to it. Since there is no flush draw on the board, no one is doing all this raising with a big draw.

THE LESSON

- Top pair, top kicker is not a guaranteed winner. Three bets on the turn or river usually mean a really big hand. Don't get married to two ladies. It's bigamy!

Now let's have some real fun with some brain teasers designed to test your grasp of the principles we've discussed in this book. Kick back and enjoy yourself!

14 GAME SCENARIOS & WINNING PRINCIPLES

These hands illustrate the principles discussed in this book. Review each one to clearly understand the situation and the action. Then answer the question about the hand before you look at the answer.

70 GAME SCENARIOS

GAME SCENARIO #1

You raise under the gun with 9♦ 9♣. Only the big blind calls (4.5 bets, two players). The flop is A♣ A♠ 7♣. He checks, you bet, and he calls (3.25 big bets). The turn is the 6♥. What do you do?

ANSWER

Bet. This may look like a "way ahead or way behind" situation and you might consider checking in case he has an ace. But an ace is just one of his possible holdings. He could have an ace, a 7, a pocket pair, or a flush draw. Since he didn't reraise before the flop, he probably doesn't have a pocket pair bigger than yours, so he is more likely to have a hand you can beat, and he will call you most of the time with those hands. If you check, you are giving up a bet; and giving a free card if he is on a flush draw is terrible. Keep in mind that with two aces on the board, he will consider it far less likely that you have an ace, and he is more likely to call you down with a hand such as 4-4. On the actual hand, the hero checked, and the villain bet after the 3♣ came on the river. The hero called and the villain showed K♠ 7♦. Checking may have cost the hero a big bet.

GAME SCENARIO #2

You are in the big blind with Q♠ Q♥. Everyone folds to the cutoff, who limps. The button and the small blind call. You raise. The cutoff and button call, and the small blind folds (7 bets, three players). The flop is K♦ 6♣ 2♠. You bet and they both call (5 big bets, three players). The turn is the 3♥. What do you do now?

ANSWER

Check. You don't want to bet after two calls on such a dry board. The dry board affects things in several ways:

There aren't a lot of hands they can call with on the flop if they don't have a king. Players don't limp very often with sixes and twos. They could have a smaller pocket pair, A-6, or A-2, but that and a king are the only likely hands they can be calling with.

With a dry board, a player with a king won't feel the same urgency to raise on the flop, as he isn't going to be afraid of draws. A king with a weak kicker might be afraid to raise the flop. With a king on the board, no one can have two overcards.

You don't have to worry about giving a free card to a drawing hand (other than A-6 or A-2).

GAME SCENARIO #3

You raise from the button with A♠ 7♦. A calling station in the small blind calls, and the big blind calls (6 bets, three players). The flop is 6♣ 4♥ 3♦. The small blind checks and the big blind bets. What do you do?

ANSWER

Raise. You may have the best hand and you could have as many as 10 outs if you don't. A 7, ace, or 5 could win the pot for you. You would rather eliminate the small blind, who is likely to call one bet with any hint of a hand. Raising gives you the option of firing again on the turn or taking a free card, depending on what comes. Finally, if you do catch a winning hand, there will be more money in the pot if you raise on the flop. On the actual hand, the hero raised and everyone folded.

GAME SCENARIO #4

The cutoff raises and you reraise from the button with A♠ A♦. Everyone else folds (7.5 bets, two players). The flop is J♦ 3♣ 2♠. He checks, you bet, he raises, and with position, you decide to wait until the turn to raise, so you just call (5.75 big bets). The turn is the J♠. He bets. If he raised you with a jack, he now has trips, so you decide to just call (7.75 bets). The river is the K♥. He checks. Now what do you do?

ANSWER

Bet. Very few players will check with a jack here, since they are afraid of missing a bet. Your aces are almost certainly the best hand. On the actual hand, the hero bet and the villain called with 8♠ 8♣.

GAME SCENARIO #5

The hijack limps, the small blind calls, and you decide to check in the big blind with A♥ 3♥ (3 bets, three players). The flop is K♠ K♥ 7♣. The small blind checks. What should you do?

ANSWER

Bet. A flop with a pair on the board and no straight or flush draw is an outstanding situation to try to steal. Here you may even have the best hand, and giving a free card would be a bad idea. Add in that one player has already checked, and this situation cries out for a bet. You only have to win 25 percent of the time to break even, and you should win a lot more often than that.

On the actual hand, the hero bet and took the pot. Note that if you had raised before the flop, it might be harder to take this pot down, since your continuation bet would get less respect. With twice as much money in the pot, it's a lot more profitable when you do take it down.

GAME SCENARIO #6

Everyone folds to you on the button and you raise with A♠ K♣. Only the small blind calls (5 bets, two players). The flop comes J♣ 9♣ 2♠. The small blind checks, you bet, and he raises (8 bets and two players). How do you respond to his check-raise?

ANSWER

Reraise. You can also play a mixed strategy here by calling some of the time. This is a very important situation that comes up frequently, and it is considered by many players to be an automatic free-card raise. You are calling anyway with 8.5 outs (6 for the overcards, 2 for the backdoor flush, 0.5 for Q-10 to a straight). By raising, you will usually get two shots at making your hand for the price of one small bet.

Let's assume you are beaten right now and your outs are all good (though this certainly isn't true if he has a hand like A-9.) If you just call, you will need to fold unless you improve on the turn. (There will be 5.5 bets in the pot and you will have six outs.) With a free card, you will see the river, which gives you a 33 percent chance of winning instead of 19 percent. A 33 percent chance of winning nine bets means your expectation is three bets. A 19 percent chance of winning eight bets is 1.5 bets. So for the cost of one small bet, you win 1.5 extra bets on average, so this is a good investment. Now, suppose the 9♣ is the 9♦ instead. You have only 6.5 outs. The raise is still worthwhile, earning you around 1.27 small bets for the cost of one small bet.

On the actual hand, the hero raised and was called. He took the free turn card, which was the 4♥. The river was the A♦ and the villain called a bet on the river. The villain had J♦ 7♦. Without the free card, the hero would not have been getting the odds to continue on the turn and would have lost the pot.

GAME SCENARIO #7

The cutoff raises and you reraise from the button with K♦ 10♦. Everyone else folds (7.5 bets, two players). The flop is K♥ 10♠ 9♣. He bets and you call (4.75 big bets). The 2♠ comes on the turn. He bets (5.75 bets). Do you fold, call or raise?

ANSWER

Raise. When he bets out on the flop, he probably doesn't have a big hand. Most players will check-raise with a really strong hand. The only question is whether to raise here or on the river. With a highly coordinated board, there are two problems that can hurt you if you wait: First, there are lots of draws out there. If you raise on the turn and he is on a draw, you will likely get called. There is less danger he will fold to a raise here. Second, plenty of scare cards could come on the river, which could make it harder for you to raise, or harder for him to call you. The scare cards might also keep him from betting the river. You are more likely to get two bets on the turn than the river.

With a strong but beatable hand in position:

- With lots of draws, tend to raise on the turn.
- With a dry board, you can afford to wait until the river to raise.

On the actual hand, the hero raised and was called. When the 9♠ came on the river, the villain bet and the hero called. The villain showed K♣ J♠.

GAME SCENARIO #8

You raise from early position with A♥ 10♥. A middle player and the big blind call (6.5 bets, three players). The flop comes K♠ Q♠ 8♠. The big blind checks. What do you do?

ANSWER

Bet. You only need to win around 13 percent of the time to break even. Unless someone has a big spade, a king or queen, they will have a hard time continuing. While the board is full of straight draws, most folks won't be drawing to a straight with three spades on the board. On the actual hand, the hero bet and everyone folded.

GAME SCENARIO #9

You raise under the gun with 7♠ 7♦. A very aggressive player reraises from middle position and you call (7.5 bets, two players). The flop comes Q♥ Q♦ 7♣. You check, he bets, you raise, and he reraises. You call (6.75 big bets). The turn brings the 2♥. You check, he bets, you raise, and he calls (10.75 bets). The river card is the 9♠. You bet and he raises (13.75 bets). Do you fold, call or reraise?

ANSWER

Call. Let's look at the math. First, we can ignore any possible bluffs. A bluff is unlikely here and if he is bluffing, he isn't calling a raise. If he has less than trips, we are only getting one bet out of him whether we raise or call. His most likely strong hands are Q-Q, Q-9s, A-Q, or 9-9. You can only beat A-Q. But how likely is each hand? Based strictly on the math, here is how many ways he can make each: Q-Q, one; Q-9s, one; 9-9, three; and A-Q, eight.

So, there are eight hands that we can beat, and only five that we lose to. However, that does not make this a raise. When we raise and lose, we lose two bets, while a win only gets us one extra bet. So a raise will lose 10 bets on average for every eight bets that we win. Of course, this math is always only approximate. He could have more hands, including K-Q, Q-2s, or even Q-7s, but those are less likely.

In addition to the math, thin value raises on the river generally don't do all that well unless you have a very aggressive image. Players with very aggressive images will get raised with more garbage, but raises on the river almost always mean business. Thin value bets are great—thin value raises aren't. In this hand, you have shown a ton of strength by check-raising the turn. Even aggressive players will get the message. He has to put you on at least A-Q and thinks he has A-Q beat. That doesn't leave much that you can beat.

On the actual hand, the hero raised and got reraised. The villain had pocket nines. The hero swore he would never play poker again, as he posted the big blind.

GAME SCENARIO #10

Two middle players limp. You call half a bet from the small blind with K♥ 7♠ and the big blind checks (4 bets, four players). The flop is 8♥ 7♦ 7♣ . What do you do?

ANSWER

Bet. These are pretty good cards to give limpers some draws, and someone could call with overcards. Also, betting is the best way to disguise your hand. Check-raising is more likely to give away that you have a 7. On the actual hand, the hero bet. He got two calls and it was raised before it got back to him, so he was able to three-bet the flop. He eventually split the pot with a 7-6 when two queens came on the turn and river.

GAME SCENARIO #11

You raise from middle position with Q♠ 10♠, and the next middle player reraises. This player three-bets 5.3 percent preflop, which is "normal." You call (7.5 bets, two players). The flop is 9♣ 8♥ 5♦. You check and he bets (9.5 bets). What do you do?

ANSWER

Call. You have as many as 10 outs, so your choices are to call or raise. In position, you might raise for a free card, but here you won't have that option. You are unlikely to steal this pot and the danger of getting reraised is pretty high. There just aren't enough hands in his distribution that you can get him to fold, and you could be far behind.

In the actual hand, the hero called. Then when a jack came on the turn, he was able to check-raise. The villain had Q-Q, so the hero actually only had four outs on the flop. But even heroes suck out sometimes. (A raise would have been a terrible play, until the jack came on the turn—and then you would have been a genius for raising!)

GAME SCENARIO #12

An early player limps, you raise from the button with A♦ 7♥, and the big blind and early limper call (6.5 bets, three players). The flop is 10♠ 7♣ 5♣. The big blind bets, and the limper folds (7.5 bets). What do you do?

ANSWER

Raise. You probably have the best hand. With a 10, the big blind is more likely to check-raise. These "donk" bets are usually weaker bets such as middle or bottom pair, or a draw. On the actual hand, the hero raised. The villain won at the showdown with 5♠ 4♣, when two more clubs came on the turn and river.

GAME SCENARIO #13

A tricky player raises from the cutoff. He likes to make plays, but isn't as smart as he thinks he is. Everyone folds to you in the big blind, where you have K♦ 9♥. As you reach for your chips to call, he says, "Why do you have to always call me from the blind?" You call (4.5 bets, two players). The flop is 7♠ 7♣ 2♥. You check and he bets (5.5 bets). What do you do?

ANSWER

When a tricky player makes an unusual statement, he is almost always trying to give the opposite impression. When he says he doesn't like that you are giving action, it means he is thrilled with your action. It's the "acting weak means he is strong" tell. It's surprisingly reliable against players like this one. Muck your hand fast as a bat out of hell! As sure at the sun will rise tomorrow, he has aces—or possibly kings or queens.

GAME SCENARIO #14

Everyone folds to you on the button, and you raise with 7♠ 5♠. The small blind folds and the big blind calls (4.5 bets, two players). The flop is 9♣ 8♦ 6♣. He bets, you raise, he reraises, and you call (5.25 big bets, two players). The turn is the A♦. He bets, you raise, and he reraises (9,25 bets). What do you do?

ANSWER

Raise. He likely has a set or a higher straight (10-7), but he could also have two pair, a pair and a draw, or even a hand like A♣ 10♣. There are a lot more hands you can beat than hands that beat you. You cap it on the turn and he calls. The river is the 4♣. He bets (14.25 bets). Now what do you do?

Call. First, he wasn't at all slowed down when you capped the turn. That makes it seem like he either has the nuts or made the nuts on the river. If his hand included a flush draw, it just got there. You are probably beat, but the pot is too big to fold a straight. On the actual hand, the villain showed 10♥ 7♣ for the bigger straight. It was terrible luck for you both to flop straights on that board, but bad things happen. You don't need to make them worse by overplaying your hand.

GAME SCENARIO #15

An early player and a middle player limp. You call from the button with A♦ 7♦, the small blind folds, and the big blind checks (4.5 bets, four players). The flop is 7♠ 6♠ 5♣. The big blind checks, the first limper bets, and the second limper calls (6.5 bets). What's your best move?

ANSWER

Fold. Sometimes you need to fold top pair, top kicker. If the turn comes a 3, 4, 8, 9 or spade you will have no idea where you are in the hand if anyone bets. You need to dodge at least 21 cards twice to get to a showdown, which doesn't even count any overcard that could give someone a bigger pair. Even worse, you might not have the best hand right now.

With only one villain taking the flop, this could be a raising hand, but with three villains, the odds are too strong that you will end up with the worst hand. On the actual hand, the hero raised and was reraised on the flop. He went to the river only to lose to 4♥ 3♥. He had been drawing almost dead all the way.

GAME SCENARIO #16

A middle player limps. The button calls and you call half a bet in the small blind with J♥ 2♥. The big blind checks (4 bets, four players). The flop is 10♣ 2♦ 2♣. You bet and only the big blind calls (3 big bets). The turn is the 3♥. You bet and the big blind calls (5 bets). The river is the 10♦. What do you do?

ANSWER

Check. There are not very many hands the villain can have. He probably has a 10, a 2, a flush draw, or a small pair. If he has a 10, a 2 or a flush draw, you cannot get any money out of him by betting. With a 10 you will get raised. With a 2, you are splitting the pot. With a busted flush he will probably fold. The only hand you want to bet into is a small pair, and if you bet and get raised, you face an ugly decision, so your best chance is to check. If you are beat, you only lose one bet, and if he is on a flush draw, you might induce a bluff.

On the actual hand the hero checked, the villain bet, and the hero called. The villain had J♣ 3♣, for a busted flush draw. With the pair of threes he picked up on the turn, you might have gotten a crying call if you had bet.

GAME SCENARIO #17

An early player limps, the cutoff and the button limp, and you call half a bet in the small blind with K♦ Q♥. The big blind checks (5 bets, five players). The flop is J♠ 10♦ 3♠. You bet, and three players call (4 big bets, four players). The turn is the Q♠. You bet, and only the button, an aggressive and tricky player, calls (6 bets, two players). The river is the 5♠. What should you do?

ANSWER

Check and call. Give him a chance to bluff at the pot. If you bet and get raised, you will probably have to call, so there is no point in risking two big bets here.

GAME SCENARIO #18

An early player limps, the cutoff and the button limp, and you call half a bet in the small blind with K♦ Q♥. The big blind checks (5 bets, five players). The flop is J♠ 10♦ 3♠. You bet and three players call (4 big bets, four players). The turn is the Q♠. You bet and only the button calls (6 bets, two players). The button is a loose, passive player. The river is the 5♠. What should you do?

ANSWER

Check. You might argue for making a bet because you could get the villain to fold a small spade, but the villain didn't come all this way to fold a flush on the river. Loose passive players like to call. If the passive player has a small spade, he will likely check behind you, and you will get a free showdown.

On the actual hand, the hero checked and the villain checked behind him. The villain had J♥ 9♥, and the hero won the pot. The villain might have called a bet, but he also might have folded with four spades on the board.

GAME SCENARIO #19

You raise from early position with J♠ J♥. A tight passive player calls from middle position, and both blinds call (8 bets, four players). The flop is 9♥ 6♦ 2♥. The blinds check, you bet, and the middle player and small blind call (5.5 big bets). The turn is the 8♦. The small blind checks, you bet, the middle player raises, and the small blind folds (8.5 bets). What's your best play?

ANSWER

Call. Aggressive players will raise you with a draw or a hand like A♦ 8♦ here, but this is a passive player. You are probably behind. On the actual hand, the player raised and the passive player capped it. The player called the turn raise and a river bet when the A♣ came on the river. The middle player showed 6♠ 6♣ for a set.

GAME SCENARIO #20

You raise from under the gun with K♠ K♥. An early player and both blinds call (8 bets, four players). The flop is 9♦ 5♠ 4♦. The blinds check to you, you bet, and everyone calls (6 big bets, four players). The turn is the 3♠. The blinds check, you bet, and only the small blind calls (8 bets, two players). The river is the 6♦. The small blind checks. Should you also check, or should you bet?

ANSWER

Check. The board has become very dangerous. If your opponent was drawing to a flush, he just got there. There are now four parts of a straight on the board, and you are losing if he has a 7 or a 2. All of this not only makes it more likely for him to have you beat, but also makes it harder for him to call you with a worse hand. On the actual hand, the hero checked, and the villain showed 7♠ 7♦ for a straight.

GAME SCENARIO #21

An early players limps, the button raises, and you reraise from the small blind with Q♠ Q♣. The big blind folds and the others call (10 bets, three players). The flop is J♣ 6♥ 6♣. You bet, and they both call (6.5 big bets, three players). The turn is the 4♦. You bet and only the limper calls (8.5 bets, two players). The river is the 10♣. What do you do?

ANSWER

Bet. This is similar to the previous hand, but there are three differences. First, there is no straight possible. There is the pair of sixes on the board, so he has you beat if he has a 6 in his hand. In the previous hand there were eight cards that make him a straight, but in this hand, there are only two sixes in the deck to make trips. Second, fewer people took the flop, making it less likely that he has a flush. Finally, you have one card of the flush suit, making it less likely that he was on a club draw. This is clearly a better place to bet than the previous hand. On the actual hand, the hero bet and the villain called with 7♥ 7♦.

GAME SCENARIO #22

Two early players and a middle player limp. The small blind calls and you raise from the big blind with A♦ J♥. Everyone calls (10 bets, five players). The flop is 8♣ 7♥ 6♦. The small blind checks. What do you do?

Check. While you will typically follow up a preflop raise with a bet on the flop, there are too many players in this hand to think that you can take down the pot with a bet. Also, the board is highly coordinated and could easily hit the kind of medium connectors and middle pairs that limpers like to play. Check and see what happens. On the actual hand, the hero checked and it was bet, raised, and reraised before it got back to him. Naturally he folded, and eventually a straight beat two pair on the river.

GAME SCENARIO #23

The hijack raises and you reraise from the cutoff with 6♦ 6♣. Only the hijack calls (7.5 bets, two players). The flop is K♠ 4♠ 3♥. He checks, you bet and he calls (4.75 big bets). The turn is the 5♣. He checks, you bet, he raises, and you call (8.75 bet). The river is the 2♥. He bets, you raise, and he reraises (13.75 bets). What do you do?

ANSWER

Raise. The only hand you are losing to is 7-6, and he is far more likely to be overplaying an ace, particularly since you hold two sixes. Also, it is very unlikely he raised the turn with 7-6, since all he would have is a gutshot draw. On the actual hand, the hero raised and won when the villain mucked A♥ 2♠.

GAME SCENARIO #24

The small blind limps and you raise from the big blind with J♥ J♣. He calls (4 bets, two players). The flop is A♠ K♠ 4♥. He checks, you bet, and he calls (3 big bets). The turn is the 10♠. He checks, you bet, and he calls (5 bet). The river is the 5♥. He checks. What do you do?

ANSWER

Check. It is hard to put him on a hand here. A good player would have raised before the flop with an ace or a king, but a good player would never limp from the small blind. On the flop it is hard to see what he can call you with except an ace, king, or flush draw. But when the spade comes on the turn, he just checks and calls. Nothing about his play makes sense. In this case, it is wise to be cautious. On the actual hand, the hero checked and the villain had 10♣ 8♦. We may have missed a bet on the river, but we should thank him for all the money he donated with a horrible call on the flop with nothing.

GAME SCENARIO #25

You raise from the button with 6♠ 5♠ and only the big blind calls (4.5 bets, two players). The flop is A♠ A♣ 2♥. He bets (5.5 bets). What do you do?

ANSWER

Raise! There is nothing wrong with a fold here, but there is no reason to believe he has an ace. If he really has an ace, he might have raised preflop or check-raised on the flop. This donk bet looks weak. Try to take it from him. On the actual hand, the hero raised and the villain folded.

GAME SCENARIO #26

A middle player and the button limp. The small blind limps, and you check in the big blind with 8♥ 2♥ (4 bets, four players). The flop comes J♥ 10♦ 9♣. Everyone checks to the button, who bets. The small blind calls (6 bets). What do you do?

ANSWER

Fold. You have a straight draw, but you are drawing to the wrong end of the straight with a one-card straight draw. The only card you will really want to see is a 7, and you could still lose to a bigger straight. The pot is small, and you don't need to get involved. On the actual hand, the hero folded. The turn was the Q♠ (which would have given you a queen-high straight). On the river, the small blind showed a king and won with a king-high straight.

GAME SCENARIO #27

Everyone folds to you in the cutoff and you raise with A♥ 7♣. A solid player in the big blind reraises, and you call (6.5 bets, two players). The flop comes 8♠ 5♥ 4♦. The big blind bets (7.5 bets). What do you do?

ANSWER

Call. Unless he has aces or has flopped a set you have at least eight outs. A 6 is an out and an ace is probably an out. If an ace is not an out (if he has a hand like A-K), a 7 is an out. While outs are worth less when you don't know which ones are good, you only need five or six outs to play, which makes this a big enough overlay. It's even possible he raised with a hand like K-Qs, in which case you are ahead. I don't think raising is a good option here, because if he has a big pair, it is too easy for him to reraise you. On the actual hand, the hero called. The turn was the 6♥ making the straight, but the river was the 7♦ and the hero lost to 9♠ 9♦, using some bad language when he lost to a higher straight.

GAME SCENARIO #28

You raise from middle position with A♠ 6♠, and the small blind reraises. He three-bets 7.3 percent preflop, which is a little high. The big blind folds and you call (7 bets, two players). The flop is A♦ 8♠ 7♦. He bets, you raise, and he calls (5.5 big bets and two players). He folds to a flop raise 25 percent of the time. The 9♦ comes on the turn. He checks, you bet, and he calls (7.5 bets). He folds to a bet on the turn 45 percent of the time. The river card is the 2♠. He checks. What do you do?

ANSWER

Check. The only hands he might pay you off with are J-J to K-K, and he most likely has a diamond, since he folds so often on the turn. He is not a player who pays off lightly. His three-betting range of the top 7 percent of his hands is roughly A-A to 8-8, A-Ks to A-10s, K-Qs or K-Js, Q-Js, A-K, or A-Q. If he has any of the suited hands without an ace and he is still playing, he has a flush. If he has an ace, you are dead.

The only hands you can beat that he is likely to call with are bigger pocket pairs. With a big ace, you might expect him to have raised the turn or bet the river, but there still seem to be more hands that beat you than hands that you can beat. He might not call you with any hands that you can beat. On the actual hand, the hero checked and won when the villain had Q♦ Q♣. It is not clear whether he would have called a river bet.

GAME SCENARIO #29

You raise from early position with 9♥ 9♠. A solid player reraises from the hijack, and everyone else folds (7.3 bets, two players). The flop is K♥ 10♥ J♣. You check and he bets (6.3 small bets). What should you do?

ANSWER

Fold. It might appear that you have two outs to a set and four outs to a straight. Throw in two outs for a backdoor flush and you have eight outs. You only need 5 to 1 pot odds to call with eight outs, but all of your outs are weak. If you catch a 9 for a set, any queen makes a better straight. If you catch two running hearts, you are losing to any hand with the A♥, Q♥ or J♥.

Your four gutshot outs are the worst of all. If a queen comes, you have the wrong end of the straight and lose to any ace. Not only are all your outs weak, you will never know if you are good or not. Plus, you have no outs to the nuts.

GAME SCENARIO #30

You raise from under the gun with A♣ K♣. An early player and the small blind call. (7 bets, three players). The flop comes K♠ J♠ 10♣. The small blind checks, you bet, and the early player raises. The small blind folds, you make it three bets, and the early player calls (11 small bets, two players). The turn is the 10♠. You bet and the early player raises (8.5 big bets). What should you do?

ANSWER

Call. You are probably beaten, but you only need to win 11 percent of the time to break even. On the actual hand, the hero folded and the villain flashed K♦ Q♥ as he raked in the pot.

GAME SCENARIO #31

An early player limps and everyone folds to you in the big blind. You check with 9♠ 3♥ (2.3, two players). The flop is 6♥ 6♦ 2♣. You both check. The turn is the 2♦. You both check. The A♣ comes on the river. What should you do?

ANSWER

Bet. With this action, you are splitting the pot if you check. This weak, passive player is probably not calling you to play the board. On the actual hand, it went check-check. The limper showed 10♥ 7♥ for a split. A bet on any street would have won the pot.

GAME SCENARIO #32

An early player raises and the cutoff, a loose passive player, calls. You call in the big blind with 7♠ 7♥ (6.3 bets, three players). The flop comes Q♦ 3♣ 6♦. You check. The opener bets, the cutoff calls, and you raise. They both call (6.1 big bets, three players). The turn is the 2♠. You bet, the opener folds, and the cutoff calls (8.1 big bets). The 8♠ comes on the river. What should you do?

ANSWER

Bet. Since your opponent has never raised, it is unlikely that he has a queen. He either has a busted draw or a pair. Unless he has a pocket pair bigger than your sevens, or he paired the river card, you probably have the best hand. Since he is passive, he is probably not going to bet a busted draw. When you probably have the best hand, you usually want to bet for value. On the actual hand, the hero bet, and the cutoff called with A♥ 6♥ for a pair of sixes.

GAME SCENARIO #33

An extremely aggressive player raises under the gun. A middle player calls and you reraise from middle position with Q♠ Q♥. Both players call and everyone else folds (10.5 small bets, three players). The flop is 10♥ 4♥ 3♣. Both players check to you, and you bet. Mr. Aggressive raises, the middle player calls, you reraise, and they both call (9.8 big bets, three players). The turn is the 2♦. They both check and you bet. They both call (12.8 big bets). The river is the 7♥. They both check. What do you do?

ANSWER

Bet. With no raises on the turn, unless someone made a flush on the river, you are probably still ahead. Many people will bet a flush here, afraid to miss a bet with their big hand. With a pot this big, you will probably get at least one crying call. You will lose your share of money making crying calls on the river in big pots; just make sure you collect the money when you have the best hand. On the actual hand, the player checked. Mr. Aggressive showed A♣ 10♣ and the middle player showed Q♦ 10♦.

GAME SCENARIO #34

You raise from early position with K♠ Q♠. A very aggressive player reraises from middle position, the small blind calls, and the big blind folds (10 bets, three players). The flop comes K♣ Q♦ 9♣. You check, and everyone checks behind you (5 big bets). The turn is the 3♦. You bet, the aggressive player calls and the small blind folds (7 bets). The J♦ comes on the river. What do you do?

ANSWER

Check. With a board this scary, you are very likely to get raised. If he was on a draw, most of his draws got there. He is very aggressive, so give him a chance to bluff at the pot if he missed. On the actual hand, the player bet and his opponent raised. He cursed under his breath and made a crying call. The opponent had Q♣ J♥. While the bet made money this time, it is still the wrong play. For it to make money, the bet required a *really* bad player who three-bet an early opener before the flop with Q-J and made a raise on a very scary board with a weak two pair.

GAME SCENARIO #35

You raise from early position with Q♦ Q♣. A tight passive player calls from middle position, and both blinds call (8 bets, four players). The flop is 9♥ 6♦ 2♥. The blinds check, you bet, and the middle player and small blind call. (5.5 big bets). The turn is the 8♦. The small blind checks, you bet, the middle player raises, and the small blind folds. (8.5 big bets). What do you do?

ANSWER

Call. Aggressive players will raise you with a draw or with a hand like A♦ 9♦ here, but this is a passive player, so you are probably behind. This is a "way ahead or way behind" situation—raising in these types of situations is a very bad idea. On the actual hand, the player raised and the passive player capped it. The player called the turn bet and a river bet when the A♣ came on the river. The middle player showed 6♠ 6♣ for a set.

GAME SCENARIO #36

A loose aggressive player raises from middle position. You reraise from the cutoff with A♠ J♥ and everyone else folds (7.5 bets, two players). The flop comes A♦ 9♠ 2♥. He bets and you call (4.8 big bets). The turn is the 8♣. He bets (5.8 big bets). What do you do?

ANSWER

Call. Because he is aggressive, there is a good chance he will bet the river as a bluff or as a value bet with a weaker ace. You can always bet the river if he checks and raise if he bets. This way you are almost always going to get a bet or two on the river. If he folds to your river bet or raise, he was probably going to fold to a raise on the turn.

One reason to raise on the turn instead of the river is if you think your opponent may have a draw. He will pay you off on the turn with his draw, but will fold his missed draw on the river. However, with this board, there don't seem to be any drawing hands he could have. On the actual hand, the player raised on the turn and the opponent folded.

GAME SCENARIO #37

A middle player raises and you decide to disguise your hand and just call from the big blind with K♠ K♥ (4.5 bets, two players). The flop comes J♦ 5♠ 2♥. You check, he bets and you check-raise. He reraises and you call. (5.3 big bets). The turn is the 8♣. You check, he bets and you check-raise. He reraises (10.3 big bets). What do you do?

ANSWER

Call. You are either way ahead or way behind, and that is a bad time to be raising. You have disguised your hand and he may not put you on a big pair, but at some point you have to respect his action. Even with a big overpair, you still have just one pair. On the actual hand, the hero raised again on the turn, the villain reraised again, and the hero called. The river was the 8♥ and the hero called another big bet. The villain showed 5♦ 5♣ for a full house. The extra raise on the turn cost the hero two big bets.

GAME SCENARIO #38

As a new player, the cutoff has posted a blind. You open from middle position with K♥ J♥. The next player raises and the cutoff caps it. The two blinds fold, and you and the original raiser call (13.6 bets, three players). The flop is 10♣ 8♦ 5♠. You both check to the cutoff, who bets (14.6 small bets). What do you do?

ANSWER

Call. You have six overcard outs, and one out for two backdoor straights. With a pot this size, you only need three clean outs. Your outs may not be very clean, but this is such a big pot, you should try to peel a card. Let's look at some possible scenarios. If he is a very aggressive player, the original raiser could have: 6-6, A-9s, A-10, K-Js, K-Q, Q-Js, or J-10s. The capper could have 7-7, A-Js, A-Q, or K-Qs. With this scenario, you have a 12 percent chance of winning. Even with the raise danger behind you, that is still a big overlay.

Most people don't play this aggressively so let's look at a tighter range. Drop the three-bettor from 10.4 percent of his hands to 7.4 percent and the capper from 6.6 percent to 4.2 percent. Now you win 9 percent of the time, and it is starting to get closer when you consider the raise danger behind you. But with that pot, you only need a 6.4 percent chance of winning to call. If the capper is a rock and will only cap with 10-10 or A-K, your win percent drops to 7 percent, at which point your call becomes marginal. While you don't love the fact that there is a player to act who could still check-raise, the pot is huge.

You should be willing to gamble a bit when the price is just one small bet.

GAME SCENARIO #39

You raise from early position with Q♦ 10♦. Only a middle player calls (5.3 bets, two players). The flop comes J♦ 6♦ 3♦. You bet and your opponent raises (8.3 small bets). What do you do?

ANSWER

Raise. You don't want to slowplay when you flop a flush. Another diamond will either kill your action or kill your hand if your opponent has the A♦ or K♦. Your opponent seemed to like the flop, so get the money in there now. Also, some players won't put you on a flush, since so many others will slowplay here. When you are out of position with a good hand, you usually want to take or keep the lead.

On the actual hand, the hero just called. The turn was the A♠. The hero was afraid that betting now would scare off his opponent so he just checked. The opponent checked behind him. The river was the 8♦. It went check-check and the villain showed 10♥ 10♣. The hero won about as little as humanly possible when flopping a flush!

GAME SCENARIO #40

A middle player and the cutoff limp. You raise from the small blind with J♥ J♦. The big blind folds and the two limpers call (7 bets, three players). The flop is 8♣ 5♦ 3♠. You bet and both players call (5 big bets). The turn is the 9♣. You bet, the first limper folds, and the next limper raises (8 bets). What do you do?

ANSWER

Call. This is a "way ahead or way behind" situation where you don't want to raise. It's hard to find a lot of hands a limper is going to get excited about on this board other than two pair or a set. A straight is unlikely, but possible. On the actual hand, the hero raised again on the turn, the villain raised again, and the hero called. The river was the 2♠ and the hero check-called another big bet. The villain showed 9♠ 8♠ (a typical limper's hand) for two pair. The extra raise cost the hero two big bets.

GAME SCENARIO #41

The first player limps and you raise from early position with A♠ Q♠. The next player calls, the small blind raises, the first player folds, and you call. Now the player behind you caps it, the small blind calls, and you call (14.4 bets, three players). The flop comes Q♣ 9♦ 5♥. The small blind bets, you raise, the next player calls, the small blind reraises, and you both call (11.8 big bets). The turn is the 10♠. The small blind bets, you call, the next player raises, and the small blind reraises (17.8 bets). What should you do?

ANSWER

Fold. There is a ton of money in the pot, but you are likely drawing dead since your opponents are both showing a ton of strength. On the flop, one player cold-called two bets and your raise did not slow down the other player. On the turn they both are betting and raising at every opportunity. Top pair, top kicker is a good hand, but not a guaranteed winner. On the actual hand, the hero called and the next player capped the betting. The river was the J♠ and everyone checked. The small blind showed A♥ A♣, and the other player showed 9♥ 9♣ for a set.

GAME SCENARIO #42

You raise from early position with 8♠ 8♣ and an aggressive player reraises. Only you call (7.5 bets, two players). The flop is K♦ K♣ Q♦. You check, he bets, and you call (4.7 big bets). The turn is the 2♣. You both check. The river is the 2♠. What should you do?

ANSWER

Bet. When an aggressive player checks, he usually has a weak hand with some showdown value. It might be a small pair or an unimproved ace. With a really weak hand or a strong hand, he will keep betting. If you bet, there is a good chance you will get a call. On the actual hand, the hero checked to induce a bluff (though this play is not too likely to work here). The villain also checked with A♠ 4♠.

GAME SCENARIO #43

The cutoff and the button limp. You call from the small blind with 9♥ 8♥. The big blind checks (4 bets, four players). The flop is J♦ 10♠ 6♠. What should you do?

ANSWER

Check. You have about as weak a two-card straight draw as possible. You have the bottom end of the straight, so your four queen outs are tainted by the possibility of a bigger straight. There are two spades on the board, tainting two more of your outs. A jack and 10 are cards that connect with a lot of limping hands, making it unlikely that a bet wins the pot right here, so just check and see how the hand develops. Stay tuned.

GAME SCENARIO #44

Now let's follow up on the previous hand with some additional action. The cutoff and button limp. You call from the small blind with 9♥ 8♥. The big blind checks (4 bets, four players). The flop is J♦ 10♠ 6♠. You check, and everyone checks to the button, who bets (5 bets). What should you do?

ANSWER

Raise. Two players checked, and on a draw-heavy board, they probably would have bet if they had anything. The button may have a hand, but he also could just be trying to pick up a pot that no one else seems to want. On the actual hand, the hero raised and only the button called. When the turn card was the 2♠, the hero followed through with a bet and picked up the pot.

GAME SCENARIO #45

An early player and the button limp. You check from the big blind with 5♣ 2♣ (3.5 bets, three players). The flop is A♦ Q♠ 7♦. It is checked around. The turn is the 7♥. Again it is checked around. The river card is the Q♦. What do you do?

ANSWER

Bet. You are playing the board and based on the action, everyone else is too. By betting you are on a freeroll. If you are called, you are still chopping the pot. If you knock out even one player, you go from winning one-third of the pot to winning half of it. On the actual hand, the hero bet and both opponents folded.

GAME SCENARIO #46

An early player limps. The game has been passive and you call from the cutoff with J♠ 10♥. The button calls, the small blind folds, and the big blind checks (4.3 bets, four players). The flop comes A♠ 8♥ 5♠, and it is checked around. The 6♠ comes on the turn. The big blind checks and the early player bets (3.2 big bets). What do you do?

ANSWER

Fold. It is rare to fold a flush draw in a multiway pot, but you should be getting pot odds of 4 to 1 to call with nine outs. In addition, you are not drawing to the nut flush. Someone with the K♠ or Q♠ could have you close to drawing dead. Also, there are still two players left to act, even though the small blind has checked twice. Of course, it is possible that the bettor is making a play at the pot. If you think he is, you should raise. You might win the pot right there and you have the spade draw to fall back on if he calls. On the actual hand, the hero folded along with the other two opponents.

GAME SCENARIO #47

A middle player limps. You call from the small blind with Q♦ 7♦ and the big blind checks (3 bets, three players). The flop comes 10♦ 9♥ 8♥. What do you do?

ANSWER

Check. You have a straight draw (8 outs), an overcard (3 outs), and a backdoor flush draw (2 outs). With 13 outs, you might be tempted to bet; however, you need to discount your outs pretty heavily. Two of your straight outs and overcard outs could make a flush. Any made straight could be splitting the pot. Further, this is a highly coordinated board that could hit a lot of hands that would limp. If you bet, you could easily get raised. This is a tiny pot with a scary board. Take the cautious approach. On the actual hand, the hero checked and it was bet and raised before it got back to him. Stay tuned.

GAME SCENARIO #48

Following up on the previous hand, a middle player limps. You call from the small blind with Q♦ 7♦ and the big blind checks (3 bets, three players). The flop is 10♦ 9♥ 8♥. You check. The big blind bets and the limper raises (6 bets). What do you do?

ANSWER

Fold. You have a straight draw (8 outs), an overcard (3 outs), and a backdoor flush draw (2 outs). That's 13 outs, but you need to discount your outs pretty heavily. The pot is small, only offering you 3 to 1, which requires 12 outs to call. You don't have enough strong outs to call.

On the actual hand, however, the hero called and everything went right. The big blind called, improving his pot odds. The turn card was the J♦, making a straight for the hero and adding a flush draw. He bet the turn and only the middle player called. The river was the 10♠. The hero bet, got raised, and called. The villain showed 10♣ 3♣ for trip tens and the hero won a big pot. In this hand, a horrible opponent rescued the hero. The villain limped with 10-3s, and then raised the highly coordinated flop with top pair and no kicker. He called the turn with his weak hand with four parts to a straight on the board. Then he raised the river on the same strong board. He lost 4.5 big bets on a hand he never should have played.

GAME SCENARIO #49

An early player and a middle player limp. You limp from middle position with 8♥ 7♥. The cutoff raises. The button and small blind fold. All the limpers call, including you (10.4 bets, five players). The flop comes 9♣ 5♥ 5♣. Everyone checks to the cutoff, who bets, and everyone folds back to you (11.4 bets). What do you do?

ANSWER

Call. You have a gutshot straight draw (4 outs) and a backdoor flush draw (2 outs). That's six outs. If the cutoff doesn't have a pair, you have six more outs, so you have somewhere between six and 12 outs, which is plenty to call with. With the size of the pot, four outs are all you need to call. You need to discount your outs, because he could have a flush draw, and he could have a pair, but he cannot have both; therefore, don't discount both your pair outs and your straight outs. This is a fairly unusual situation where it is impossible for the villain to have both a flush draw and a pair, but usually, one opponent will only be able to hurt some of your outs.

On the actual hand, the hero called. The turn was the 7♦, giving him a pair. The hero checked and called a bet by the villain. The river was the 10♦. The hero checked and called again. The villain showed A♣ K♥ and the hero won a pot of almost 10 big bets. As it turned out, the hero had all 12 outs. The villain probably should not have bet the river; He had showdown value and was unlikely to get a better hand to fold.

GAME SCENARIO #50

An aggressive player raises from middle position. You reraise from the cutoff with 9♠ 9♣, and only the opener calls (7.5 bets, two players). The flop is 10♦ 8♦ 2♠. He checks, you bet, and he raises. You call (7.75 big bets, two players). The turn is the 5♠. He bets and you call (9.75 bets, two players). The river is the 6♦. He checks. What do you do?

ANSWER

Bet. Here's a good example of making a thin value bet. You could be losing to a flush or a straight, but your nines block the most likely straights. You could also be losing to a pair of tens, and he may have slowed down because he is afraid you have a flush; however, most aggressive players will bet top pair here. There are enough hands he will call you with that you should fire here. On the actual hand, the hero checked and the villain showed J♥ 8♥.

GAME SCENARIO #51

Two early players limp. Because the game has been very loose, you don't think a raise will knock many players out, so you just call with 9♥ 9♣. Three more players call, including both blinds (6 bets, six players). The flop is 8♠ 8♥ 4♦. Both blinds check, the first limper, who is a loose passive player, bets. The next limper folds (7 bets). What do you do?

ANSWER

Fold. A passive player is not leading into a field of five other players without having an 8. Even if he doesn't have an 8, there are still three more players behind you who could have one. On the actual hand, the hero called to the river, and the limper showed 10♦ 8♦.

GAME SCENARIO #52

A loose player raises under the gun, a very loose player calls, and the aggressive player in the cutoff reraises. You call from the big blind with Q♥ 9♥, and the other two players call (12.5 bets, four players). The flop is 8♥ 4♠ 4♥. Everyone checks to the cutoff. He bets, you call, the UTG player calls, and the very loose player folds (7.75 big bets, three players). The turn is the 8♠. Everyone checks to the cutoff, who bets (8.75 bets). What do you do?

ANSWER

Raise. Usually you should fold a flush draw with two pair on the board, but it isn't very likely that either of these players has an 8 or 4 and the pot is very big, so a call seems indicated— but this is a good spot to try to semibluff. You are representing a hand that is stronger than you're drawing to, but you'll lose the minimum if there's a bigger flush draw out there and you hit. On a good day, you will get a better flush draw to fold. You can also check down if called and then a Q or 9 hits. If you get three-bet on the turn, you can safely fold. On the actual hand, the hero called as did the opener. The river was the K♥, and the hero lost to the cutoff, who had A♥ 10♥.

GAME SCENARIO #53

You raise from the hijack with A♠ A♥, the small blind calls, and the aggressive big blind reraises. You reraise, and they both call (12 bets, three players). The flop comes J♥ 8♥ 3♦. They check to you, and you bet. The small blind raises, the big blind reraises, you call, and the small blind calls (10.5 big bets, three players). The turn is the 5♠. The small blind checks, the big blind bets, and you raise. Both players call. (16.5 bets, three players). The river is the 9♠. The small blind bets and the big blind calls (18.5 bets). What do you do?

ANSWER

Call. The pot is too big to fold, and you might even consider raising. It is unlikely the small blind has Q-10 offsuit for a straight, since he was not getting the right price to draw to an inside straight; however, he could have Q♥ 10♥ or another big hand. If he flopped two pair or a set, he might have been waiting for the right time to make a play. With a set, he probably would have raised the turn, but with two pair, he could be afraid of a bigger two pair with this action. He has to put you on a big pair, and he is still betting. You are probably better off just calling rather than raising. Stay tuned.

GAME SCENARIO #54

You raise from the hijack with A♠ A♥, the small blind calls, and the aggressive big blind reraises. You reraise, and they both call (12 bets, three players). The flop comes J♥ 8♥ 3♦. They check to you, and you bet. The small blind raises, the big blind reraises, you call, and the small blind calls (10.5 big bets, three players). The turn is the 5♠. The small blind checks, the big blind bets, and you raise. Both players call. (16.5 bets, three players). The river is the 9♠. The small blind bets and the big blind calls (18.5 bets). You notice that the small blind only has one-third of a bet left. What do you do?

ANSWER

Raise. The small blind may have you beat, but he cannot cost you much and you probably have the big blind beat. On the actual hand, the hero called, the small blind showed K♥ J♦, and the big blind showed K♠ K♦. A raise would have won some more money, but the hero didn't notice the small blind's short stack.

GAME SCENARIO #55

A player leaves when it is his turn to post the small blind, so there are two big blinds, and you post a small blind of 60 percent of a bet on the button. An early player raises, the hijack calls, and you call with 7♣ 5♣, along with both blinds (10 bets, five players). The flop is K♦ 7♥ 5♥. Everyone checks to the hijack, who bets. You raise and everyone calls (10 big bets, five players). The turn is the 2♥. Everyone checks to you. What do you do?

ANSWER

Check. When two players call two bets cold on the flop, there is an excellent chance that one has a flush draw. If you bet and get raised, you are not getting the right price to play on. Take a free card and maybe you will get lucky on the river. If someone bets the river, you can call. On the actual hand, the hero checked, and the river was the beautiful 5♦. The small blind bet, the big blind called, and the hero raised. The small blind grumbled as he called the raise and then mucked his hand when the hero showed his full house. The hero got lucky, but he gave himself that chance.

GAME SCENARIO #56

You raise from early position with A♥ A♦. The next player, the cutoff, and the small blind call (9 bets, four players). The flop is K♠ 3♣ 2♦. The small blind checks, you bet, the next two players call, and the small blind folds (6 big bets). The turn is the 10♠. You bet, the next player raises, and the cutoff folds (9 big bets). What do you do?

ANSWER

Call. When you are way ahead or way behind, you usually don't want to make risky raises, and you should rarely put in the third bet on the turn or river with only a pair, even if it is aces. On the actual hand, the hero raised and it was capped. The river was the 8♦ and the hero called another bet. The villain had 10♦ 2♣ for two pair. The villain played horribly in calling two bets before the flop, but that doesn't make the hero's reraise on the turn a good play.

GAME SCENARIO #57

You raise from early position with A♥ Q♥. Two middle players and the big blind call (8.5 bets, four players). The flop comes A♦ 10♠ 8♦. The big blind checks and you bet. The first middle player calls and the second one raises. The big blind calls (14.5 bets). What do you do?

ANSWER

Call. There is too much money in the pot and too many draws to fold top pair, good kicker. Too many players are in the pot to get too frisky and raise with one pair. You are unlikely to get any draws to fold in a big pot. On the actual hand, the hero called and so did the middle player. The turn was the 5♠, everyone checked to the raiser, who bet. Everyone called. The river was the 4♥ and everyone checked. The raiser had A♣ J♠, the small blind had Q♠ 9♠, and the third player had A♠ 6♠. The hero won the pot with the best kicker.

GAME SCENARIO #58

You raise from middle position with A♦ 8♦, the next player calls, and the cutoff reraises. Everyone else folds (10.4 bets, three players). The flop is A♣ J♣ 6♣. You both check to the cutoff, who bets. You call and the other middle player folds (5.2 big bets and two players). The turn is the 6♥. You check, he bets, and you call (7.2 bets and two players). The river is the K♥. What do you do?

ANSWER

This is a close decision, but I recommend a bet. The cutoff's most likely hands are a bigger ace or a pocket pair. For most ace hands (other than an A-K, A-Q or A-J), the river card just killed his bigger kicker. If he has an ace, you are splitting the pot, but a bet gives you a chance to take it all. If he has a big pair, he will probably check the river. If his pocket pair happens to be kings or jacks, you are dead, but otherwise you are likely to cost yourself a bet by checking.

Of course, it is not impossible that he has a flush. Are you going to call a raise? If so, you should probably check, since there are probably more hands he will raise with—including sets, flushes, two pair, and A-K and A-Q—than hands where you will win an extra bet by betting. If you are confident enough about this player to fold to a raise, you should bet. On the actual hand, the hero checked and the villain checked with Q♠ Q♣. His bet on the turn was a mistake. He should have checked, but if you check the river, you reward him for his mistake.

GAME SCENARIO #59

A fairly aggressive player raises from the button. You call from the big blind with 5♠ 4♣ (4.5 bets, two players). The flop is 4♠ 4♦ 3♣. You check, he bets, and you raise. He calls (4.25 big bets, two players). The turn is the J♥. You bet, he raises, and you call (8.25 bets, two players). The 9♣ comes on the river. You check, and he bets. What do you do?

ANSWER

Raise. His betting pattern is consistent with pocket jacks, since he needs to fear your having trip fours; however, there are a lot more hands he can have. While it is true that he won't call your raise with many hands, he might have played this way with A-J or a big pocket pair. You might get a call if he has those hands. On the actual hand, the hero called and the villain showed K♠ K♣.

GAME SCENARIO #60

An early player limps, the cutoff and the button limp, and you call half a bet in the small blind with K♦ Q♥. The big blind checks (5 bets, five players). The flop is J♠ 10♦ 3♠. You bet, and three players call (4.5 big bets, four players). The turn is the Q♠. You bet and only the loose passive player on the button calls (6.5 bets, two players). The river is the 5♠. What should you do?

ANSWER

Check and call. As a passive player, the button is unlikely to bluff, but he is also likely to check behind you with a medium to small spade. While betting might earn another bet, it is more likely to cost you a bet. The only time you should bet is if you think there is a chance he will fold a small spade. On the actual hand, the hero checked and the villain checked behind him. The villain had J♥ 9♥, and the hero won the pot. The villain might have called a bet, but he might have folded with four spades on the board. If you do bet, you should fold to a raise since a passive player won't raise here without a good flush.

Everyone folds to the button, who raises. He is a good player, but not overly aggressive. The small blind calls and you reraise from the big blind with A♣ Q♥. They both call (6 bets, three players). The flop is 10♣ 8♥ 4♠. The small blind checks, you bet, the button raises, the small blind calls. With 11 bets in the pot, you call (6 big bets, three players). The turn is the 5♦. The small blind checks, you check, the button bets, and the small blind calls (8 bets). What do you do?

ANSWER

Fold. The button probably doesn't have a big pair since he didn't reraise before the flop, so his most likely holding is something like A-10, K-10, Q-10 or J-10. If he has A-10 or Q-10, you are in trouble. Also, you have to worry about the small blind. He called two bets cold on the flop and called on the turn. He has either a straight draw or a pair. If he has J-9, a queen isn't an out. Since you have to discount your overcard outs, you don't have the price to continue.

GAME SCENARIO #62

A middle player raises, you reraise from the cutoff with Q♠ Q♣, and a very aggressive player calls from the button. The blinds fold (10.6 bets, three players). The flop is 7♠ 5♦ 2♣. The middle player checks, you bet, and they both call (6.8 big bets, three players). The turn is the J♥. The middle player checks, you bet, and they both call (9.8 bets, three players). The river is the K♣. The middle player checks. What do you do?

ANSWER

Check. While you usually want to keep betting when no one raises, you have to wonder what your two opponents have been calling you with *and* what they will call you with on the river that you can beat. With such a dry board, their most likely holdings are two overcards or a medium pair. If either has two overcards, they either have A-K or A-Q. With A-K, you just lost. With A-Q, you are unlikely to get a call. While they might call you on the river with a hand such as 10-10, they have been hoping all along that you have A-K and have to be afraid that you just got there. Also notice that a very common hand when someone calls three bets cold before the flop (like the button did) is A-K. Finally, by checking, you give the aggressive button a chance to bet a weaker hand. On the actual hand, the hero bet and everyone folded.

GAME SCENARIO #63

An early player raises, a middle player calls, and you reraise from the cutoff with K♠ K♦. The button and both blinds call (18 bets, six players). The flop is A♣ Q♥ 6♠. Everyone checks to you. What do you do?

ANSWER

Check. With six players you are not the favorite. Aces only win against five villains 43 percent of the time—you don't have aces and an ace has come on the flop, so you are a solid dog. With 18 bets in the pot, there is almost no chance you will win the pot with a bet. Don't let the fact that four players checked fool you. On the actual hand, the hero checked, the button bet, the early player raised, the next player called, and the hero folded. The button had A♥ 10♥, and the early player had A♦ 3♦. Note that if there had not been a raise, the hero would have been getting almost the right price to draw to his 2.5-outer. With the implied odds, a call of only one bet would have been a good idea, but the raise killed those pot odds.

GAME SCENARIO #64

An early player and a middle player limp. You take the cheap play from the small blind with 9♥ 7♦ and the big blind checks (4 bets, four players). The flop is 9♦ 9♣ 7♣. What should you do?

ANSWER

Bet. It is hard to play a big hand out of position. If you check-raise the flop, you show a lot of strength with this board. If you check-call the flop, it could get checked around on the turn. There is a flush draw out there, there could be straight draws, and this hand might have hit some limpers. Since so many people check here with a 9, your bet is deceptive. With a small pot, you can slowplay more often, but with bad position you are better off betting. On the actual hand, the hero checked and called against two players.

GAME SCENARIO #65

A solid player raises from the hijack, and you reraise from the big blind with A♣ K♦. He calls (6.5 bets, two players). The flop is K♥ 7♣ 5♣. You bet and he calls (4.25 big bets, two players). The turn is the 3♣. You bet and he calls (6.25 bets). The river brings the 6♣. You bet and he raises (9.25 bets). What do you do?

ANSWER

Call. It is hard to put a solid player on a 4 after his preflop raise, but a solid player isn't reraising you here with just the Q♣. A raise will either win you one bet or lose you two (unless you are planning to fold to a reraise). Here's the question: Which is more likely? (1) A solid player raised from the cutoff with a 4 in his hand, or (2) A solid player raised on the river with the third-best flush or worse. I think (1) is more likely than (2), and if you are wrong, you lose two bets instead of gaining one. On the actual hand, the hero raised and was reraised. He called and the villain showed 4♠ 4♣ for the straight flush.

GAME SCENARIO #66

You raise from middle position with J♠ J♦. The button and both blinds call (8 bets, four players). The flop is Q♣ Q♥ 9♦. The small blind checks and the big blind bets (9 bets). What do you do?

ANSWER

Raise. The big blind probably isn't betting a queen, as he's more likely to check-raise with that hand. Donk bets like this are usually weak. On the actual hand, the hero just called and folded when the button raised. The big blind showed 9-3 at the showdown and the button had A-9.

GAME SCENARIO #67

You raise from the button with Q♠ 9♠, and a tight aggressive player calls from the big blind (4.4 bets, and two players). The flop comes 8♠ 8♣ 5♦. He checks, you bet and he calls (3.2 big bets). The turn is the 6♣. He checks. What do you do?

ANSWER

Bet. Since he is tight, he probably has somewhat high cards for his preflop call. He could easily be calling the flop with overcards, and he will fold to a bet on the turn. If you get raised, you have two overcards and a gutshot to fall back on. On the actual hand, the hero checked. The river was the 2♥ and the villain bet. The hero folded.

GAME SCENARIO #68

You raise from the button with J♠ J♥. Only a loose-aggressive player in the big blind calls (4.5 bets, two players). The flop is Q♥ 8♣ 3♦. He checks, you bet, and he calls (3.25 big bets). The turn is the A♣. He checks. What do you do?

ANSWER

Check. This is a classic "ace on the turn" situation. If you are behind, you will save a bet. If you are ahead, the ace makes it hard for him to call the turn. You give him a chance to bluff the river, and you make it more likely that he will call a river bet. On the actual hand, the hero checked the turn. The river was the 7♦. The villain bet and the hero called. The villain showed J♦ 10♣. You might argue that by checking, you gave him a free card to hit his gutshot draw and risked losing the whole pot. However, this is a small pot. The risk of losing is more than offset by the chance of gaining an extra bet.

GAME SCENARIO #69

A very loose-aggressive player opens under the gun. You have seen him open from any position with any two cards. Although he plays crazy before the flop, he plays well once the flop comes down. A tight player calls and you call from the big blind with 8♣ 6♣ (6.6 bets, three players). The flop is A♥ 9♥ 4♥. You check, the wild man bets, the tight player calls. With 8.6 bets in the pot, you make a very loose (horrible) call. The turn is the 8♠. You check, the wild man bets, the tight player folds, and you call. The river is the 6♠. You check and the wild man bets. What do you do?

ANSWER

Call. This is an example of not making marginal bets or raises when faced with a tricky player. You will usually need to call if you get raised, so you basically are risking two bets to win one. For this to be right, you need the following factors to be true two-thirds of the time: (a) you have the best hand; (b) he will call your raise. In other words, to raise here you need to be confident that you have the best hand. In the actual hand, the hero raised, and the villain reraised. The hero called and the villain showed 6♥ 3♥.

GAME SCENARIO #70

You raise from middle position with A♣ J♠. An aggressive button reraises, and a tight player with a short stack caps it in the small blind. The big blind folds and both you and the button call (13 bets, three players). The flop comes K♦ J♥ 10♣. The small blind bets, you call, and the button raises. You call and the small blind calls all-in. The main pot is 8.9 big bets and the side pot is 0.4 big bets. The turn is the 7♣. You check and the button bets (10.3 bets). What do you do?

ANSWER

Call. You are probably behind, but you could have as many as nine outs. You only need around 4.5 outs to call; however, you may be up against a made straight or a set with this action, so your outs are definitely shaky. But I don't see discounting your outs to the point where you don't have 4.5 of them. On the actual hand, the hero called and then called a bet after the 9♣ came on the river. The aggressive villain showed A♠ A♦, and the tight all-in player showed Q♦ Q♣ for a straight. The hero actually only had five outs, which was still enough to call the turn.

15 SOME HOLD'EM ODDS

Occasionally it is useful to know the probabilities of certain events. Here are the odds of winning a showdown between two hands.

ODDS OF WINNING A SHOWDOWN BETWEEN TWO HANDS			
HAND	**EXAMPLE**	**1ST HAND WINS**	**2ND HAND WINS**
Pair vs. Pair	A-A vs. 5-5	82%	18%
Pair vs. lower suited connectors	K-K vs. 8-7s	77%	23%
Pair vs. suited over and under	10-10 vs. A-2s	68%	32%
Pair vs. higher suited connectors	7-7 vs. K-Qs	51%	49%
Pair vs. unsuited connectors	7-7 vs. K-Q	54%	46%
Suited connectors vs. suited connectors	J-10s vs. 6-5s	63%	37%
High low vs. two in middle	A-2 vs. Q-8	58%	42%
High low vs. middle suited connectors	A-2 vs. Q-Js	53%	47%
Domination	A-10s vs. A-2	70%	30%
Two high vs. two low	K-10 vs. 6-4	64%	36%
Interlaced cards	Q-7 vs. 10-5	63%	37%
Best vs. worst	A-A vs. 7-2	89%	11%

SOME HOLD'EM ODDS

If you are suited, you will make a flush by the river 6.4 percent of the time. You will flop a flush less than 1 percent of the time and flop a draw 11 percent. With an unpaired hand, you will flop at least a pair 32.4 percent of the time. Think of it as one time out of three. You will flop two pair 2.02 percent of the time.

PREFLOP HANDS CHART WITH IMPROVEMENT ODDS			
HAND OR OUTCOME	**PERCENTAGE**	**PROBABILITY**	**ODDS AGAINST**
Pair preflop	6%	1 in 17	16:1
Suited cards preflop	24%	1 in 4.2	3.2:1
Suited connectors (2-3, K-Q, etc.)	4%	1 in 25	24:1
A-A or K-K preflop	0.9%	1 in 111	110:1
A-K preflop	1.2%	1 in 83	82:1
A-Ks preflop	0.3%	1 in 332	331:1
Ace in hand preflop	16%	1 in 6.25	5.25:1
A-A, K-K, Q-Q, J-J	1.8%	1 in 56	55:1
Flop being all one rank (J-J-J or Q-Q-Q)	0.24%	1 in 425	424:1
A-A versus K-K preflop (heads-up)	0.004%	1 in 22560	22559:1
A-K dealt preflop and hitting an A or K by the river	50%	1 in 2	even
Q-Q versus A-K heads up to river	56%	1 in 1.78	14:11 favorite
Two cards preflop jacks or higher	9%	1 in 11	10:1
Dealt any unsuited cards, such as 7-2	0.9%	1 in 110	109:1
Four flush completing (two cards to go)	39%	1 in 2.6	3:2
Open-ended straight flush draw completing to flush or straight by river	54%	1 in 1.85	

PREFLOP HANDS CHART WITH IMPROVEMENT ODDS

HAND OR OUTCOME	PERCENTAGE	PROBABILITY	ODDS AGAINST
Open-ended straight completing (J-10 with Q-9-4-8-6 flop)	34%	1 in 2.9	~2:1
Two pair on flop improving to full house	17%	1 in 5.8	~5:1
Three of a kind (set) on flop improving to full house or quads	37%	1 in 2.7	~3:2
Pocket pair improving to three of a kind on flop	12%	1 in 8	7:1
No pair preflop improving to a pair on the flop	32%	1 in 3.125	~2:1
Being dealt two suited cards	24%	1 in 4	3:1
If you have suited cards, flush will flop	0.84%	1 in 119	118:1
If you have suited cards, flush draw will flop	11%	1 in 9	8:1
If you have suited cards, flush by the river	6.4%	1 in 16	15:1
One pair on flop improving to two pair or three of a kind by river	22%	1 in 4.7	~4:1
Pocket pair improving to three of a kind after flop	9%	1 in 11	10:1
Two overcards improving to a pair by river	26%	1 in 3.9	~3:1
Two overcards and a gutshot improving to pair or straight	43%	1 in 2.3	4:3
Gutshot straight draw hitting by river	17%	1 in 6	5:1
Gutshot and pair improving to two pair or better	39%	1 in 2.6	3:2
Backdoor flush draw hitting (5♠ 6♠ with flop 7♠ A♦ 9♥ K♠ J♠)	4%	1 in 24	1.9 outs
One-way runner-runner straight (357 - 46)	0.74%	1 in 135	

SOME HOLD'EM ODDS

PREFLOP HANDS CHART WITH IMPROVEMENT ODDS			
HAND OR OUTCOME	**PERCENTAGE**	**PROBABILITY**	**ODDS AGAINST**
2-way runner-runner straight (356 - 47, 24)	2.96%	1 in 34	1.4 outs
3-way runner-runner straight (456 - 34, 37, 78)	4.44%	1 in 23	2 outs
Backdoor flush and gutshot improving to one by river (A♣ 4♣ with flop 3♥ 5♣ K♦)	21%	1 in 4.8	3.8:1
Backdoor flush and two overcards improving to pair or flush	30%	1 in 3.3	2.3:1
Five players on flop, that someone has an A when one is on board	58%	1 in 1.7	
Four players on flop, that someone has an A when one is on board	47%	1 in 2.1	
Three players on flop, that someone has an A when one is on board	35%	1 in 2.9	
Two players on flop, that someone has an A when one is on board	23%	1 in 4.3	
3 of one suit on board and another coming (Q♥ 10♥ 2♥) if you have one	39%	1 in 2.6	3:2
Five players in with board paired, chance of one of them having trips	43%	1 in 2.4	
Four players in with board paired, chance of one of them having trips	34%	1 in 3	
Three players in with board paired, chance of one of them having trips	26%	1 in 4	
Two players in with board paired, chance of one of them having trips	17%	1 in 5.8	

Don't fall in love with a big pair. Sometimes aces lose, especially against a lot of opponents. Here are your odds of winning with pocket aces against different numbers of opponents.

ODDS OF WINNING WITH POCKET ACES	
NUMBER OF OPPONENTS	**ACES WIN**
1	83%
2	68%
3	59%
4	50%
5	43%

G GLOSSARY

Animal

    A very aggressive player who loves to bet and raise, with or without a hand.

Backdoor Draw

    A draw to a straight or flush that needs two more cards to complete. For example, if you have three cards of the same suit, you have a backdoor flush draw.

Big Bet

    The larger of the two betting limits in a limit hold'em game. In a $25/$50 game, a big bet is $50.

Blank

    A card on the turn or river that has no apparent value.

Button

    The player with the dealer button, who acts last on the flop, turn or river.

Calling Station

    A player who uses any excuse to call all the way to the river. Often they seem to think that everyone who bets against them is bluffing.

Cap

    The maximum number of bets allowed on a round. Also can be used as a verb to mean putting in the last raised allowed on a round, as in "John capped it on the turn."

Card Dead

Not getting any good hands for a period of time. For example, "I was card dead for the last three hours."

Chasing

Calling with a weak hand in the hope of improving even though the pot odds don't justify continuing.

Cheap Kill

In a kill game, when you are the "killer" because you won two hands in a row and were going to post the blind anyway, the extra amount you have to post is known as a "cheap kill" since you are only posting the blind anyway.

Chop

To split a pot because of a tie at the showdown. Also, to split the blinds without seeing a flop when no one else has entered the pot.

Clean Out

An out that will almost certainly win when it comes. If there are four spades on the board and you have the ace of spades, any spade is a clean out. Technically, the only clean outs are spades that don't pair the board or make a straight flush possible.

Connectors

Two cards that are close in rank such as 8-7 or 8-6, either suited or unsuited.

Cutoff

The player to the dealer button's immediate right who acts just before the button.

Dangerous Board

Community cards with a lot of straight or flush possibilities.

Discount an Out

To reduce the value of an out because of the chances that you may improve your hand and still lose.

Donk Bet

A bet into a previous round aggressor. For example, if the button raised before the flop, and the big blind bets on the flop rather than checks to the button, he is making a donk bet.

Donkey

A bad player.

Double Gutshot

A hand with two different inside straight draws. For example, when you have 9-6 and the board is 7-5-3, either an 8 or 4 will make you a straight.

Expectation or Expected Value

Statistical terms for the average return of a contest or course of action. It is what your average return would be if you played the same situation over many times.

Fold Equity

The increase in expectation from betting or raising based on the possibility that everyone else will fold. When you check or call, your expectation is based solely on the probability you have the best hand, but with a bet or raise, the possibility that everyone folds adds to your expectation.

Full-Kill Game

A game that, when you win two pots in a row, you must post a blind double the normal big blind, and the limits go up for that hand. So if the game is $8/$12, the kill would be $16 with the limits $16/$32.

Gutshot

A gutshot or inside straight draw is a hand with four cards to the straight and only cards of one rank will complete the straight. An example is a board of K-9-7 with a hand of 10-6, where only an 8 will complete the straight.

Gypsy

To enter the pot before the flop by just calling the big blind. Also known as a limp.

Half-Kill Game

A game that, when you win two pots in a row, you must post a blind 150 percent larger than the normal big blind, and the limits go up for that hand. So if the game is $8/$12, the half-kill would be $12 with the limits $12/$24.

Hijack

The seat to the right of the cutoff seat, two seats to the right of the button.

Insta-Call

A call made without delay or hesitation. The caller almost beats the bettor's chips into the pot.

Kill

In a kill game, to win two pots in a row, which triggers an increase in the blinds and the stakes for the following deal.

Kill Game

A game that, when you win two pots in a row, you must post a blind that is larger than the big blind, and the limits go up for that hand.

Killer

In a kill game, the player that wins two pots in a row, triggering an increase in the blinds and the stakes for the following deal. The "killer" is the player that must post the larger blind.

LAG

Loose and aggressive player.

Leg Up

In a Kill Game, when you win a pot, the dealer will typically post a button in front of you indicating that if you win the next hand, you trigger the "kill," and an increase in the blinds and stakes or the following deal.

Limp

To enter the pot before the flop by just calling the big blind. Also known as a gypsy.

Loose (player)

A player who likes to play a lot of hands and will generally play weaker hands.

Maniac

A very loose, very aggressive player.

Meta Game

A strategy designed to maximize your profit over a long period of time. The long period may be the rest of the session, or longer. The idea is that you make a play that might not gain the maximum profit in a specific hand if you think this play will allow you to make more money on future hands.

Monster

A very strong hand.

Muck

To fold. Giving up your hand without showing it when there is a showdown. Also, the pile of discarded and unused cards on the table.

Overcard

A card of higher rank than any cards on the board. When you are playing overcards, both the cards in your hand are higher than any card on the board.

Overlay

A winning wager. In the long run, the payoff from the wager more than compensates for the risk. Statistically, it is a bet with a positive expectation.

Out

A card that will improve your hand to one that is likely to win.

Pair Plus Draw

A pair plus an open-ended straight draw or a flush draw.

Rag

A low value card that doesn't coordinate with the board. If the flop is K-Q-J, a 5 on the turn is a rag. Also used to designate a bad hand, such as K-3 (king-rag).

Rainbow

Three or four cards on the board of different suits.

Rock

A tight player.

Set

Three of a kind where two of those cards are in your hand.

Small Bet

The smaller of the two betting limits in a limit hold'em game. In a $25/$50 game, a small bet is $25.

Steaming

Getting angry or frustrated over losses in a way that negatively affects your play.

Strong Draw

In the context of small connectors, no pair and a draw with at least 12 outs.

Strong Hand

In the context of small connectors, two pair or better, but does not include a pair or three-of-a-kind on the board. (A board of Q-Q-7 does not qualify as giving you a strong hand when you have 8-7. This is treated as a pair.)

TAG

Tight and aggressive player.

Tainted Out

An out that doesn't always give you the best hand.

Thin

Marginal. A "thin" bet is a bet where you only have slightly over a 50 percent chance of winning if you are called. It could also be called a bet with small positive expectation. Also, few chances of winning. A player with very few outs is said to be "drawing thin."

Three-bet

To make a second raise on a round of betting. For example, if someone bets $10 and another player raises to $20, if you raise to $30 you are "three-betting." Before the flop, if one person raises, the next raiser is three-betting.

Tight (player)

Someone who usually only plays strong hands and will often fold without a strong hand.

Trips

Three of a kind where only one of the three cards is in your hand. While this is often a strong hand, it is not usually as strong as a set.

Two-card Draws

When you need to use both hole cards to complete a drawing hand.

UTG

Short for "under the gun," meaning first to act before the flop.

Value

Betting because you believe you will have the best hand more than half the time when you are called.

GREAT CARDOZA POKER BOOKS
ADD THESE TO YOUR LIBRARY - ORDER NOW!

HOLD'EM WISDOM FOR ALL PLAYERS *By Daniel Negreanu.* Superstar poker player Daniel Negreanu provides 50 easy-to-read and right-to-the-point hold'em strategy nuggets that will immediately make you a better player at cash games and tournaments. His wit and wisdom is great reading; even better, it makes for killer winning advice. Conversational, straightforward, and educational, this book covers topics as diverse as the top 10 rookie mistakes to bullying bullies and exploiting your table image. 176 pages, $14.95.

PLAYING NO-LIMIT HOLD'EM AS A BUSINESS *by Rob Tucker.* A serious player's manual for making big money in cash games. The author shows how to stop bluffing your money away and start walking away with consistent profits - both online and in live cash games. Tucker's easy-to-implement system teaches you how to wait for big hands with which to trap opponents and avoid all the marginal and high-risk trouble situations that lead to losses. 320 pages, $19.95.

PLAYING SIT & GO POKER AS A BUSINESS *by Rob Tucker.* This is the only book that shows players how to earn cash by playing in satellites for big buy-in no-limit hold'em tournaments like the World Poker Tour, European Poker Tour and the World Series of Poker. Tucker, who has won 18 World Poker Tour main event seats in two years using this exact same method, shows how to survive until the top two places of a single-table sit-and-go and either win the valuable main event seat or negotiate a deal for a huge cash profit. You'll learn how to play aggressively in the short-stacked supersatellites, more conservatively in the deeper-stacked satellites, and when and how to negotiate deals. Dozens of hand examples, table graphics, and clear explanations demonstrate how decision making is guided by the objective of playing heads-up. 192 pages, $19.95

HOW TO WIN NO-LIMIT HOLD'EM TOURNAMENTS *by McEvoy & Don Vines.* Learn the basic concepts of tournament strategy and how to win big by playing small buy-in events, graduate to medium and big buy-in tournaments, adjust for short fields, huge fields, slow and fast-action events. Plus, how to win online tournaments. You'll also learn how to manage a tournament bankroll and get tips on table demeanor for televised tournaments. See actual hands played by finalists at WSOP and WPT championship tables with card pictures, analysis and useful lessons from the play. 376 pages, $29.95.

CARO'S MOST PROFITABLE HOLD'EM ADVICE *by Mike Caro.* When Mike Caro writes a book on winning, all poker players take notice. And they should: The "Mad Genius of Poker" has influenced just about every professional player and world champion alive. You'll journey far beyond the traditional tactical tools offered in most poker books and for the first time, have access to the entire missing arsenal of strategies left out of everything you've ever seen or experienced. Caro's first major work in two decades is packed with hundreds of powerful ideas, concepts, and strategies, many of which will be new to you— they have never been made available to the general public. This book represents Caro's lifelong research into beating the game of hold em. 408 pages, $24.95

OMAHA HIGH-LOW: Play to Win with the Odds *by Bill Boston.* Selecting the right hands to play is the most important decision to make in Omaha. This is the *only* book that shows you the chances that every one of the 5,278 Omaha high-low hands has of winning the high end of the pot, the low end of it, and how often it is expected to scoop all the chips. You get all the vital tools needed to make critical preflop decisions based on the results of more than 500 million computerized hand simulations. You'll learn the 100 most profitable starting cards, trap hands to avoid, 49 worst hands, 30 ace-less hands you can play for profit, and the three bandit cards you must know to avoid losing hands. 248 pages, $19.95.

GREAT CARDOZA POKER BOOKS
ADD THESE TO YOUR LIBRARY - ORDER NOW!

DANIEL NEGREANU'S POWER HOLD'EM STRATEGY *by Daniel Negreanu.* This power-packed book on beating no-limit hold'em is one of the three most influential poker books ever written. Negreanu headlines a collection of young great players—Todd Brunson, David Williams. Erick Lindgren, Evelyn Ng and Paul Wasicka—who share their insider professional moves and winning secrets. You'll learn about short-handed and heads-up play, high-limit cash games, a powerful beginner's strategy to neutralize pro players, and how to mix up your play, bluff and win big pots. The centerpiece, however, is Negreanu's powerful and revolutionary small ball strategy. You'll learn how to play hold'em with cards you never would have played before—and with fantastic results. The preflop, flop, turn and river will never look the same again. A must-have! 520 pages, $34.95.

POKER WIZARDS *by Warwick Dunnett.* In the tradition of Super System, an exclusive collection of champions and superstars have been brought together to share their strategies, insights, and tactics for winning big money at poker, specifically no-limit hold'em tournaments. This is priceless advice from players who individually have each made millions of dollars in tournaments, and collectively, have won more than 20 WSOP bracelets, two WSOP main events, 100 major tournaments and $50 million in tournament winnings! Featuring Daniel Negreanu, Dan Harrington, Marcel Luske, Kathy Liebert, Mike Sexton, Mel Judah, Marc Salem, T.J Cloutier and Chris "Jesus" Ferguson. This must-read book is a goldmine for all serious players, aspiring pros, and future champions! 352 pgs, $19.95.

SUPER SYSTEM *by Doyle Brunson.* This classic book is considered by the pros to be the best book ever written on poker! Jam-packed with advanced strategies, theories, tactics and money-making techniques, no serious poker player can afford to be without this hard-hitting information. Includes fifty pages of the most precise poker statistics ever published. Features chapters written by poker's biggest superstars, such as Dave Sklansky, Mike Caro, Chip Reese, Joey Hawthorne, Bobby Baldwin, and Doyle. Essential strategies, advanced play, and no-nonsense winning advice on making money at 7-card stud (razz, high-low split, cards speak, and declare), draw poker, lowball, and hold'em (limit and no-limit). This is a must-read for any serious poker player. 628 pages, $29.95.

SUPER SYSTEM 2 *by Doyle Brunson.* SS2 expands upon the original with more games and professional secrets from the best in the world. New revision includes Phil Hellmuth Jr. along with superstar contributors Daniel Negreanu, winner of multiple WSOP gold bracelets and 2004 Poker Player of the Year; Lyle Berman, 3-time WSOP gold bracelet winner, founder of the World Poker Tour, and super-high stakes cash player; Bobby Baldwin, 1978 World Champion; Johnny Chan, 2-time World Champion and 10-time WSOP bracelet winner; Mike Caro, poker's greatest researcher, theorist, and instructor; Jennifer Harman, the world's top female player and one of ten best overall; Todd Brunson, winner of more than 20 tournaments; and Crandell Addington, no-limit hold'em legend. 704 pgs, $29.95.

CARO'S BOOK OF POKER TELLS *by Mike Caro.* One of the ten greatest books written on poker, this must-have book should be in every player's library. If you're serious about winning, you'll realize that most of the profit comes from being able to read your opponents. Caro reveals the secrets of interpreting *tells*—physical reactions that reveal information about a player's cards—such as shrugs, sighs, shaky hands, eye contact, and many more. Learn when opponents are bluffing, when they aren't and why—based solely on their mannerisms. Over 170 photos of players in action and play-by-play examples show the actual tells. These powerful ideas will give you the decisive edge. 320 pages, $24.95.

GREAT CARDOZA POKER BOOKS
ADD THESE TO YOUR LIBRARY - ORDER NOW!

THE POKER TOURNAMENT FORMULA *by Arnold Snyder.* Start making money now in fast no-limit hold'em tournaments with these radical and never-before-published concepts and secrets for beating tournaments. You'll learn why cards don't matter as much as the dynamics of a tournament—your position, the size of your chip stack, who your opponents are, and above all, the structure. Poker tournaments offer one of the richest opportunities to come along in decades. Every so often, a book comes along that changes the way players attack a game and provides them with a big advantage over opponents. Gambling legend Arnold Snyder has written such a book. 368 pages, $19.95.

POKER TOURNAMENT FORMULA 2: Advanced Strategies for Big Money Tournaments *by Arnold Snyder.* Probably the greatest tournament poker book ever written, and the most controversial in the last decade, Snyder's revolutionary work debunks commonly (and falsely) held beliefs. Snyder reveals the power of chip utility—the real secret behind winning tournaments—and covers utility ranks, tournament structures, small- and long-ball strategies, patience factors, the impact of structures, crushing the Harringbots and other player types, tournament phases, and much more. Includes big sections on Tools, Strategies, and Tournament Phases. A must buy! 496 pages, $24.95.

CHAMPIONSHIP NO-LIMIT & POT-LIMIT HOLD'EM *by T. J. Cloutier & Tom McEvoy.* New edition! The bible for winning pot-limit and no-limit hold'em gives you the answers to your most important questions: How do you get inside your opponents' heads and learn how to beat them at their own game? How can you tell how much to bet, raise, and reraise in no-limit hold'em? When can you bluff? How do you set up your opponents in pot-limit hold'em so that you can win a monster pot? What are the best strategies for winning no-limit and pot-limit tournaments, satellites, and supersatellites? Inspired advice you can bank on from two of the most recognizable figures in poker. 304 pages, $19.95.

CHAMPIONSHIP HOLD'EM *by T. J. Cloutier & Tom McEvoy.* New edition! Hard-hitting hold'em the way it's played *today* in limit cash games and tournaments. Get killer advice on how to win more money in rammin'-jammin', kill-pot, jackpot, shorthanded, and full table cash games. You'll learn the thinking process for preflop, flop, turn, and river play with specific suggestions for what to do when good or bad things happen. Includes play-by-play analyses, advice on how to maximize profits against rocks in tight games, weaklings in loose games, experts in solid games, plus tournament strategies for small buy-in, big buy-in, rebuy, satellite and big-field major tournaments. Wow! 392 pages, $19.95.

OMAHA HIGH-LOW: Play to Win with the Odds *by Bill Boston.* Selecting the right hands to play is the most important decision to make in Omaha. This is the *only* book that shows you the chances that every one of the 5,278 Omaha high-low hands has of winning the high end of the pot, the low end of it, and how often it is expected to scoop all the chips. You get all the vital tools needed to make critical preflop decisions based on the results of more than 500 million computerized hand simulations. You'll learn the 100 most profitable starting cards, trap hands to avoid, 49 worst hands, 30 ace-less hands you can play for profit, and the three bandit cards you must know to avoid losing hands. 248 pages, $19.95.

HOW TO BEAT SIT-AND-GO POKER TOURNAMENTS by Neil Timothy. There is a lot of dead money up for grabs in the lower limit sit-and-gos and Neil Timothy shows you how to go and get it. The author, a professional player, shows you how to reach the last six places of lower limit sit-and-go tournaments four out of five times and then how to get in the money 25-35 percent of the time using his powerful, proven strategies. This book can turn a losing sit-and-go player into a winner, and a winner into a bigger winner. Also effective for the early and middle stages of one-table satellites.176 pages, $14.95.

Order now at 1-800-577-WINS or go online to: www.cardozabooks.com

POWERFUL WINNING POKER SIMULATIONS
A MUST FOR SERIOUS PLAYERS WITH A COMPUTER!
IBM compatible CD ROM Win 95, 98, 2000, NT, ME, XP

These incredible full color poker simulations are the best method to improve your game. Computer opponents play like real players. All games let you set the limits and rake and have fully programmable players, plus stat tracking, and Hand Analyzer for starting hands. Mike Caro, the world's foremost poker theoretician says, "Amazing... a steal for under $500... get it, it's great." Includes free phone support. "Smart Advisor" gives expert advice for every play!

NEW! Windows Versions More Features!

1. TURBO TEXAS HOLD'EM FOR WINDOWS - $59.95. Choose which players, and how many (2-10) you want to play, create loose/tight games, and control check-raising, bluffing, position, sensitivity to pot odds, and more! Also, instant replay, pop-up odds, Professional Advisor keeps track of play statistics. Free bonus: Hold'em Hand Analyzer analyzes all 169 pocket hands in detail and their win rates under any conditions you set. Caro says this "hold'em software is the most powerful ever created." Great product!

2. TURBO SEVEN-CARD STUD FOR WINDOWS - $59.95. Create any conditions of play; choose number of players (2-8), bet amounts, fixed or spread limit, bring-in method, tight/loose conditions, position, reaction to board, number of dead cards, and stack deck to create special conditions. Features instant replay. Terrific stat reporting includes analysis of starting cards, 3-D bar charts, and graphs. Play interactively and run high speed simulation to test strategies. Hand Analyzer analyzes starting hands in detail. Wow!

3. TURBO OMAHA HIGH-LOW SPLIT FOR WINDOWS - $59.95. Specify any playing conditions; betting limits, number of raises, blind structures, button position, aggressiveness/passiveness of opponents, number of players (2-10), types of hands dealt, blinds, position, board reaction, and specify flop, turn, and river cards! Choose opponents and use provided point count or create your own. Statistical reporting, instant replay, pop-up odds high speed simulation to test strategies, amazing Hand Analyzer, and much more!

4. TURBO OMAHA HIGH FOR WINDOWS - $59.95. Same features as above, but tailored for Omaha High only. Caro says program is "an electrifying research tool...it can clearly be worth thousands of dollars to any serious player. A must for Omaha High players.

5. TURBO 7 STUD 8 OR BETTER - $59.95. Brand new with all the features you expect from the Wilson Turbo products: the latest artificial intelligence, instant advice and exact odds, play versus 2-7 opponents, enhanced data charts that can be exported or printed, the ability to fold out of turn and immediately go to the next hand, ability to peek at opponents hand, optional warning mode that warns you if a play disagrees with the advisor, and automatic mode that runs up to 50 tests unattended. Tough computer players vary their styles for a great game.

---

6. TOURNAMENT TEXAS HOLD'EM - $39.95

Set-up for tournament practice and play, this realistic simulation pits you against celebrity look-alikes. Tons of options let you control tournament size with 10 to 300 entrants, select limits, ante, rake, blind structures, freezeouts, number of rebuys and competition level of opponents. Pop-up status report shows how you're doing vs. the competition. Save tournaments in progress to play again later. Additional feature allows quick folds on finished hands.
